A Pleasant Vintage of Till Eulenspiegel

A pleasant vintage of
Till Eulenspiegel

born in the country of Brunswick. How he spent his life. 95 of his tales.

Translated from the edition of 1515, with Intro=
duction and Critical Appendix, by Paul Oppenheimer
Wesleyan University Press, Middletown, Connecticut
M. C M. lxxij.

Acknowledgement is gratefully made to the
Princeton University Library, from whose copy of
the Schröder facsimile of the Grieninger edition
of 1515 the woodcuts in this volume were reproduced.

ISBN: 0-8195-4043-9
Library of Congress catalog card number: 73-184361
Manufactured in the United States of America
First edition

For Julie

Contents

xi

xiii

Preface

I wish to thank two scholars for their considerable help in preparing this translation. Professor W. T. H. Jackson of Columbia University, whose delightful and inspiring seminars first led me into medieval studies, has been kind enough to read the manuscript and to make numerous major and minor suggestions for its improvement. Professor Howard Schless, also of Columbia, has helped immensely, both with suggestions for improvement and with thoughtful and exciting teaching over the years. I want finally, and especially, to thank my wife Linda, who typed and helped edit and who offered so much excellent advice along the way.

Introduction

Toward the close of the fifteenth century, at around the time when Caxton was publishing Malory's adventures of King Arthur and his knights, and shortly after the first printing of Dante's *Divine Comedy*, a writer of Brunswick, Germany, possessed of a cunning sense of humor as well as a fishy eye for human pomposity, began to put together a book whose queer anti-hero was destined to become as famous as its author was to remain anonymous. The book described the escapades of Till Eulenspiegel, a professional buffoon and vagabond who, if he ever actually lived, was thought to have died in 1350 — and while it offered the world neither the lyricism of Malory's prose nor the majesty of Dante's vision of man, it was in its own way to exert a vast and happy influence on Western literature and life. For Till Eulenspiegel — jester, clown, rogue, sadist, skeptic, beggar, satirist, actor, thief, liar, savior, and even philosopher — was to become as perfect a mirror of a late medieval, and perhaps also very modern, German existentialist personality as of the everlasting foolishness of the lives of most men and women everywhere.

Eulenspiegel's adventures, written first in a Low German version which has never been found, were apparently quite popular from the start — so popular in fact that another anonymous but obviously gifted writer, known to this day simply as "N.," translated them into Middle High German in 1500, rewriting and no doubt changing the original considerably as he went along. His version seems to have met with even greater success. In 1515, Johannes Grieninger of Strassburg, an early and excellent printer who managed to produce one-hundred-thirty-nine different books in thirty-six years, on subjects ranging from alchemy through theology, history, liquor-making, and the classics, published N.'s *A Pleasant Vintage of Till Eulenspiegel* as a quarto with eighty-six fine woodcuts by an unknown artist — thereby setting the stage for Eulenspiegel's career as an international, as well as a German, folk-hero. For that is what Eulenspiegel rapidly became. Grieninger published a second, slightly revised edition of the book in 1519; and thereafter followed a prolific series of editions and versions of Eulenspiegel's adventures, by other translators, publishers, and adaptors, in High German, Modern German, Dutch, Danish, French, Swedish, Flemish, Hungarian, Slovak, Spanish, and Norwegian. Literally dozens of books either based upon, centered around, or influenced by Eulenspiegel's fascinating life have appeared during the past five centuries; his impact, both directly and indirectly, on the arts of drama, fiction, and even music has been considerable; and every German and student of German and medieval culture has in one way or another been exposed to his wild, often boisterous, and usually refreshing exploits — whose shrewd earthiness has always captured much of the vitality, variety, charm, and ruthlessness of the waning Middle Ages, a period that many people are still taught to regard as an intermission of blank piety in human affairs.

Which leads to three interesting facts. The first is that most Germans and students of German culture, despite what they may think, have never read Eulenspiegel's adventures. The second is that Eulenspiegel has been consistently misrepresented, often in the silliest fashion, in the versions of his tales that have become popular. And the third is that Eulenspiegel's tales have never really been translated into English. These three facts, which need some explanation, are some of the chief reasons for this book, which presents the first translation into English of Grieninger's edition of 1515, the earliest and most important collection of Eulenspiegel's adventures known to us. In the next few paragraphs I wish to outline, primarily for the reader who is unfamiliar with Eulenspiegel and the significance of his history, some perhaps helpful ideas about him: for this is a book whose value lies as much in its rare, detailed pictures of daily life among ordinary people in the late Middle Ages as in its possible artistic and intellectual pleasures.

Now, it will seem perfectly clear to the most casual

xviii

reader of these tales, first, that *A Pleasant Vintage of Till Eulenspiegel* is a very odd little book indeed; and second, that Eulenspiegel is obviously a much more interesting character than most people, who have been taught to think of him as a merely childish hero of children's fables, have generally understood. His popularity and influence alone, which must be regarded as rather unusual in the history of literature, suggest this — and the tales themselves amply confirm it. The book purports to present the whole of Eulenspiegel's life, from his birth to his death, in ninety-six brief chapters (actually, this is a typographical error of Grieninger's: there are only ninety-five). N.'s intentions, as he tells us in his "Foreword," are quite simple: they are to win "favor and esteem" and "to create a happy feeling in hard times, so my readers and listeners may experience good, pleasant entertainment and fun." But a reading of the tales themselves, especially at one sitting, suggests that N., whoever he was, probably had in mind purposes both more profound and more enjoyable than creating merely an entertainment.

For there is, at the outset, the character of Eulenspiegel himself to be considered. "Eulenspiegel" means literally "owl mirror" and, metaphorically, and also more to the point, "wise mirror" or "wise reflection" — and while some scholars have questioned whether he ever understood the meaning of his name, it seems clear that he understood it very well. In Chapter 40 there appears, for example, the following:

> Now, Eulenspiegel had this custom whenever he did some mischief where he was not known: he took chalk or coal and drew an owl and a mirror over the door, and underneath wrote, in Latin, *Hic fuit* [He was here.]

So Eulenspiegel apparently conceived of himself as a "wise" or "sharp" or "crafty" reflection. But of what? Of human absurdity perhaps? In most of his tales, he encounters a middle-class, usually urban employer of some sort: a woolweaver who needs apprentices, a baker who needs a baker's boy, a tanner, a landlord, a tailor, a carpenter, a merchant, a furrier, and so on. Generally, the employer, to whom

Eulenspiegel hires himself out, sometimes for money and sometimes for sheer fun, balloons with pomposity or glitters with cruelty — and Eulenspiegel either deflates him with a trick or dupes him into public embarrassment. Often, too, he exposes the hypocrisy of various priests, doctors, university professors, and politicians. Eulenspiegel has no scruples about lying, posing as somebody he is not, and stealing. Nor does he always do so for moral reasons. In a large number of his adventures he behaves as a sadist, with no moral interest whatever; and the pleasures of these episodes — for there are pleasures here as well — seem to lie in two aspects of his rather unusual psychology: his seemingly infinite ability to get away with whatever he does, and his indifference to conventional middle-class loyalties. For while Eulenspiegel clearly wishes to survive, and is always ready to take any job at all to do so, he never confuses an employer with a divinity and never barters a chance for some fun to win mere public praise. Praise, in fact, interests him as much as love — which is only to say, not at all.

But it is precisely Eulenspiegel's indifference to love and sex that is so surprising. Most of the jest or *Schwank* books of the same late medieval period contain heroes, often similar in type to Eulenspiegel, who have many experiences of both. For example, *The History of Father vom Kalenberg*, one of the jest-cycles that N. seems to have used as a source for a number of the tales that he ascribes to Eulenspiegel, contains not only episodes in which the dishonest priest-hero seduces various women, but also woodcuts showing him in bed with the women he seduces. *A Pleasant Vintage of Till Eulenspiegel* provides nothing comparable — a fact which becomes the more significant once it is noticed that while Eulenspiegel ignores sex and love, he delights in shit. In a great many of his adventures he uses either his own or other people's excrement as a weapon, an instrument of revenge, or a device for embarrassment. In Chapter 24, he wins the title of champion buffoon from the King of Poland by eating his own excrement with a spoon; in Chapter 91, he humiliates a devious priest by forcing him to drench his hands in excrement camouflaged with coins. Of course, the tales of Father vom Kalenberg, as well as *The History of Father Amis,* another nearly contemporary jest-cycle from which N. apparently borrowed some of his stories, also contain incidents in which the hero uses human excrement as a weapon; and readers familiar with earlier medieval tales, such as Chaucer's "Miller's Tale," will be aware that medieval authors entertained none of the prejudices of many modern authors against depicting farts, bowel movements, and human excrement for the sake of comedy and psychological illumination. But the point here is that, unlike these other medieval figures, Eulenspiegel seems to enjoy human excrement to the exclusion of sex and love — and that, as a result, his life seems to reflect a satirically excremental and sardonic vision of mankind. Readers may here be reminded, and appropriately so, of Swift's Gulliver, whose similarly excremental view of human behavior causes him, as writers such as Norman O. Brown have pointed out, to douse a fire in the palace of the Lilliputian Queen by urinating on it and often to use his own excrement as a satirical weapon.

Nor is Eulenspiegel's seriousness as a genuinely adult satirical figure by any means limited to this excremental vision — which ought, incidentally, to be taken as a measure of N.'s originality. The vision is complicated and deepened by Eulenspiegel's obvious fascination with language and by his determination to reveal its ultimate silliness. In more than half of his adventures he makes a point of following his employer's instructions literally — with disastrous results. What usually happens is that the employer, like anybody else, uses figures of speech and slang, rather than logically precise language, when he gives his instructions: he assumes, as do most people in their conversational lives, that he will be understood despite the sloppiness and purely psychological content of his speech. But Eulenspiegel has no patience with sloppiness or psychology: he is bent on taking people at their word, convinced always that they really mean what they say. And people rarely do. Thus, in Chapter 46, he brews a dog named "Hops" in a beermaker's kettle, because he has been told to boil some hops; in Chapter 23, he has his horse shod with gold shoes and silver nails, because the King of Denmark has told him to get his horse the "best" shoes possible; and in Chapter 68, he relieves himself of a great pile of excrement in a bathhouse, because the place had, after all, been advertised as a "House of Cleansing." Such behavior might be considered simply silly or childish if it occurred only once or twice. But a large, grim, and clever satire begins to emerge through its incessant repetition. And one begins to gather as well that Eulenspiegel and N., his creator, are both deeply concerned with showing us the essential clumsiness of the sort of language that we all speak and cannot seem to do without.

It is in this sense that Eulenspiegel and N. may be seen as early linguistic philosophers: indeed, their fascination with the influences of language and grammar on human reality rather closely parallels that of modern linguistic philosophers such as Bertrand Russell and Ludwig Wittgenstein. Two other pertinent facts ought also to be mentioned. The first is that while N. introduces an enormous number of slang phrases and figures of speech into his paragraphs of conversation, he very rarely uses them in his paragraphs of description — something which is not only rather unusual for any writer but also a likely proof that his focus on the unavoidable lies of conversation is deliberate. The second fact is that there is nothing terribly astonishing about N.'s interest in language. German itself was experiencing profound alterations during the early sixteenth century. These changes had indeed begun to make themselves felt, in various ways and at varying rates, in different parts of Germany as early as the thirteenth century; but their sharp acceleration during the late 1400s and early 1500s may be traced to at least three related events: the rapid expansion of the urban middle-class, which in fact peoples N.'s book; the invention and wide application of movable type, which for the first time allowed the middle-class to enjoy printed books and which stimulated a new middle-class literature; and, in 1521, Martin Luther's translation of the *Bible*, which sought not only to make the texts of Christianity available to everybody, but also to standardize the German language and to give it a pungent, clear style. These major changes in morphology, syntax, spelling, pronunciation, and attitudes toward written expression had been occurring more slowly among the German-speaking peoples than among the English or the French, whose languages had earlier experienced similar developments owing to the earlier centralization of government and intellectual life in England and France. It may be suggested, therefore, that N.'s interest in language is simply what we should expect of any literate German of his time. But it must be added that N.'s interest runs far deeper than the usual, and that it is clearly bound up with his passion for discovering what can be honest, real, and true between men and women. Indeed, Eulenspiegel himself, as N. presents him to us, is a character obviously struck by the puzzles of the words "true" and "truth." In a great many of his adventures he remarks that he has either told the truth, or followed his master's instructions truthfully, or simply said what was true — but to no avail. In his world, it seems, truth is as elusive as compassion.

All of this may begin to account for Eulenspiegel's extraordinary popularity. For Eulenspiegel is clearly a far more complicated character than the heroes of other jestbooks, such as Father Amis and Father vom Kalenberg — and while they may present in miniature his excremental vision and his obsession with linguistic clarity, they do not develop and elaborate these themes, as does Eulenspiegel, into a grand mockery of the human experience. And indeed, it is man as a comical and foolish creature, rather than simply a corrupt society, that N. and Eulenspiegel want finally to reveal to us. For Eulenspiegel's is a book that belongs to what might be called the literature of middle-class escape, in which the hero, or anti-hero, succeeds in triumphing over the dull repetitiousness of much middle-class life, while implicitly acknowledging the futility of having been born a man in a universe that insists on cruelty, injustice, and death. At a later date, Marlowe's Faustus, Shakespeare's Falstaff, and Mark Twain's Huckleberry Finn, who may be considered aesthetic though not direct descendants of Till Eulenspiegel, represent similar quests for escape, in drama and the novel. And in fact most countries, at one time or another, no doubt give birth to their Eulenspiegels — their mythical buffoons (however much they may have their inception in actual history) who manage through inpertinence, cunning, and laughter to turn reality upside down for a while.

Unfortunately, the prudishness of generations of translators and adaptors has so far kept Eulenspiegel's full satirical complexity all but hidden. Only rarely — and never into English — have all of his tales been translated together. Rarer still — and never into English — has their translation been from Grieninger's first edition, the book now before us. In most cases, translators and adaptors have worked from editions published years later — editions that progressively toned down or eliminated Eulenspiegel's scatology and presented him as a merely childish character. An exception was Ben Jonson, who certainly knew of Eulenspiegel, probably read his adventures, and even mentioned an "Howleglass" in his *Masque of the Fortunate Isles* (1626). More typical, though, has been the treatment accorded Eulenspiegel by Charles Theodore Henry de Coster, whose *Ulenspiegel* (Brussels, 1867) transforms N.'s work into a collection of Victorian moral fables and Eulenspiegel himself into a sentimental clown. Ironically, it is de Coster's view of Eulenspiegel that has become the popular one, persisting to this day among many Germans and almost everyone else who has heard of him. Again, a notable and modern reflection of Eulenspiegel's true spirit appears not in literature at all, but in music. Richard Strauss' celebrated tone-poem *Till Eulenspiegel's Merry Pranks* embodies perfectly Eulenspiegel's foolishness, seriousness, courage, and scorn.

Strauss' choice of the rondo form for his composition is, moreover, entirely right for N.'s essentially picaresque seminovel, which contains many minor climaxes and many unconnected episodes, but no main climax and no main plot. The abrupt twists and turns of the music also echo well N.'s style, with its mixture of informality, roughness, slang, lightness, and, here and there, formal speech. I have attempted to capture this style, which often lacks polish and grace, in my translation — while also striving both to make the English as modern as possible and to preserve something of the sixteenth-century flavor of N.'s Middle High German dialect. For while Eulenspiegel is in spirit and outlook as modern a figure as many heroes and heroines of many twentieth-century comic novels — as daring, perverse, egotistical, impudent, absurd, and delightfully irresponsible as many of them — he is also very much a creature of his own age, and interesting precisely because of this. Small attention indeed has been paid even by scholars to the possible importance of folk-books such as Eulenspiegel's to the history of ideas and to our knowledge of how men actually lived in the Europe of five-hundred years ago. N., through his wild and crafty anti-hero, has opened a window on that world — a world which, as can be seen in many of Eulenspiegel's adventures, was making the awkward, painful transition from an agricultural to an urban economy, and from medieval convictions that the universe must be harmonious to more modern suspicions that it might be ultimately chaotic.

A Pleasant Vintage of Till Eulenspiegel

Foreword

Fifteen hundred years after Christ's birth, as one reckons, I, N., have been asked by various persons to bring together (for their sake) these accounts and tales and to describe how in times past a clever, sly and roguish son of a farmer was born in the Duchy of Brunswick and named Till Eulenspiegel — what he thought up and did in foreign and German countries.

For this (my trouble and work) they were willing to pay me favor and esteem. I answered that I would be willing to do this, and more, but did not know how to finish something like it with intelligence and understanding. So I made many excuses to them, with a friendly request to release me from writing about Eulenspiegel (the things he did in various states, which might have annoyed them) but they had no intention of accepting my answer. So according to my small understanding, I have committed myself and taken it on, with God's help (without which nothing may be done); have begun with diligence; and would like to beg everyone's pardon, so my narration may put no one in a bad mood or embarrass anyone: that would be far from my desire.

My only ambition is to create a happy feeling in hard times, so my readers and listeners may experience good, pleasant entertainment and fun. Also there is in this my plain writing no art or elegance, because I am, I am sorry to say, unacquainted with Latin writing and am a simple layman. My writing will best merit reading (providing that of the Lord's service not be hindered by it) as the mice bite under the benches, and the hours grow short, and the baked pear tastes good with the new wine.

And so I ask everybody: where my writing about Eulenspiegel seems either too long or too short, that he improve it, so I do not earn ingratitude.

And so my foreword ends. I now present the beginning, Till Eulenspiegel's birth, with the addition of various fables of Father Amis and Father vom Kalenberg.

3

1. How Till Eulenspiegel was born, how he was baptized three times in one day, and who his godfathers were.

Eulenspiegel was born near a forest called the Elm,[1] in the district of Saxony, in the village of Kneitlingen;[2] and his father was named Claus Eulenspiegel and his mother Anna Wibeken. Well, when she had recovered from the birth of the child, they sent it to Ambleben, to the village, for baptism, and had it named Till Eulenspiegel — with "Till" from the citizen of Ambleben who became his godfather. Now, Ambleben is the castle that was destroyed as a wicked thieves' castle by Magdeburg, with the help of other states, somewhat more than fifty years ago.[3] The church and the village nearby were now in charge of the worthy Abbot Arnolf Pfaffenmeier of Sunt.[4]

---

1. J. M. Lappenberg, whose *Dr. Thomas Murners Ulenspiegel* (Lepizig, 1854) is the first and finest critical edition of Grieninger's text of 1519 (Lappenberg was unaware of the existence of Grieninger's

what sort of rare trick he would demonstrate or what sort of marvelous sport he would carry out.

Well, when Eulenspiegel was sitting on the rope and his performance was at its best — for his mother was indoors and could not do much about it — she crept up secretly anyhow, back in the house, to the lattice-work to which the rope was tied, and sliced the rope in two, so Eulenspiegel, her son, fell into the river, amid huge ridicule, and took quite a bath in the Saale. The farmers now roared with laughter, and the young boys called after him "Heh-heh, have a good bath," and so on. "You've been asking for a bath for a long time."

This greatly annoyed Eulenspiegel, and he paid no attention to the water, but to the mocking and screaming of the boys — and thought how he might get even with them and pay them back for this. Meanwhile, he washed himself off as well as he could.

A short time after this, Eulenspiegel decided to avenge the hurt and mockery he had at his ducking. He stretched the rope out from another house, over the Saale, and let the people know he planned to walk the rope. The crowd, young and old, soon assembled for it.

Eulenspiegel now told the boys that each one should give him his left shoe: he planned to show them a fine performance on the rope with their shoes. The boys believed this, thinking it all true. The old men did too.

So the boys began to take off their shoes and give them to Eulenspiegel. Well, from the boys there were almost two equal piles; that is, twice sixty: half of the shoes were for him. So he tied them onto a string and climbed onto the rope with it. When he was on the rope, and had the shoes with him on it, the old men and boys looked up to him, for they thought he intended to do some exceptional thing on it; but the boys became a little anxious, since they wanted to have their shoes back again.

Well, Eulenspiegel sat on his rope, making his preparations. He then called down from the rope, "Everybody watch out, and everybody look for his own shoe again." Then he sliced the string in two and threw all the shoes from the rope to the ground, with one shoe tumbling over the other. The boys and old men at once rushed to them. Well, one pointed out his shoe here, the other there. And one said, "This shoe is mine." The other said, "You're lying. It's mine." So they grabbed one another by the hair and began to beat one another. One lay underneath, another on top; one screamed, the other wept, the third laughed. And this lasted till the old men took part in the face-slapping too, and pulled one another's hair.

Well, Eulenspiegel was sitting on the rope, laughing and calling, "Heh-heh! Now look for your shoes, as I had to finish my bathing yesterday." Then he ran off the rope and left the boys and old men to themselves.

After that — because of the shoes — he dared not come near those boys or the old men, but sat in the house with his mother and mended Helmstädt shoes. His mother now became quite happy, and thought he might still turn out all right. But she did not know that he had now made even more of a rogue of himself — so he dared not come out of the house, and so on.

5. How Eulenspiegel's mother tried to persuade him to learn a trade—with which she intended to help him.

Well, Eulenspiegel's mother was happy that her son was so quiet. But she reproved him for not wishing to learn any trade. He kept silent, though, so his mother continued to admonish him.

Eulenspiegel then said, "Dear Mother, anything a man takes up will provide for him all his life."

And his mother said, "I certainly have my doubts about that. — I've had no bread in my house for two weeks."

Eulenspiegel said, "That has nothing to do with my statement. But a poor person who has nothing to eat should fast well for Saint Nicholas, and if *he* has something, then he'll eat by Saint Martin's Eve.[1] And that's the way we're going to eat too."

---

1. Pope Nicholas I died on November 13, 867; the saint's day of Pope Martin falls on November 12. Pope Nicholas (not to be confused

12

with Nicholas, the patron-saint of scholars, who was Bishop of Myra in Lycia and who died in 326) was devoted to fasting. Pope Martin was known for his philanthropy — this extending even to his dividing his coat among the poor. Eulenspiegel's idea, therefore, is that one should fast with the fasting and eat with the generous. See Lappenberg, p. 230.

6. How Eulenspiegel cheated a baker out of a sack of bread at Stassfurt, in the city, and brought it home to his mother.

"Dear God, help!" thought Eulenspiegel. "How'll I keep my mother quiet? Where'll I find bread for her house?"

So he went out of the village where his mother lived, toward Stassfurt, to the city. There he noticed a rich baker's establishment, went into the baker's house, and asked whether he would send his master ten shillings' worth of rye and white bread. Then he named the Lord of someplace, and said, moreover, that his master was at Stassfurt, in the same city, and named an inn at which he was staying. The baker was supposed to send a boy with him to the inn, where he would give him the money.

The baker said, "Yes."

Now, Eulenspiegel had a sack which had a hidden hole, and he let him count the bread into the sack. Then the baker sent a boy with Eulenspiegel to pick up the money. But when

Eulenspiegel had gone a crossbow's shot from the baker's house, he let one white loaf drop out of the open hole into the mud. Eulenspiegel then set down his sack and said to the boy, "Oh, I couldn't bring this dirty bread to my master. Quick — run home with it and bring me another loaf. I'll wait for you here."

The boy ran off and got another loaf — while Eulenspiegel left and went to the outer city, to a house. A cart from his village was there, on which he laid his sack. Well, he walked beside it and was led to his mother's house.

Well, when the baker's boy returned, Eulenspiegel was gone with the bread, so the boy ran back to tell the baker. The baker was soon at the inn Eulenspiegel had named to him. There he found no one and realized he had been tricked.

Eulenspiegel arrived home, brought the bread to his mother, and said, "Look here. Now, eat these while you've got something — and fast with Saint Nicholas when you haven't."

7. How Eulenspiegel ate the breakfast bread, or rolls, with other boys; and how he had to overeat, and was beaten into doing so.

Now, there was a custom in the village in which Eulenspiegel lived with his mother: whenever a householder slaughtered a pig, the children of his neighbors went to his house, and there ate a soup or broth called the breakfast bread.[1]

A farmer lived in that district, in the same village, who was very stingy with his food and who still dared not refuse the children their breakfast bread. So he thought up a scheme to make them sick of breakfast bread — and sliced the fatty rind of the bread into a milk-jug.[2]

---

1. The term *weckbrot*, literally "waking bread," refers here, as can be seen, not to bread at all, but to the breakfast itself, which in this case consisted of a soup. The modern German *Abendbrot*, literally "evening bread," but actually "supper," is comparable.

2. It is not at all clear that either Grieninger or N. knew what was going on at this point. Obviously bread has no "fatty rind;" then too, as has just been pointed out in n. 1, it is not bread that is being discussed. A plausible guess is that the malicious householder sliced

When the children arrived, boys and girls with Eulenspiegel along as well, he let them in and closed the door. Then he poured out the soup, or breakfast bread. Now, there were far more of these pulpy pieces than the children wanted to finish eating. But if one walked away from it and was full, the householder came along with a whip and beat him about the thighs — so everybody had to overeat. This householder was also well aware of Eulenspiegel's trickiness, so he watched him. Whenever he beat one of the others about the thighs, he beat Eulenspiegel even harder. He continued this till they had been forced to eat all the pulpy pieces and breakfast bread.

Now, this pleased them as well as grass might a dog; so afterwards no one had any desire to go to that stingy man's house to eat breakfast bread or butcher's soup any more.

---

some of the fat of his pig into the milk-jug. The taste would certainly have been awful enough to account for the children's reaction.

8. How Eulenspiegel caused the stingy householder's chickens to play tug-of-war over bait.

The next day, when the man was going out, Eulenspiegel met him.

He asked, "Dear Eulenspiegel, when would you like to come over for breakfast bread?"

And Eulenspiegel said, "When your chickens play tug-of-war over bait — four to a bit of bread."

And he said, "Well, that way you'll be a long time coming."

And Eulenspiegel said, "But what if I come before it's fatty-soup-time again?" And with that he walked away by himself.

Now, Eulenspiegel watched till he got his chance and the man's chickens went feeding along the lane. Eulenspiegel had twenty or more strings with him, and had tied each, two and two, in the middle. He fastened a bit of bread onto the end of each one, took the strings, and laid them

18

down concealed, with the bits of bread in the open. Well, the chickens pecked here and there, and gulped down the bits of bread, with the ends of the strings in their throats. They could not swallow them, though, for another chicken was pulling at the other end. So each one held back the other and could neither swallow it nor get it out of his throat, because of the size of those pieces of bread. And so more than two hundred chickens stood there, each one choking opposite the other, and playing tug-of-war over bait.

9. How Eulenspiegel crawled into a beehive; how two men came by night, intending to steal it; and how he made them tear each other's hair and let the beehive drop.

It happened that Eulenspiegel once went with his mother to the dedication of a church in a village. Well, Eulenspiegel drank till he became drunk, so he went off to look for a place to sleep pleasantly and also have no one do anything to him.

Now, he found a pile of honey standing behind the place in the courtyard, and nearby were lying many beehives that were empty. So he crawled into an empty hive that was next to the honey, thinking he would sleep a little. But he slept from noon right through to midnight. Well, his mother thought he had gone home, because she could not see him anywhere.

Now, during that same night two thieves came, intending to steal a beehive, and talked there together: "I've always heard the beehive which is heaviest is best." So they lifted the baskets and hives, one after the other, and came to the hive in which Eulenspiegel lay (that was heaviest), and said, "This is the best beehive." So they took it up on their necks and carried it off.

Meanwhile, Eulenspiegel awoke and heard their intentions. Well, it was quite dark, so one man could barely see the other, and Eulenspiegel reached out of the hive and grabbed the first man by the hair, giving him a good pull. At this he became angry with the man behind him, thinking he had pulled him by the hair, and began to curse him. The man behind him said, "You've been dreaming or falling asleep. How could I grab you by the hair? I can hardly hold the beehive with my hands."

Eulenspiegel laughed and thought, "This game'll turn out all right." And he waited until they had gone the length of a field. Then he gave the man behind a good pull of the hair also, so he cringed. He now got just as angry, and said, "I've been walking and carrying enough to break my neck, and you're saying that I'm grabbing you by the hair. But you're grabbing me by the hair enough to tear my scalp."

The first man said, "You're lying in your throat. How could I grab you by the hair? I can hardly see the road before me. Also, I know you just grabbed me by the hair."

They walked on with the beehive this way, roaring as if they were going to fight with each other. Not long afterwards, when their quarreling was most violent, Eulenspiegel pulled the first man again, causing his head to bang back against the beehive. He now got so angry that he let the beehive fall and hit the man in the darkness behind him — in the head with his fists. The man behind him also let go of the beehive, plunged into the hair of the man ahead of him, and they tumbled over one another. Well, the one lost the other — not knowing where he was — and they lost themselves in the darkness, leaving the beehive lying there.

Well, Eulenspiegel looked out of the basket. Then, when he saw it was still dark, he slept again, and stayed lying in there till it became bright day. He then crawled out of the beehive but did not know where he was. So he followed a road till he came to a palace. There he hired himself out as a page-boy.

10. How Eulenspiegel became a page-boy; and how his squire taught him that whenever he found the plant hemp, he should shit on it; so he shat on mustard, and thought hemp and mustard were the same thing.

Soon afterwards Eulenspiegel approached a country squire at a castle and pretended he was a page-boy. Well, presently he had to ride over open country with his squire. Now, along the paths stood hemp, which is called, in the area of Saxony in which Eulenspiegel was at the time, 'henep.'

So his squire said, as Eulenspiegel was leading his horse for him, "Do you see that plant standing there? That's called 'henep.'"

Eulenspiegel said, "I see it all right."

So his squire said, "Wherever you find it, shit on it. For with that plant we bind and hang robbers and those who, without serving a Lord, support themselves from the saddle — with the fiber that's spun from those plants."

22

Eulenspiegel said, "Sure, that's a good thing to do."

The courtier or squire rode here and there with Eulenspiegel, into many cities, and helped to rob, steal, and take, as was his custom. But one day it happened that they were at home and at rest. Well, when it was getting toward mealtime, Eulenspiegel went into the kitchen. There the cook said to the boy, "Go down to the cellar. An earthen jug or pot is standing there, with senep (as in the Saxon speech) in it. Bring that up to me."

Eulenspiegel said, "Yes," but had never in his life seen any senep — or mustard. So when he found the jug with the mustard in the cellar, he thought to himself, "What's the cook want with this? I imagine he wants to tie me up with it." Then he thought further, "My squire's told me that whenever I find a plant like this I ought to shit on it." So he crouched over the jug, filled it up, and brought it to the cook.

What happened? The cook suspected nothing, quickly prepared the mustard in the little dish, and sent it to the table. The squire and his guest dipped into the mustard — and it had a rather awful taste. The cook was sent for and asked what sort of mustard he had made. The cook tasted the mustard too, spat it out and said, "This mustard tastes as if it had been shat on."

Eulenspiegel now began to laugh. So his squire said, "Why're you laughing so shamelessly? Do you think we can't taste what it is? If you don't believe it, come and taste this mustard too."

Eulenspiegel said, "I'm not going to eat it. Don't you know what you told me in open country on the road? — If I should see that plant, I should shit on it? One takes care of robbers with it, by hanging and throttling? Well, when the cook sent me to the cellar for the senep, I obeyed your command."

The squire at once said, "You worthless scoundrel, this is the end of you! The plant I showed you is called henep or hemp — and the one the cook asked to be brought is called senep or mustard.[1] You did this from sheer mischief!"

---

1. There appears to be an error in Grieninger's text at this point. He repeats "senep" and "senff" in place of "henep" and "haff," when he must clearly want the latter words. I have made the necessary changes.

And he took up a club and tried to beat him. But Eulen-spiegel was clever: he ran out of the castle and did not come back.

11. How Eulenspiegel hired himself out to a priest; and how he ate his roast chickens from the spit.

In the district of Brunswick lies a village, in the Bishopric of Magdeburg, called Buddenstedt.[1] Eulenspiegel arrived at the priest's house there. The priest hired him as a servant. But he did not know him. So he told him he would have happy days and pleasant service with him, eating and drinking the best — as well as his maid — and all he would be asked to do he could do with half-time labor.

Eulenspiegel said "Yes" to this (he intended to stick closely to it); then he saw that the priest's maid had only one eye.

Well, the priest's maid presently took up two chickens and stuck them on the spit to roast. She told Eulenspiegel to sit down and roast them. Eulenspiegel was agreeable and turned the chickens over. But when they were almost

---

1. This is in Brunswick, between Schöningen and Helmstädt.

roasted, he thought, "The priest definitely said, when he hired me, that I'd eat and drink as well as he and his maid — and that appears to be nonsense as far as these chickens are concerned. In that case the priest's words won't be true, and I won't eat any of these chickens. I ought to be clever enough to make him keep his word." So he broke one from the spit and ate it without bread.

Well, when it was nearing mealtime, the priest's maid (who was one-eyed) came to the fire, planning to baste the chickens. But she saw just one chicken on the spit, and said to Eulenspiegel, "Well, there were two chickens. Where's the one chicken gone?"

Eulenspiegel said, "Woman, open your other eye too — then you'll see both chickens."

Now, when he mocked the woman that way for her one eye, she became very angry and furious with Eulenspiegel. She ran to the priest and told him how his splendid servant had made fun of her for her one eye, how she had put two chickens on the spit, and how when she looked in on him to see how he was roasting them, she had found just one chicken.

The priest went to the fire in the kitchen and said to Eulenspiegel, "Why're you making fun of my maid? Besides, I see very well that there's just one chicken stuck on the spit, and there were definitely two of them."

Eulenspiegel said, "Yes, there were definitely two of them."

The priest said, "Well, where's the other chicken?"

Eulenspiegel said, "It's stuck there all right. Open both your eyes and you'll see perfectly that one chicken's stuck on that spit. I said so to your maid, but she got angry."

Well, the priest began to laugh, and he said, "My maid can't open both eyes: she's got just one."

Eulenspiegel said, "You're saying that; I'm not saying it."

The priest said, "It's all over. But it remains a fact that one chicken's gone."

Eulenspiegel said, "Yes, one's gone and the other's still stuck there. I've eaten the other, since you promised earlier I was supposed to eat and drink as well as you and your maid.

Well, it made me unhappy that you might be thought to have lied — that you might be thought to have eaten both chickens so there'd have been none of it for me. So you'd not be a liar in what you said, I ate one chicken."

Well, the priest was satisfied with that, and said, "My dear servant, that's one roast I didn't get. But from now on, act according to the wishes of my maid, as she sees fit."

Eulenspiegel said, "Yes, dear Father, just as you've told me."

So after that, whatever the maid told Eulenspiegel to do, he half-did. If he were to fetch a bucketful of water, he brought one half-full; and if he were to fetch two logs for the fire, he brought one. Were he to give the bull two bundles of hay, he gave him just one — and so on in many things, till she noticed that he was doing this to irritate her. She decided to say nothing to him, however, and complained about him to the priest.

So the priest told Eulenspiegel, "Dear servant, my maid's complaining about you. Now, I've clearly ordered you to do everything she wants."

Eulenspiegel said, "Yes, sir. I've also not done anything other than you've told me to. You told me I could do your business with half-time work, but your maid ought to see well with both eyes. She sees, though, with only one eye, and sees only half: therefore, I did half-work."

Well, the priest began to laugh. But his maid became angry, and said, "Father, if you plan to keep this fool and rogue as a servant any longer" — she intended to leave him. So the priest, against his will, had to give Eulenspiegel his notice. But he helped the farmers in choir-singing, since the sexton or sacristan of the same village had recently died. Then afterwards, because the farmers could not do without a sexton, the priest came to an agreement with the farmers to take on Eulenspiegel.

12. How Eulenspiegel became a sexton in a village, at Buddenstedt; and how the priest shat in his church, so Eulenspiegel won a barrel of beer.

When Eulenspiegel became a sexton in the village, he could sing out, as was fitting for a sacristan. Well, the priest was now furnished with a sacristan.

Once the priest was standing before the altar, dressing himself and preparing to hold mass. Eulenspiegel was standing behind him and was arranging the priest's vestment properly. The priest now loosed so huge a fart that it resounded through the church.

Eulenspiegel then said, "Sir, what's this? Do you serve Our Lord with this sort of incense smoke here before His altar?"

The priest said, "What're you talking about? This church is mine all right. I've even got the right to shit in the middle of this church."

Eulenspiegel said, "It'll cost either you or me a barrel of beer if you do it."

"All right," he said. "It's a bet."

So they bet with one another. The priest then said, "You think I'm not brave enough?" And he turned around and shat a great pile in the church. Then he said, "Look, my dear sacristan, I've won the barrel of beer."

Eulenspiegel said, "No, Father. First we've got to measure whether it's in the middle of the church, as we said before."

Well, Eulenspiegel measured it, and it was far from being in the middle of the church. So Eulenspiegel won the barrel of beer.

But the maid became angry, and said, "You won't let that cunning servant go till he brings you into utter disgrace."

13. How Eulenspiegel played a trick during Easter matins that caused the priest and his maid to tear the hair of and battle with their farmers.

When it was getting close to Easter, the priest said to Eulenspiegel his sacristan, "It's a custom here that at Easter, during the night, the farmers always hold an Easter play: 'How Our Lord Rises From His Tomb.'" Well, he had to help with it, because it was only right for the sacristan to arrange and direct it.

Eulenspiegel thought, "How can the play of the Marys possibly take place with these farmers?" So he told the priest, "Now, there's certainly no farmer here who's educated; so you'll have to lend me your maid for this. She can read and write well."

The priest said, "Yes, yes. Just take whoever can help you with it. Besides, my maid's been in many of these."

His maid was delighted, and she wanted to be the angel in the tomb because she knew the lines by heart. Eulenspiegel then looked for two farmers, and got them, too. Now, he wanted the three of them to be the three Marys, so Eulenspiegel taught one farmer his lines in Latin. Well, the priest was Our Lord God, Who was supposed to rise from the tomb.

Eulenspiegel now approached the tomb with his farmers dressed as the three Marys. At this point, the maid, as the angel in the tomb, spoke her lines in Latin, *"Quem queritis?"* — "Whom seek ye here?"[1]

And the farmer who was the first Mary replied as Eulenspiegel had taught him: "We're looking for a priest's old, one-eyed whore."

When she heard this — that she was being laughed at for her single eye — she became furious with Eulenspiegel, sprang out of the tomb, and tried to attack him in the face with her fists. But she struck carelessly here, hitting one of the farmers, so one of his eyes swelled up. When the other farmer saw this, he lunged out also, hitting the maid on the head as well, so her wings fell off. When the priest saw this, he let his van fall, came to help his maid, grabbed the hair of one of the farmers, and they pulled one another in front of the tomb. When the other farmers saw this, they ran forward and there was a tremendous uproar. Well, the priest was lying at the bottom with his maid; and the two farmers (the two Marys) were also lying underneath — so the farmers had to pull them apart from one another.

But Eulenspiegel had taken note of these events and gotten himself out of there in time. He ran out of the church, walked out of the village, and did not come back.

God knows where they found another sacristan.

---

1. Grieninger spells *quaeritis* as above.

14. How Eulenspiegel announced that he intended to fly from the roof at Magdeburg, and dismissed his onlookers with abusive language.

Soon after the time when Eulenspiegel was a sacristan he arrived in Magdeburg and did lots of clever things. Well, his name became known there for the first time, so people knew Eulenspiegel as a name to speak of.

He was now challenged by the best citizens of the city to provide some trick. He said he was willing to do so — and that he intended to go up on the town hall and fly off the roof. There now arose such a clamor in the city that young and old gathered at the market-place, intending to watch this.

Well, Eulenspiegel stood on the roof of the town hall, flapping his arms, and acting as if he really planned to fly. The people stood there, opening their eyes and mouths and thinking he was really going to fly. Eulenspiegel then laughed and said, "I thought there was no greater fool or buffoon in the world than I. But I see very well that this whole city's utterly full of fools. Now, if you'd all told me that you intended to fly, I wouldn't have believed it — and you think I'm a fool. How am I supposed to fly? I'm still neither goose nor bird; after all, I've got no feathers, and without feathers or plumes nobody can fly. So you see very well it's all been a lie."

Then he turned, ran off the roof, and left the crowd, one part cursing, the other part laughing and saying, "There goes a charlatan; but still he spoke the truth."

15. How Eulenspiegel pretended to be a doctor, and doctored the doctor of the Bishop of Magdeburg, who was tricked by him.

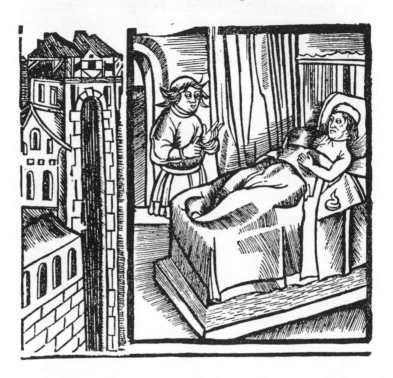

At Magdeburg was a Bishop called Bruno,[1] a Count of Quer-furt, who heard about Eulenspiegel's pranks and had him summoned to Greuenstein. Well, the Bishop liked Eulenspiegel's tricks and gave him clothes and money; and his servants liked him very much and had a lot of fun with him.

Now, the Bishop had a doctor[2] staying with him who thought himself very learned and wise — with the result that the Bishop's royal household disliked him. Well, this doctor's attitude was that he did not enjoy having fools around him.

---

1. N. probably has in mind here Burchard III, Archbishop of Magdeburg from 1307 to 1325. See Lappenberg, pp. 235–237.

2. While Eulenspiegel plays the part of a doctor of medicine in this tale, the Bishop's "doctor" is probably a learned man who had received a degree of some sort. He is in any case no physician.

And the doctor told the Bishop and his advisors, "One ought to keep wise people among the Lords of courts, and not retain such clowns, for various reasons."

The knights and the royal household agreed on this much: that this was not a fair opinion of the doctor's. If somebody did not enjoy foolishness, he could easily leave; nobody had to participate.

The doctor argued against this. "Fools for fools, and wise men for wise men. If Princes had wise people with them, wisdom would lie before them; but because they have fools with them, they learn foolishness."

Some then said, "Who are the wise? — Those who claim they are wise? One can easily come across people like that — who have been duped by fools. It's very good for Lords and Princes to keep all sorts of people at their courts. For with fools they drive away many brooding thoughts; and where Lords are, there fools like to be." So the people of the court approached Eulenspiegel, arranged certain schemes with him, and asked him to think up an idea (they wanted to help him with it, and the Bishop did too) so the doctor might be repaid for his "wisdom" — for he had heard it also.

Eulenspiegel said, "Of course, you Lords and Princes: if you'd like to help me, this doctor shall be taught a lesson."

They agreed on it. Well, Eulenspiegel traveled over open country for four weeks, considering how he might handle the doctor; and once he had thought the thing through, he returned to Greuenstein and disguised himself, pretending he was a doctor, because the Bishop's doctor was often physically ill and took a lot of medicine for it. The knights now informed the doctor that a physician of medicine had arrived.

The doctor did not recognize Eulenspiegel, went to visit him at his inn, and after some conversation, took him along with him to the palace. Well, they reached an understanding with each other; and the doctor said to his physician, if he could help him with his sickness, he would reward him well. Eulenspiegel replied with such words as doctors then used, and deceived him into spending one night at his house so he might better observe his constitution: "For I very much want to give you something before you go to sleep, to make you sweat." Well, through the sweat he intended to discover what his infirmity was.

The doctor allowed all this to be said to him, thought it all true, and climbed into bed with Eulenspiegel. For he thought nothing other than what Eulenspiegel told him must be true. Well, Eulenspiegel gave the doctor a strong laxative, and the doctor thought he was supposed to sweat from this, not knowing it was a strong laxative.

Eulenspiegel found a hollowed-out stone, deposited a pile of his shit in it, and placed the hollowed-out stone, with the filth, on the bed between the wall and the doctor. And the doctor lay closest to the wall, with Eulenspiegel lying forward on the bed. Well, the doctor lay there, and turned toward the wall. Then the filth which was lying in the hollowed-out stone, stank right under his eyes, so he had to turn back toward Eulenspiegel. But as soon as the doctor turned toward Eulenspiegel, Eulenspiegel released a quiet fart, so he stank horribly. The doctor then turned back again; but now the filth in the hollowed-out stone attacked the doctor again, stinkingly. He kept this up with the doctor for almost half the night.

Well, at that point the laxative began to work, and acted sharply, quickly and powerfully — causing the doctor to make himself utterly unclean and to stink most terribly. Eulenspiegel now said to the doctor, "What's this, worthy Doctor? Your sweat's been stinking terribly for a long time. What's wrong with you that you sweat such a sweat? It stinks quite foully."

The doctor lay there and thought, "I smell it all right." And indeed he was so full of the smell that he could barely speak.

Eulenspiegel said, "Just lie still. I want to go to get a light, so I can see how bad your condition may be." As Eulenspiegel was pulling himself up, he let still another weighty shit fall, and said, "Ah, such pain! I, too, am getting weak. I've gotten this from your sickness."

The doctor lay there, and was so sick he could barely raise his head; but he thanked God his physician had left him, so he might get a bit of air. For whenever the doctor had tried to get up during the night, Eulenspiegel had told him he must not get up, saying he must first sweat enough.

Eulenspiegel now really got up, left the room, and ran away. Meanwhile, daylight arrived. The doctor now saw the hollowed-out stone, with the filth, standing beside the wall, and was so sick that his face was soiled with stink.

Well, the knights and people of the court looked in on the doctor and wished him a good morning. The doctor spoke feebly, could not answer well, and lay in his room on a bench, on a pillow. So the court people got the Bishop over to the room, and he asked him how things had gone with his physician.

The doctor said, "I've been hounded by a knave! I assumed he was a doctor of medicine, but he's really a doctor of knavery!" And he told them exactly what had happened to him.

Well, the Bishop and all the people of the court began to laugh, and they said, "This happened exactly according to your own words. For you said, 'One should not bother with fools, for the wise man becomes foolish among fools.' But you'll see that one man will be made wise through fools: for your physician was Eulenspiegel. You didn't recognize him, and you believed him. You were tricked by him. But we, who tolerated his foolishness, knew him well. However, we didn't want to warn you — since and because you wanted to appear so wise. Ah, nobody's wise enough to recognize fools too. And if there were no fools — how would the wise be recognized?"

Well, the doctor was silent and complained no more.

16. How Eulenspiegel made a sick child shit at Peine—and earned great thanks.

One sometimes shies away from true, proven doctors because they want a small sum of money; but one must often give just as much to tramps.

So it happened once in the Bishopric of Hildesheim. Eulenspiegel arrived there once as well, and went to an inn where the innkeeper was not at home. Now, Eulenspiegel was well known around there. Well, the innkeeper's wife had a sick child, so Eulenspiegel asked the innkeeper's wife what was wrong with her child and what illness it had.

Well, the innkeeper's wife said, "The child can't go to its stool. If only it could go to its stool, things would be better for him."

Eulenspiegel said, "There's good advice to follow for that."

The woman said that if he helped him, she would give him whatever he wanted.

Eulenspiegel said he would take nothing for this: for him this was an easy art. "Wait a little while. It'll soon happen."

38

hundred guilders and promise them to him. The director of the hospital promised him the money, providing he helped his patients. So Eulenspiegel swore that if he could not make these sick people healthy, he need not give him a single penny. This pleased the director so well that he immediately gave him twenty guilders.

Well, Eulenspiegel went into the hospital, taking two assistants with him, and asked the patients, each one separately, what was wrong with them. Finally, as he was leaving each patient, he made him swear an oath and said, "What I now reveal to you, you must keep secret and reveal to no one." The sick people, with a great oath, assured Eulenspiegel of this. Then he told each one in private, "If I'm to help you back to health and get you on your feet — that won't be possible unless I burn one of you to a powder and give that to the others to drink down. That I'll have to do. Therefore, whoever is sickest among you all and cannot walk — I'll burn him to the powder, so I can help the others with him. To get you all up, I'll take the director of the hospital and stand at the door of the hospital and shout in a loud voice, 'Whoever isn't sick in there — let him come out here.' — Don't go to sleep when I do!"

He told this to each one individually — that the last one out would have to pay the reckoning. Everyone listened carefully to these little speeches; and on the appointed day they rushed forward, with their sick and lame legs, for no one wanted to be last. When Eulenspiegel called out to them, according to his promise, they began to charge out of the place, some who had not been out of their beds in ten years. And since the hospital was quickly vacant, he demanded his payment from the director, telling him he had to hurry off to another town. The director gave him his money, with great thanks, and he rode away.

But in three days the sick people returned, groaning with their illnesses. So the director of the hospital asked them, "What's this? I brought you the greatest master physician, who helped all of you enough to walk out of here by yourselves."

They now told the director that Eulenspiegel had

warned them that whoever was last through the door when he called "time" he planned to burn to a powder. Well, the director of the hospital realized he had been tricked by Eulenspiegel, but he was gone. And he could do nothing to him. So the sick people stayed on at the hospital again, and that money was lost.

18. How Eulenspiegel bought bread because of the proverb "One gives bread to him who has it."

Honesty provides bread.

After Eulenspiegel had tricked the doctor, he arrived in "Half-City"[1] and walked around the market-place. Now, when he saw it was hard winter, he thought, "The winter is hard and the wind blows bitterly as well. You've often heard 'One gives bread to him who has it.'" So he bought bread for two shillings, took a table, and went to stand in front of the Cathedral of Saint Stephan to offer his bread for sale. Well, he sustained this foolish illusion until a dog came and took a loaf from the table and ran into the courtyard with it. Eulenspiegel ran after the dog.

Meanwhile, a sow with ten young piglets arrived and knocked over the table. Well, each of them took a loaf in its mouth and ran off with it. Eulenspiegel then began to laugh and said, "Now I see clearly that those words people say are

---

1. Halberstädt.

43

false: 'One gives bread to him who has it.' For it's been taken from me." And he went on, "Oh, Half-City, Half-City, the name of you then! Your beer and food taste good enough, but your penny-purses are made of pigskin."

So he want off toward Brunswick again.

19. How Eulenspiegel hired himself out as a baker's boy to a baker—and how he baked owls and long-tailed monkeys.

When Eulenspiegel returned to Brunswick, to the baker's establishment, there was a baker[1] living nearby who called him into his house and asked him what sort of journeyman he was. He said, "I'm a baker's boy."

The baker said, "I've got no boy at present. Would you like to work for me?"

Eulenspiegel said, "Yes."

When he had been with him two days, the baker told him to bake during the evening because he could not help him till morning. Eulenspiegel said, "Yes, but what'll I bake?"

The baker was a playful man, but he grew annoyed and said to him jokingly, "You're a baker's boy and you ask what you're supposed to bake? What does one usually bake? —

---

1. Grieninger has "weaver" here – by mistake, I should guess.

Owls and long-tailed monkeys!" And with that he went off to sleep.

So Eulenspiegel went into the bakery and made of the dough nothing but owls and long-tailed monkeys, till the bakery was full of them, and baked them.

His master arose the next morning, intending to help him. But when he came into the baking room, he found, instead of either breakfast bread or wheat bread, only owls and long-tailed monkeys. Then his master began to get angry and said, "Ah! What've you been baking here?"

Eulenspiegel said, "What you told me to bake — owls and long-tailed monkeys."

The baker said, "What'll I do with this foolish stuff? This bread isn't any use to me. I certainly can't turn it into money." And he grabbed him by the neck and said, "Pay me for my dough."

Eulenspiegel said, "All right. If I pay you for the dough, then the goods that were baked from it ought to be mine."

The baker said, "What do I care about these goods? Owls and long-tailed monkeys can't do my business any good."

So he paid him for his dough, put the baked owls and long-tailed monkeys into a basket and carried them out of the house to the inn "At The Wild Man." Eulenspiegel then thought to himself, "You've often heard that one can't bring anything so peculiar to Brunswick that one can't make money with it." Now, at that time it was the day before Saint Nicholas Eve. So Eulenspiegel went to stand in front of the church with his little enterprise, sold all the owls and long-tailed monkeys, and made much more money from them than he had been forced to give the baker for the dough.

The baker found out about this. It annoyed him, and he ran to Saint Nicholas Church, intending to charge him for the fire-wood and the costs of baking the things. But Eulenspiegel was already gone, so the baker's trouble went for nothing.

20. How Eulenspiegel sifted flour into the courtyard by moonlight.

Eulenspiegel wandered around the country and came to Uelzen,[1] to the village, where he became a baker's boy again. When he was at home with his master, his master arranged everything so he could bake, and Eulenspiegel was supposed to sift the flour during the night, to have it ready by morning.

Eulenspiegel said, "Master, you ought to give me a light, so I can see to sift."

The baker said to him, "I'm not giving you any light. To this day I've never given my baker's boys any lights. They've had to sift in the moonlight. Well, you'll have to do so too."

Eulenspiegel said, "If they've sifted that way, I'll do so too."

The baker went to sleep, intending to sleep for several hours. Meanwhile, Eulenspiegel took the sifter, held it out of the window, and sifted the flour into the courtyard, where

---

1 A town south of Lüneburg. See Lappenberg, p. 240.

the moon shone, according to its light. When the baker arose and wanted to start baking, Eulenspiegel was still standing there and sifting. The baker saw that Eulenspiegel was sifting the flour into the courtyard, which was utterly white with flour. The master said, "What the devil! What are you doing here? Didn't that flour cost enough, that you're sifting it into that filth?"

Eulenspiegel said, "Come now, master! Be satisfied. It's been done both in and by moonlight — and there isn't much lost, only a handful. I'll quickly gather that up again. It doesn't hurt the flour one little bit."

The baker said, "While you're gathering up the flour — during that time — no dough's being made. It'll take too long to bake."

Eulenspiegel said, "My master, I've got a good idea. We want, after all, to bake as quickly as our neighbor. His dough is lying in the hutch. If you want it, I'll get it quickly — and I'll put our flour in its place."

The master became angry and said, "You ought to get the devil! Oh, get over to the gallows and drag a thief here."[2]

"Yes," he said. So he went to the gallows. The skeleton of a thief was lying there, having fallen down.[3] He lifted it on his neck, carried it home, and said, "What do you want this for? I've no idea what it's good for."

The baker said, "Didn't you bring anything else!"

Eulenspiegel said, "There wasn't anything else there."

The baker became furious and said with some heat, "You've insulted my lords' judiciary and robbed their gallows. I'll complain about this to the mayor — you should see how I will."

So the baker went out of his house to the market-place. And Eulenspiegel followed him. But the baker was in such a hurry that he did not look behind him and so did not notice

---

2. While "get over to the gallows" is reminiscent of such expressions as "go to the gallows," the likelihood — made more plausible by the addition of "and drag a thief here" — is that the baker was being more clumsily sarcastic than colloquial.

3. Thieves and other criminals were often left hanging as a warning until they fell. See Lappenberg, p. 240.

that Eulenspiegel was following. Well, the bailiff or mayor was standing there in the market-place. The baker went up to him and at once began to make his complaint. But as soon as his master began his complaining, Eulenspiegel quite nimbly took a place just beside him, opening both his eyes widely. When the baker caught sight of Eulenspiegel, he became so enraged that he forgot what he wanted to complain about, and said furiously to Eulenspiegel, "What do you want?"

Eulenspiegel said, "I don't want anything. But you said I should see how you were going to complain about me to the mayor. If I'm supposed to see it, I've got to open my eyes widely — so I can see it."

The baker said to him, "Just get out of my sight! You're a knave."

Eulenspiegel said, "That's what I'm often called. And if I'm sitting in your 'sight,' then I'll have to crawl out of your nostrils when you close your eyes."

The mayor walked away from him, seeing well enough that this was foolishness, and left both of them standing. When Eulenspiegel saw this, he ran after him and said, "Master, when are we going to bake? The sun isn't shining any more." Then he ran off, and left the baker standing.

21. How Eulenspiegel always rode on a reddish-gray horse, and was not happy where there were children.

Eulenspiegel was always happy in company. But as long as he lived, there were three sorts of things he avoided. First, he rode no gray horse, but always a reddish-gray horse, for the sake of foolishness.[1] Second, he never enjoyed staying where there were children, because people worried more about their needs than his. Third, he did not like going to an inn where there was an old, generous innkeeper. For an old, generous innkeeper kept no watch over his goods and was usually a fool; there, too, was not his sort of company: for in his sort of company there would also be money around to be won, and the like.

---

1. One possibility here is that the foolishness of the reddish-gray horse derived from its mottled appearance, motley being a traditional and conventional part of the costume of many professional medieval and renaissance jesters and buffoons. Enid Welsford, in *The Fool: His Social and Literary History* (Murray Hill, New York, 1936), p. 339, provides some interesting comments on the subject of fools' clothing.

He also crossed himself every day against healthy food, against great good luck, and against strong drink. For healthy food was just weeds, no matter how healthy it might be too. He also crossed himself against food from the pharmacist's shop: no matter how healthy it is, it is also a sign of sickness. It was the same with great good luck. For if a stone falls from a roof, or a beam from a house, one could well say, "Had I been standing there, the stone or beam would have killed me. That was my great good luck." Such good luck he could well do without. And the strong drink was water. For while water may drive huge mill wheels with its strength, many people of the best company will also drink their deaths from it.

22. How Eulenspiegel hired himself out as a tower bugler to the Count of Anhalt; and how, when enemies were coming, he failed to sound his horn; and how, when there were no enemies, he sounded it.

Not long afterwards, Eulenspiegel went to the Count of Anhalt,[1] to whom he hired himself out as a tower bugler.[2] Now, the Count had many enemies, so during this period, both in the town and at his castle, he kept many knights and people of his court — and these had to be fed all day. So Eulenspiegel, waiting in the tower, was forgotten and no food was sent to him.

---

1. Lappenberg (p. 241) argues that this must have been Count Bernhard II, who acquired the title "Prince of Anhalt" in 1318.

2. Count Bernhard II was (according to Lappenberg, p. 241) descended from the Bernburgers. A tower, still referred to as "Eulenspiegel's," and thought to be more than eleven hundred years old, still stands in Bernburg.

Well, that very day it happened that the Count's enemies raced up to the town and in front of his castle, took his cows, and drove them off. Now, Eulenspiegel was lying in the tower and looking through the window, but he gave no alarm, either by bugling or shouting. But the noise reached the Count, and he rushed after them with his men.

Some of them looked up to the tower and saw that Eulenspiegel was lying in the window and laughing. So the Count called up to him, "How can you lie in the window that way — so unmoved?"

Eulenspiegel called down to him, "Before eating, I don't shout and don't like shouting."

The Count called up to him, "Don't you intend to sound the signal for the enemy?"

Eulenspiegel called back, "I don't need to sound the signal for any enemy. The field's already full, and some have gone off with your cows. If I sound the signal for more enemies, they'll beat you to death. — Go on, now! All's well."

The Count hurried after his enemies and busied himself with them; but Eulenspiegel and his food were forgotten again.

Well, for a while the Count was content. For he also took a quantity of bacon from his enemies, and cut it up for boiling and baking. Up in the tower, Eulenspiegel thought how he too would like to obtain some of this loot, and paid careful attention to the hour when mealtime would come. Then he began to shout and sound his horn. "Enemy, ho! Enemy, ho!" The Count ran hastily from the table (on which the food was lying) with his men, laid on harness, took weapons in hand, soon rushed out through the gate into the field, and looked for the enemy.

In the meanwhile, Eulenspiegel ran smartly and rapidly down from the tower and arrived at the Count's table. And he took boiled and baked things from the table — and whatever he pleased — then quickly returned to the tower.

Well, when the knights and footsoldiers got outside, they saw no enemies. So they all said, "The tower watchman did this out of roguishness." So they returned home to the gate,

53

and the Count called up to Eulenspiegel, "Have you gone foolish and crazy?"

Eulenspiegel said, "Utterly without evil design."

The Count said, "Why did you sound 'Enemy, ho!' that way, when there was no one there?"

Eulenspiegel said, "Since there were no enemies, I had to call some over."

Then the Count said, "You're scratching *yourself* with your rogue's nails. When the enemy's there, you don't want to sound the signal; and when no enemy's there, you sound the enemy. This might well be called treason." So he dismissed him, engaged another tower bugler in his place, and Eulenspiegel had to follow them on foot, as a footsoldier.

This was most annoying to him, and he would have been glad to get away from there; but he certainly could not get away through fair play. So whenever they moved out against the enemy, he delayed in all sorts of ways and was always last through the gate. But when they had finished their business and turned toward home, he was always first inside the gate.

So the Count asked him how he was supposed to understand him: whenever he went out with him against the enemy, he was always last, and on going home he was first.

Eulenspiegel said, "You shouldn't be angry at that. For while you and your royal household were all eating, I was sitting up in the tower and getting thin. As a result, I've become quite feeble. If I'm now supposed to be first against the enemy, I'll have to make up that time and rush up here, so I'm both the first at the table and last to leave it. Once I become strong again, I'll be first and last against the enemy."

"So now I hear," said the Count, "that you plan to go on with this for the entire length of time you spent sitting in the tower?"

Eulenspiegel said, "Everybody's right about something, depending on how you take him."

The Count said, "You won't be mine for long," and let him go. Eulenspiegel was happy about this, since he had little enthusiasm for fighting with enemies all day.

23. How Eulenspiegel had his horse shod with gold shoes, for which the King of Denmark had to pay.

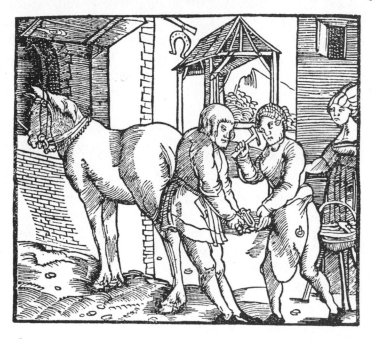

So fine an entrepreneur was Eulenspiegel that his cleverness came to the attention of a number of princes and lords, and he was widely talked about. He greatly pleased these princes and lords; and they gave him clothes, horses, money, and food. Well, he went to the King of Denmark,[1] who liked him very much and who told him that if he would do some sort of trick, he would have his horse shod for him with the very best horseshoes.

Eulenspiegel asked the King whether he should take him at his word. The King said, "Yes," for he kept his word.

Eulenspiegel rode his horse to the goldsmith and had his horse shod with gold shoes and silver nails. Then he went to the King and said he wanted him to pay for the shoeing. The King said, "Yes," and told his accountant to pay for the shoeing. The accountant thought it was an ordinary horseshoeing

---

1. This may have been King Christopher II, who died in 1332. See Lappenberg, p. 242.

— until Eulenspiegel brought him to the goldsmith and the goldsmith asked for one hundred Danish marks. The accountant had no intention of paying it, left, and reported the matter to the King. The King had Eulenspiegel summoned and said to him, "Eulenspiegel, what an expensive horseshoeing you've gotten! If I had to have all my horses shod in this way, I'd soon have to sell both country and people. It wasn't my intention to have the horse shod with gold shoes."

Eulenspiegel then said, "Gracious King, you said they would be the best horseshoes, and that I ought to take you at your word."

The King said, "You're the most valuable of all the people at my court: you do what I tell you!" And he began to laugh — and paid the one hundred marks.

Eulenspiegel then went to have the gold shoes taken off and settle with the smith. And he had iron shoes put on his horse, and stayed with the King to the end of his days.

24. How Eulenspiegel, with great roguishness, triumphed over the King of Poland's jester.

At that time His Highness Casimir[1] was King of Poland. Staying with him was an adventurer of rare humor and buffoonery who could also play the fiddle well. Well, Eulenspiegel, who was also in Poland, went to the King, and the King had heard a great deal about Eulenspiegel, who was a well liked guest with him. For the King had seen him, heard of his adventures before this, and so liked his entertainer very much.

Well, Eulenspiegel and his fool met, and then things were as they often say: two fools in one house seldom go well together. The King's jester had no liking for Eulenspiegel and at the same time did not wish to be thrown out himself. The King noticed this, so he had them both summoned to

---

1. This may have been Casimir III (1330–1370). See Lappenberg, p. 243.

57

his chamber. "Come on!" he said. "Whichever of you makes the wildest performance — which the other cannot repeat after him — I'll give him new clothes and twenty guilders. And let's do it now."

So the two set about their buffoonery, and performed many comical tricks, with funny faces and strange speeches. And whatever one could think up for the other — and whatever the King's fool did — Eulenspiegel imitated. And whatever Eulenspiegel did, this same fool also imitated. The King laughed, as did all his knights, and they saw all sorts of wild acts.

Eulenspiegel now thought, "Twenty guilders and a new wardrobe — that would be rather nice. I shall therefore do something I would otherwise find unpleasant." For he saw clearly what the King's attitude was — that it was all the same to him who won the prize, and by what means.

So Eulenspiegel walked to the middle of the room, lifted his behind, shat a pile right in the center, took a spoon, and divided the filth in half, down the middle. Then he called the other fool over and said, "Fool, come here and do some lapping up after me now, since I intend to do it before you." And he took the spoon, scooped half the filth into it, and ate it up. Then he offered the spoon to the clown and said, "Look here, you eat the other part; and after that you make a pile too, divide it up also, and I'll eat after you."

The King's fool then said, "No, not that too. Put that spoon away. Am I supposed to be debased for the rest of my life? I don't eat from you, or from me, that way."

So Eulenspiegel won the championship of buffoonery, and the King gave him the new clothes and the twenty guilders. And Eulenspiegel rode off and took the King's prize with him.

25. How Eulenspiegel was banished from the Duchy of Lüneburg, and how he cut open his horse and stood inside it.

Eulenspiegel practiced his extraordinary buffoonery in the province of Lüneburg at Celle. So the Duke of Lüneburg banished him from the province — and if he were found anywhere around there, he was to be seized and hanged. But Eulenspiegel did not avoid the province on that account. If his path led him that way, he rode or walked through the district anyhow.

There came a time, then, when he wanted to ride through Lüneburg. The Duke was coming toward him, and when he realized it was the Duke, he thought, "It's the Duke, and if you're careless, they'll catch up with you with their nags and put you off your horse. Then comes the angry Duke and hangs me from a tree." Then he thought of a good idea: he dismounted from his horse, quickly sliced open its stomach, shook out its bowels, and took a standing position in its trunk. When the Duke and his knights got closer, they saw that Eulenspiegel was standing in his horse's stomach.

The Prince rode up to him and said, "Is it you? What're you doing in this carcass here? Don't you know I've banished you from my territory — and if I find you in it, I'm going to have you hanged from a tree?"

But he said, "Gracious Lord and Prince, I haven't done anything so awful that it's worth a hanging."

The Duke said to him, "Come over here to me and explain your innocence. — And what do you mean by this, that you're standing in a horse's skin?"

Eulenspiegel approached him and answered, "Gracious and high-born Prince, I worried about your displeasure and feared terribly for myself, but all my life I've heard a man is entitled to be left in peace — in his four-poster."

Well, the Duke began to laugh, and he said, "Will you stay out of my territory from now on?"

Eulenspiegel said, "Gracious Lord, as your princely Grace wishes."

The Duke rode away from him and called, "Stay as you are."

But Eulenspiegel quickly jumped out of the horse — and he said to his dead horse, "Thanks, my dear horse, that you've helped me out of this and saved my life. And that, in addition, you've made me a respectable man again. Just lie here. It's better that ravens eat you than they might have eaten me." And he continued on foot.

26. How Eulenspiegel bought some land from a farmer in the province of Lüneburg, and sat in it, in a tumbrel.

After this, Eulenspiegel passed that way again. Well, he went into a village near Celle, and waited for the moment when the Duke might again be riding toward Celle. A farmer was going into a field there. Now, Eulenspiegel had gotten himself another horse and a tumbrel, and drove up to the farmer and asked him whose field it was.

The farmer said, "It's mine, and I've inherited it."

Eulenspiegel then asked how much he would have to give him for a cartful of earth from his field.

The farmer said, "I'll take one shilling for it."

Eulenspiegel gave him a shilling coin, filled the cart full of earth from the field, crawled into it, and drove up to the castle at Celle on the Aller. When the Duke came riding by, he noticed that Eulenspiegel was sitting in the cart — and was sitting in earth up to his shoulders.

So the Duke said, "Eulenspiegel, didn't I banish you from

my land? — If I found you in it, I intended to have you hanged?"

Eulenspiegel said, "Gracious Lord, I'm not in your land. I'm sitting in my land, which I bought for a shilling. And I bought it from a farmer who told me it was his inheritance."

The Duke said, "Get yourself and your earthy empire out of my earthy empire, and don't come back — or I'll have you hanged, *along* with horse and cart."

Eulenspiegel quickly leaped out of the cart and jumped on his horse. He rode out of that district, leaving his cart standing before the castle. And that is why Eulenspiegel's earthy empire still stands there in front of the bridge.

27. How Eulenspiegel painted for the Landgrave of Hesse, doing it in white, so whoever was illegitimate could not see it.

Eulenspiegel set amazing things going in the country of Hesse. When he had roamed the country of Saxony through and through, and was almost too well known — so he was no longer quite able to get away with his mischief-making — he went into the country of Hesse, and arrived, near Marburg, at the court of the Landgrave. Well, the Lord asked what he could do. He answered, saying, "Gracious Lord, I am an artist." This made the Landgrave happy, for he thought he was a performer and could do alchemy. So he asked whether he was an alchemist.

Eulenspiegel said, "No, gracious Lord. I am a painter — the equal of whom will not be found in many lands. For my work surpasses the work of others."

The Landgrave said, "Let's see something."

Eulenspiegel said, "Yes, gracious Lord." Now, he had

various paintings on canvas and *objets d'art,* which he had bought in Flanders. He pulled these out of his sack and showed them to the Landgrave. The Lord liked these, and said to him, "Dear master, what would you take to paint our chamber here — of the arrival of my wife, the Landgrave of Hesse,[1] how she initiated my friendship with the King of Hungary, and other Princes and Lords, and how long all this has lasted? And we would want to have this thing done as sumptuously as possible."

Eulenspiegel replied, "Gracious Lord, if your Grace were to let me do it, it would probably cost four hundred guilders."

The Landgrave said, "Master, just let it be well done for us: we intend to reward you well for it."

So Eulenspiegel took it on — and of course the Landgrave had to give him one hundred guilders right away, so he could buy paints and hire assistants. But when Eulenspiegel, with three assistants, was ready to start the job, he instructed the Landgrave to allow no one other than his helpers into the room while he was working — so he would not be disturbed in his art. The Landgrave permitted him this. However, Eulenspiegel came to an agreement with his assistants. He suggested to them that they keep silent and let him do everything — they were not to work — and that they would receive their pay anyhow: their greatest labor would consist of playing backgammon. His assistants were glad they were to earn the same pay for doing nothing.

This lasted for one week or four — till the Landgrave decided to see what master and company might be painting and whether it would really be as good as the samples. So he said to Eulenspiegel, "Ah, dear master, we very much wish to see your work. We request that we be allowed to go into the room with you to view your painting."

Eulenspiegel said, "Yes, gracious Lord. But I must tell Your Grace one thing: whoever enters with Your Grace and

---

1. This may refer to Elizabeth, wife of Ludwig VI, Count of Thüringen, and the daughter of Andreas II, King of Hungary. Elizabeth died in 1227. See Lappenberg, p. 224.

views the painting — if he is not of proper and legitimate birth, he won't be able to see my painting."

The Landgrave said, "Master, it must be something great."

Meanwhile they were walking into the room. Eulenspiegel had spread a long linen cloth across the wall where he was supposed to have been painting. Well, Eulenspiegel now drew this back a little, pointed at the wall with a small white stick, and began to speak. "Look, gracious Lord. This man — he was the first Landgrave of Hesse and a pillar of Rome, who afterwards became Kaiser and had as his Princess and Lady mild Justinian's daughter, a Duchess of Bavaria. Look here, gracious Lord. Adolphus was born of him. Adolphus sired William the Black; William sired Ludwig the Pious — and so on, to Your Princely Grace. And indeed I know this much: no one can censure my work, so artistic is it and with such beautiful colors."

The Landgrave saw nothing other than the white wall before him and thought to himself, "Maybe I'm supposed to be the son of a whore, but I don't see anything there other than a white wall." Nonetheless, he said (wishing to be fair), "Dear master, we are well satisfied — but we aren't sophisticated enough to judge." And with that he left the room.

When the Landgrave approached the Princess, she asked him, "Ah, gracious Lord, what is your master painter painting? You've seen it. How do you like his work? I myself have but little faith in it: he looks like a charlatan."

The Prince said, "Dear Lady, I like his work enormously. You do him an injustice."

"Gracious Lord," she said, "may we not also view it?"

"Yes, with the master's permission."

She had Eulenspiegel summoned before her, and requested that she might also see the painting. Eulenspiegel then told her what he had told the Prince: whoever was illegitimate would not be able to see his work. Then she, along with eight ladies-in-waiting and a female court jester, went into the room. Eulenspiegel now drew back the cloth, as before, and told the Princess too about the arrival of the Landgrave's wife, one section after the other. But the Princess and the ladies-in-waiting remained silent; no one praised or condemned the painting. Everyone was afraid she might be illegitimate, either on her father's or mother's side. But at last the court jester roused herself and said, "Dear master, maybe I'll have to remain a whore's daughter for the rest of my life, but I don't see any painting there."

Then Eulenspiegel thought, "This isn't good at all. If fools start telling the truth, then I, in truth, will have to do some traveling." And he tried to laugh it off.

In the meantime the Princess returned to her Lord, and he asked her how she liked the painting. She answered him, saying, "Gracious Sir, I like it as much as Your Grace. But our jester doesn't like it. She says she sees no painting. Our ladies-in-waiting say the same — and I am afraid there may be knavery in the thing."

The Prince looked into his heart and realized he had been tricked. Nonetheless, he had Eulenspiegel informed that if he were to pay for his thing, everyone at court would have to see his work. For the Prince said he wished to see who among his noblemen might be legitimate or illegitimate.

Well, Eulenspiegel went to his assistants and dismissed them. Then he charged the steward another hundred guilders and got it. And then he left at once. The next day the Prince asked after his painter — he was gone. So the Prince, with all the people of his court, went into the room to discover whether anyone could see the painting. But no one could say he saw anything. And since they all remained silent, the Landgrave said, "We now see we have been tricked. Oh, I never wanted to be troubled with Eulenspiegel; he came to us anyhow. We can forget easily enough about the two hundred guilders, though: you can't stop him from being the knave he is. And so he had better avoid our principality."

But Eulenspiegel was gone from Marburg and had no wish to engage in any further painting.

28. How Eulenspiegel disputed with the students at the University of Prague, in Bohemia, and emerged victorious.

Eulenspiegel traveled through Bohemia to Prague when he left Marburg. Now, at that time good Christians were still living there — before the days when Wickliff brought his heresy from England to Bohemia and it was spread further by John Huss.[1] Well, Eulenspiegel described himself as a great master there in the answering of great questions — to which any other master would be able to offer neither explanation nor reply. He had this written into announcements and posted them on the church doors and at the lecture halls.

This irritated the rector. The students, professors, and masters of arts were annoyed over it, as was the whole university. So they met to find a means by which they could

---

1. Huss (1370–1415) received a Master of Arts degree from the University of Prague in 1396. See Kamil Krofta, "John Huss," *The Cambridge Medieval History*, VIII (Cambridge, 1959), p. 46.

present Eulenspiegel with problems he would not be able to solve. If he came through badly, they would be able, with some justice, to seize him and put him to shame. And it was arranged and agreed among them (and they also concluded and ordained it) that the rector ought to present the questions. So they had Eulenspiegel notified through their attendants that he should appear the next day to answer problems and questions, which would be given to him in writing before the whole university, if he wished to be tested and desired to have his skill found to be genuine. Otherwise he could not be accepted.

Eulenspiegel, by way of reply, told these attendants, "Inform your superiors that I shall do this thing, and that I yet hope to come through it a clever fellow — as I have till now."

The next day all the professors and learned men gathered. Eulenspiegel also arrived, bringing with him his innkeeper, various other townspeople, and various good acquaintances, in case of any sudden attack that might befall him from the students. And when he entered their meeting, they told him to climb up on a chair and to answer the questions which would be placed before him.

Well, the first question the rector put to him was that he should state, and prove with true facts, how many currents of water there were in the sea. If he could not solve and answer this question, they would condemn and punish him as an uneducated corruptor of his art.

He made a quick answer to this question. "Worthy Lord Rector, tell the rest of the water, which runs from all ends of the sea, to stand still, and I shall measure, prove and report the truth about it. For that will be easy to do."

It was impossible for the rector to stop the water — so he left this subject and excused him from any measuring. But the rector stood there, rather embarrassed, and put his next question. "Tell me, how many days have passed from Adam's time till today?"

He answered briefly. "Only seven days. And when they've passed, then seven more days commence. This lasts till the end of the world."

The rector gave him the third question. "Tell me now, how or where is the center of the world located?"

Eulenspiegel answered, "It's right here. I'm standing in exactly the center of the world. And to see whether that's true, have it measured with a string. And if I'm off by even a straw's length, I'll admit I'm wrong."

Rather than measuring it, the rector chose to concede Eulenspiegel this question. Then, with true fury, he offered Eulenspiegel the fourth question. He said, "Tell me, how far is it from the earth to Heaven?"

Eulenspiegel replied, "That's quite nearby. If one speaks or calls from Heaven, one easily hears it down here. Just climb up there. I'll call softly from down here. You'll certainly hear it in Heaven. Of course, if you don't hear it — I'll admit I'm wrong."

The rector was satisfied with this, and asked the fifth question. "How wide is Heaven?"

Eulenspiegel soon answered him. "It's a thousand fathoms wide and a thousand ells[2] high. I can't be wrong about that. If you don't want to believe it, take the sun, moon and all the stars of Heaven, and measure them together. You'll find I'm right, even though the idea doesn't appeal to you."

What could they say? Eulenspiegel was never at a loss for an answer, and they had to admit he was right about everything. But he did not wait long after he had defeated these learned men with quackery. For he was afraid they might offer him something to drink to trip him up. So he took off the long academic robe, left, and went toward Erfurt.

---

2. Probably about 250 feet, though the ell, as a unit of measure, varied considerably from place to place.

29. How Eulenspiegel taught an ass to read from an old psalter at Erfurt.

After he had played this trick in Prague, Eulenspiegel had a great longing for Erfurt — for he was worried that they might be rushing after him. When he arrived in Erfurt, at which there is a remarkably large and famous university, Eulenspiegel posted his announcements there as well. Now, the students of the university had heard a great deal about his tricks and wondered what they ought to set him as a problem, so things would not go for them as they had gone for those with him at Prague and they would not be humiliated.

Well, they decided to give Eulenspiegel an ass to teach — for at Erfurt there are many asses, old and young. They sent for Eulenspiegel and told him, "Master, you've posted learned announcements that you can teach any creature to write and read in a short time. Well, the Lords of the University are here and plan to offer you a young ass for teaching. Will you dare teach him too?"

He said, "Yes," but he would need time for it, since an ass was a speechless and unintelligent creature. So they agreed on twenty years with him. Eulenspiegel thought, "There are three of us. If the rector of the University dies, I'm free. If I die, who will hold me accountable? If my pupil dies, I'm free in any case." So he took it on, and agreed on five hundred old groschen to do it. Of this they gave him some gold in advance.

Well, Eulenspiegel led the ass away with him, and moved into the inn "At The Tower," where at that time there was a unique innkeeper. He engaged a stall for his pupil alone and acquired an old psalter. This he placed before him, in the manger, and between each of the pages he laid oats. The ass was made aware of these — and tossed the pages over with its mouth, to get at the oats; but when it found no more oats, it screamed, "Eee — aa, eee — aa!"

When Eulenspiegel noticed this, he went to the rector and said, "Lord Rector, when would you like to see a bit of what my pupil's doing?"

The rector said, "Dear Master, can he, too, accept teaching?"

Eulenspiegel said, "He's extremely clumsy in his skill, and it's very hard for me to teach him. Nonetheless, with much effort and work, I've accomplished enough so he recognizes some letters and vowels and can name them. Would you like to go with me to hear and see this?"

Now, his good pupil had been fasting during this time — till three in the afternoon. When Eulenspiegel arrived, with the rector and several masters, he placed a new book before his pupil. As soon as he discovered it in the manger, he tossed the pages back and forth, looking for the oats. When he did not find any, he began to scream, in a loud voice, "Eee — aa — eee — aa!"

Eulenspiegel then said, "Look, dear gentlemen, the two vowels 'e' and 'a.' These he can do so far. I am hoping he may yet do nicely."

Well, the rector died shortly afterwards. Eulenspiegel now released his pupil, letting him go where his nature took him. Then Eulenspiegel moved away with the money he had kept. And he thought, "If you had to make all the asses in Erfurt wise, you'd need many lifetimes." He had, moreover, no desire to do so, and let the place remain as it was.

Eulenspiegel came into the province of Thüringen, near Nienstetten, into the village, and asked about an inn. The innkeeper, a woman, approached him and asked him what sort of fellow he was.

Eulenspiegel said, "I'm not a journeyman. Instead I practice telling the truth."

The woman said, "I like harboring the truth, and I'm especially well disposed to those who tell the truth."

Now, as Eulenspiegel was looking around him, he noticed that the lady was squinting; and so he said, "Squint-eyed lady, squint-eyed lady, where shall I sit and where shall I put my staff and sack?"

The innkeeper said, "Aaah — may nothing good ever happen to you! In all my life nobody's ever mentioned to me that I'm squint-eyed."

Eulenspiegel said, "Dear innkeeper, if I'm always to tell the truth, I can't keep silent about it."

The woman was pleased with this and laughed over it.

Since Eulenspiegel was staying there overnight, he began to talk with the innkeeper, and they happened to discuss the fact that he knew how to wash furs. Now, this very much delighted the woman, so she asked him whether he would like to wash pelts: she would tell her neighbors about it, and they would bring all their pelts for him to wash. Eulenspiegel said, "Yes." The woman called all her neighbors together, and the women brought all their pelts.

Eulenspiegel said, "You'll have to have milk for this."

The women became enthusiastic, since they had a yearning for fresh furs, and got all the milk they had in their houses. Eulenspiegel than placed three kettles on the fire, poured the milk into them, stuck the pelts in as well, and let them boil and cook. When it looked all right to him, he said to the women, "You'll have to go to the woods and bring me white linden wood from young trees. And strip it, because when you come back I'm going to lift the pelts out. They'll be soaked enough by then, and I want to wash them through — and for that I'll need the wood."

The women willingly left for the woods, and their children ran along with them. Well, they took them by the hands and jumped and sang, "Oh-ho, good new pelts! Oh-ho, good new pelts!"

But Eulenspiegel stood there laughing and said, "Ah, wait, your pelts aren't ready yet."

As soon as they were off in the woods, Eulenspiegel dipped the pelts under once more, left the kettle standing with their pelts, left the village and went off: he had no intention of returning to wash their pelts. Well, the women came back with the linden wood, did not find Eulenspiegel, and guessed he might be gone. So they tried, each before the other, to take their pelts out of the kettles; but these had been so ruined by the washing that they fell apart. So they left the pelts standing, hoping he might come back to wash them out for them.

But he thanked God he had gotten out of there unhurt.

31. How Eulenspiegel wandered around with a death's-head, fascinating people with it, and profited greatly by doing so.

Eulenspiegel had made himself known in all countries through his malicious tricks; and where he had once been he was no longer welcome, so it happened that he disguised himself so he would not be recognized. Nonetheless, it finally became clear to him that he could no longer trust himself to make his living by idleness — despite his having been a cheery fellow from his youth up and having gotten money enough through all sorts of clever games. And now that his roguery was becoming known through all countries, and his profits were declining, he reflected on what he might undertake — to support himself in idleness anyhow — and had the idea of doing himself up as a wandering monk and riding, with relics, through the surrounding country. So, with a student, he dressed himself to look like a priest, took the head of a dead man, had it mounted in silver, and arrived in the country of Pomerania, where priests care more about drinking than praying.

Now, wherever there might be a dedication of a church in a village, or a wedding, or some other gathering of the country people, Eulenspiegel offered himself to the priest as one who could pray and preach religion to the farmers so well that they would allow themselves to be hypnotized — and of whatever he might receive in offerings he intended to give him half. The uneducated priests agreed to this — as long as they got some money.

Well, when all the people were in the church, he mounted the pulpit, said something from the Old Testament, tossed in the New as well, with Noah's Ark and the Golden Bucket, in which the bread of Heaven lay — and said, moreover, that this was the greatest holiness. Then at the same time he began to speak of the head of Saint Brendan, who had been a holy man.[1] He had his head right there — and it had been commanded of him that he use it to collect for the building of a new church — and to do so with purest goodness, never (on pain of death) taking any offerings from any woman who might be an adulteress.

"And whoever here may be such women, let them stand back. For if they offer me something — those who are guilty of adultery — I won't take it, and they will be put to shame before me. So — know yourselves!"

And he offered the people the head to be kissed, a smith's head, perhaps, that he had taken from a church graveyard, and gave the farmers and their wives the blessing. Then he stepped down from the pulpit and stood in front of the altar. Well, the priest began to sing and ring his bells. So both guilty and innocent wives approached the altar with their offerings, hurrying so much they gasped for breath. And he took the offerings, from guilty and innocent alike, scorning

---

1. Saint Brendan of Ireland (484–577?) is, in legend at least, reputed to have discovered America long before the Norsemen. Geoffrey Ashe, in *Land to the West* (The Viking Press, New York, 1962), examines the legend of Brendan through investigations of both Irish history and the medieval European versions of Brendan's possible voyage.

none. Well, so firmly did the foolish wives believe in his sly, roguish business that they considered any women impious who might still be holding back. And those women who had no money offered a gold or silver ring — and each one eyed the other to see if she gave too; and those who had given thought they had confirmed their honor and destroyed their evil reputations. There were also those who offered two or three times, so that the people could see them do so and get them out of their malicious gossip. Well, he received the most splendid donations, the likes of which had never been heard of before. And when he had taken up the donations, he commanded, on pain of excommunication, that all those who had given him something never behave with deceit, for they were free of it — since if there had been any such deceitful wives there he would not have taken any offering from them. Well, those wives were thoroughly satisfied.

And wherever Eulenspiegel went, he preached, and became rich through doing so. And the people took him for a pious preacher, so well was he able to conceal his knavery.

32. How Eulenspiegel made the city patrol of Nürnberg follow him over a narrow bridge and fall into the water.

Eulenspiegel was inventive in his roguishness. After he had traveled widely with the head, greatly deceiving people, he arrived in Nürnberg, intending to spend the money he had won with his relic. But when he had lived there for a while, and had seen all aspects of the city, he was unable to abandon his nature and had to perpetrate a clever trick there too.

Now, he saw that the city patrol slept, with armor on, in a large chamber beneath the city hall. And Eulenspiegel had made himself well acquainted with the roads and narrow bridges of Nürnberg — and had especially examined the narrow bridge between the hog market and the "Little House," which it is dangerous to cross during the night, for many innocent girls out to get wine have been assaulted there. Well, Eulenspiegel delayed his little prank until people had gone to sleep and all was quiet. Then he broke three planks from this same bridge and threw them into the river (called the

78

Pegnitz). He walked up to the city hall, began to swear, and beat on the plaster with an old knife till the sparks flew.

When the watchmen heard this, they were soon up and running. As Eulenspiegel heard them coming after him, he ran ahead of the watchmen, took flight toward the hog market, and once there, had them still behind him. He arrived, barely ahead of them, at the place where he had thrown away the three planks, and managed, as best he could, to get across the bridge. But once he had made it across, he called in a loud voice, "Ha, ha! What're you waiting for, you weak-hearted scoundrels?" When the watchmen heard this, they raced toward him, quite without thinking, for each one wished to be first. As a result, they fell, one after the other, into the Pegnitz. And the passage-way across the bridge was so narrow that they started to quarrel with each other all along it. So Eulenspiegel called out, "Ha, ha, aren't you running yet? Tomorrow you might run after me some more. You'd have arrived at this bath early enough — tomorrow morning. Even if you hadn't wanted to go hunting half as much, you'd still have arrived here on time." Well, one broke a leg, another an arm, the third received a gash on his head — with the result that none of them got out of there unhurt.

When he had accomplished this deception, he did not stay at Nürnberg too long and went traveling again. He had, after all, no desire for this to become known about him, since he might be flogged, for the people of Nürnberg would probably not take it as a joke.

33. How Eulenspiegel ate for money at Bamberg.

Through cunning, Eulenspiegel earned money for a meal at Bamberg, after he left Nürnberg and was quite hungry. For he arrived there at the house of a lady innkeeper whose name was Mrs. Königen. She was a cheerful innkeeper and told him he was welcome there, since she saw by his clothes that he was a rare guest.

When he wanted his morning meal, the woman asked him how he wished to have it: whether he preferred to sit at the table for complete meals, or whether he wished to eat *à la carte*. Eulenspiegel answered that he was a poor fellow, and asked her whether, for the sake of God, she would give him something to eat.

The woman said, "Friend, at the butchers' stalls, or at the bakers' stalls, I am given nothing free: I've got to pay for it. Therefore, I've also got to have money for the food."

Eulenspiegel then said, "Ah, woman, I too like to eat for money. For what — or how much — should I eat and drink here?"

The woman said, "At the Gentlemen's Table for twenty-four pennies, at the next table there for eighteen[1] pennies, and with my servants for twelve pennies."

Eulenspiegel then replied, "Woman, the most money would serve me best." And he seated himself at the Gentlemen's Table and soon ate his fill. When he felt good, and had eaten and drunk well, he told the innkeeper that she should conclude their business, for he had to be on his way so he would not have too much of a bill.

"Dear guest," said the woman, "give me the meal's price of twenty-four pennies, and go where you wish. May God speed you."

"No," said Eulenspiegel. "You must give me twenty-four pennies, as you said. For you said, at this table one eats a meal for twenty-four pennies. Well, I understood that to mean that I should earn money for it — for things have been getting hard enough for me. I've been eating till the sweat's broken out on me — and if life and limb had depended on it, I couldn't have eaten any more. So give me my hard-earned reward."

"Friend," said the woman, "it's true you've eaten enough for three men. But that I should also pay you for it — the two things don't at all rhyme together. But this meal is finished and you may as well go. However, I won't give you any money for it: that's lost. And I'll ask no money of you. Don't come back to me again. For if I had to feed my guests this way all year round, and raise no more money than from you, I'd have to give up house and home that way."

So Eulenspiegel took his leave of that place, without earning much thanks.

---

1. An error? Grieninger has twenty-eight here.

34. How Eulenspiegel traveled to Rome and visited the Pope, who took him for a heretic.

Eulenspiegel was dedicated to cunning roguishness. After he had tried all sorts of tricks, he thought of the old saying, "Go to Rome, pious man: come back worthless."[1] So he traveled to Rome, to give his mischief a chance there too, and took lodgings with a widow. She saw that Eulenspiegel was a handsome man and asked him where he was from. Eulenspiegel said he was from the district of Saxony, was an Easterner, and that he had come to Rome to speak to the Pope.

The woman then said, "Friend, you can easily see the Pope — but to speak to him, that I don't know. I was brought up and born here, and am of the best lineage — but have never yet been able to exchange words with him. How could you do it so fast? I'd give easily a hundred ducats to talk to him."

---

1. An old Italian and German saying indeed, with various versions. See Lappenberg, p. 249.

82

Eulenspiegel said, "Dear Innkeeper, if I get the chance to bring you before the Pope — so you *can* speak to him — will you give me the hundred ducats?"

The woman was quick to promise him the hundred ducats, on her honor, if he could bring it about. But she thought it would be impossible for him to do such a thing, for it would cost him a lot of trouble and work.

Eulenspiegel said, "Dear Innkeeper, if it does happen, I'll ask for the hundred ducats."

She said, "Yes." But she thought, "You're still not even near the Pope."

Eulenspiegel waited. For every four weeks the Pope had to read a mass in the chapel called Jerusalem, at Saint John in Lateran. Well, after the Pope had finished his mass, Eulenspiegel pushed himself forward in the chapel, as close to the Pope as he could. And when he held the low mass, Eulenspiegel turned his back on the sacrament. The Cardinals observed this. And when the Pope said the blessing over the communion cup, Eulenspiegel turned his back again. When the mass was over, they told the Pope that a certain person, a handsome man, had been at mass and had turned his back to the altar during low mass.

The Pope said, "It's important to inquire about this, for it concerns the Holy Church. For if disbelief were not punished, it would be a sin against God. If the man has done this, it may well be feared that he has come into disbelief and is not a good Christian." And he ordered that he be brought to him.

They approached Eulenspiegel then and told him to appear before the Pope. So at the appointed hour Eulenspiegel went to stand in front of the Pope. The Pope now asked him what sort of man he was. Eulenspiegel said he was a good, Christian man. The Pope asked what sort of beliefs he held. Eulenspiegel said he held the same beliefs as his lady-innkeeper — and named her, for she was a woman who was well known there. So the Pope brought the woman before him. The Pope asked the woman about the nature of her beliefs. The woman said she believed in the Christian religion and in what the Holy Christian Church allowed her and forbade her. She held no other beliefs.

Eulenspiegel was standing nearby; and he began to bow, with much ceremony, and said, "Most Gracious Father, Thou Servant Among All Servants, I hold the same beliefs as well. I am a good, Christian man."

The Pope said, "Why do you turn your back on the altar during the low mass?"

Eulenspiegel said, "Most Holy Father, I am a poor, great sinner and was so glaring in my sins that I wasn't worthy — till I had confessed my sins."

The Pope was satisfied with this, released Eulenspiegel, and went to his palace. But Eulenspiegel went to his inn and asked his innkeeper for the hundred ducats. She had to give them to him. Well, Eulenspiegel remained the same person now as before — and was not much improved by his trip to Rome.

35. How Eulenspiegel cheated the Jews at Frankfurt-on-the-Main out of a thousand guilders, by selling them his excrement as prophet's berries.

No one should mind if the cunning Jew has his eye closed.[1]

When Eulenspiegel returned from Rome, he traveled to Frankfurt-on-the-Main, where it was just fair-time. So Eulenspiegel walked here and there and observed the sorts of merchandise everybody had for sale. Then he spotted a young, clever man, wearing fine clothes, who had a very small shop, with musk from Alexandria, which he sold at a cost far beyond its possible value.

Eulenspiegel thought, "I'm also a lazy, clever scoundrel who doesn't like to work. If I could support myself as easily as this fellow, it would please me very much." So he lay without sleeping that night, and thought and speculated on business. In the meantime, a flea bit him in the behind. He quickly fumbled about for it, and found several small knots

---

1. *i.e.*, does not see and gets cheated.

on his behind. Then he thought, "These must be the little rough sources (which one calls 'Lexander'[2]) from which the musk comes."

When he got up the next day, he purchased gray and red taffeta, wrapped the little knots in it, found a seller's bench, bought some spices for it, and went to stand in front of the town hall with his stall. Many people came up to him, inspected his curious shop, and asked him the nature of the odd things he had for sale there. For it was an unusual commodity: it was wrapped, like musk, into a little bundle, and smelled most strangely. But Eulenspiegel gave no one accurate information about his merchandise — until three rich Jews approached him to ask about his wares. He told them it was prophet's berries — and whoever put one of them into his mouth, and then stuck one in his nose, would speak the truth from that time on. The Jews withdrew to consult for a while. Eventually, the old Jew said, "With this we'll be able to prophecy when our Messiah is to come — something that would be of no small comfort to us Jews."

So they decided they would buy up all these wares, no matter what they might have to pay for them. They then returned to Eulenspiegel and said, "Merchant, what in a word, would one of these prophet's berries cost?"

Eulenspiegel thought quickly and said, "Indeed, whenever I've got merchandise, Our Lord bestows buyers on me. These delicacies please Jews especially." And he added, "I'll give one for a hundred guilders — and if you don't wish to pay them, you dogs, take off and leave the filth behind."

As they did not wish to anger Eulenspiegel — and as they wanted to obtain his wares — they soon paid him the money, took one of the berries, and quickly went home. Then they had all the Jews, old and young, rung[3] into *schule*. When they had met, the oldest Rabbi (named Alpha)[4] stood up and told how, by the will of God, they had acquired a prophet's berry, which one of them was to take into his mouth to be able to prophecy the coming of the Messiah.

---

2. There is evidently a pun involved here: on "Alexandria," the source of musk, and the Low German expression for "it licks itself," "leckts selbander."

86

And so salvation and comfort might come to them from it, they ought to prepare themselves with fasting and praying; then after three days, one Isaac would consume it with great reverence.

And so it happened.

When the man had it in his mouth, Moses asked him, "Well, dear Isaac, how does it taste?"

"Servant of God! — We've been cheated by that Goi! — This is nothing other than human filth."

So they all tasted the prophet's berry — until they saw the "wood" out of which the berry had grown.

But Eulenspiegel was gone; and he enjoyed himself enormously for as long as the Jews' money lasted.

---

3. Actually, "klopfen," or "knocked," it being the custom then to dispatch someone to Jewish homes to knock on the doors to summon the people to synagogue.

4. Lappenberg (p. 250) believes this is a version of "Kaiphas."

36. How Eulenspiegel bought chickens at Quedlinburg, and left the farmer's wife one of her own chickens as a pledge for the money.

People were not always as sophisticated as they are now — especially country people.

Once Eulenspiegel arrived in Quedlinburg. It was just market-time, and Eulenspiegel had few provisions. For as he won his money, so it left him again — and he wondered how he might acquire provisions. Well, a countrywoman was sitting in the market place, and she had a basketful of good chickens for sale. So Eulenspiegel asked what a pair of them would cost.

She answered him, "By the pair, two Stevens-shillings."

Eulenspiegel said, "Won't you sell them for less?"

The woman said, "No."

So Eulenspiegel took the chickens with the basket and walked off toward the castle gate.

The woman ran after him and said, "Sir — buyer — how am I to understand this? Don't you intend to pay me for my chickens?"

Eulenspiegel said, "Yes, with pleasure. I'm the Abbess' scribe."

"I'm not asking about that," said the woman. "If you want to keep the chickens, pay for them. I hope never to have to do with your Abbot or Abbess. My father taught me that I should not buy from or, still less, sell to or give credit to those before whom one must bow or raise one's cap. So pay me for the chickens, do you hear?"

Eulenspiegel said, "Woman, you're of small faith. It wouldn't be good if all merchants were as you are: good comrades would have to go about poorly dressed. But so you'll be sure of your money — take this one chicken as a pledge till I bring you the basket and the money."

The good woman fancied herself well taken care of, and took one of her chickens as a pledge. But she had been fooled. For Eulenspiegel — and the chickens and the promised money — did not appear. It happened to her as it does to those who are most meticulous in their supervision of what is theirs: they are the first to be cheated.

So Eulenspiegel left that place — and left the woman furious over the single chicken she had taken for her chickens.

Eulenspiegel was at Hildesheim, and he bought a good red sausage at the butcher's stall and went on to Egelsheim. He was well known to the priest there, and it was on a Sunday morning when he arrived. As he wished to eat presently, Eulenspiegel went into the parsonage and asked the girl cooking there to roast the red sausage for him.

The girl said, "Yes."

So Eulenspiegel went into the church. There, early mass was just finished, and another priest was taking over the high mass, which Eulenspiegel heard to its end.

In the meantime, the priest went home and said to his servant girl, "Isn't there anything cooked, so I can eat a little?"

The girl said, "Nothing's ready, except a red sausage that Eulenspiegel brought: that's cooked. He'd planned to eat it after he returned from church."

The priest said, "Hand me the sausage. I'd like to eat a bit of it."

The girl handed him the sausage.

The priest enjoyed the taste of the sausage so much that he ate it all. And he said to himself, "God bless me, it tasted good. The sausage was good." And he said to the girl, "Give Eulenspiegel bacon[1] and cabbage, as he's used to eating. That's much better for him."

Now, after the service was let out, Eulenspiegel went back to the parsonage, intending to eat his sausage. And the priest greeted him, thanked him for his sausage, told him how good it had tasted, and presented him with bacon and cabbage. Eulenspiegel kept quiet, ate what had been cooked there, and left on Monday.

The priest called after Eulenspiegel, "Listen, when you come back, bring two sausages with you — one for you and one for me. I'll pay you back whatever you have to spend for them. Then we'll really enjoy ourselves — till our mouths get messy."

Eulenspiegel said, "Yes, Father, that's what'll happen. I'll certainly be thinking of you when I get the sausages." And he went back to Hildesheim.

Now, it happened, as he had hoped it would, that the commercial pig-slaughterers[2] were carrying a sow to their slaughters' burial place. So Eulenspiegel asked the slaughterer whether, for money, he would make two red sausages from his sow — and paid him some silver pennies for it right there. The slaughterer did so, making him two fine sausages. And Eulenspiegel took them, boiled them half through, as was customary with such sausages, and went back to Egelsheim the following Sunday. But it happened that the priest was holding early mass; so he went over to the parsonage, brought his sausages to the cook, and told her to roast them for breakfast. The priest was to have one and he the other. Then he went into the church.

---

1. The bacon of the time consisted simply of the meatless fat behind the ribs of the pig. It was both the cheapest and the poorest tasting part of the animal.

2. *i.e.*, those who slaughter pigs for products other than food.

Well, the girl placed the sausages on the fire and roasted them. When the mass was over, the priest noticed Eulenspiegel and immediately left the church for the parsonage, where he said, "Eulenspiegel is here. Did he bring the sausages too?"

She said, "Yes, two sausages finer than almost any I've ever seen; and they're both just about roasted." And she went over and took one out of the hot fire. Now, she was as greedy for the sausages as the priest — so they both sat down to eat together. But as they were eating the sausages so lustily, their mouths began to drip with filth. Another man saw and heard the priest saying to his servant girl, "Oh, my dear girl! How your mouth froths!"

But the girl answered the priest, "Oh, dear sir! Your mouth is just the same!"

And just at that moment, Eulenspiegel came in from church. So the priest said to him, "Look here, what kind of sausages did you bring? Look how messy my mouth and my servant girl's mouth are!"

Eulenspiegel laughed. "God bless you," he said. "What's happening to you is exactly according to your wishes when you called after me to bring two sausages from which you planned to eat till your mouth got messy. But I paid no attention to the kind of mess — as long as vomit didn't follow it. I understand, though: that'll soon come. For those two sausages were made from a dead sow; so I had to boil them clean with soap. The mess comes from that."

The girl began to gag, and vomited all over the table. The priest did the same. And he said, "Get out of my house, you rogue." And he grabbed a club to beat him with.

Eulenspiegel said, "This doesn't become a pious man. You told me to bring these two sausages. Well, you've eaten both of them, and now you plan to beat me. First pay me for the sausages; I'll forget about the third one."

The priest became furious and almost crazy with rage and said he himself ought to have eaten his moldy sausages made from the corpse of a sow, and not have brought such things into his house.

Eulenspiegel said, "I certainly haven't made you sick

against your wishes. Besides, I wouldn't want these sausages. I might have liked the first one, though. That one you ate against my wishes. Since you've gobbled up the first, good sausage — eat the bad ones too." And he said, "Adieu! Good night!"

38. How Eulenspiegel, with a false confession, talked the priest of Küssenbrück out of his horse.

Eulenspiegel did not refrain from terrible mischief at Küssenbrück,[1] a village in the Asseburg jurisdiction. A priest was living there too, who had a very pretty girl as his maid and a little, pretty, smart horse — both of which the priest liked — the horse as much as the girl.

The Duke of Brunswick[2] was in Küssenbrück at that time and had asked the priest, through other people, to let him have the horse: he would give him whatever would satisfy him for it. The priest continually refused the prince, for he had no desire to give up his horse. And the prince was also not permitted to have the horse simply taken away, since the law there was under his own administration of Bruns-

---

1. Grieninger has "Ryesseburg." Küssenbrück is a village south of Wolfenbüttel.

2. This must have been either Henry the Strange, who died in 1322, or his son Henry II. See Lappenberg, p. 253.

wick. Well, Eulenspiegel heard about the matter, thought it over, and told the prince, "Gracious Lord, what will you give me if I get that horse away from the priest of Küssenbrück?"

"If you can do it," said the Duke, "I'll give you the coat I'm wearing." Well, it was a red camlet coat, woven with pearls.

Eulenspiegel accepted the challenge, and rode out of Wolfenbüttel to take lodgings with the priest in the village. Now, Eulenspiegel was well known at the priest's house, for he had often stayed with him before and was welcome to him. When he had been there about three days, he pretended to be ill, complained loudly of pain, and lay down. The priest and his cook, the girl, were unhappy about this, but had no idea what they ought to do about it. Finally Eulenspiegel became so sick that the priest addressed him, exorting him to confess and receive God's mercy. Eulenspiegel was quite inclined to do so — as long as the priest himself would confess him and question him as sharply as possible. So the priest told him to consider well the state of his soul, for he had done many tricky things during his lifetime; therefore he should prove himself true, so God would forgive him his sins.

Eulenspiegel spoke most pitiably, telling the priest he knew of nothing he had done — aside from one sin, one he dared not confess to him. He would rather he got another priest: he would confess it to him. For he feared that were he to confess it to him, he would become quite angry. When the priest heard this, he reflected there might be some secret here; and since he wanted to find out what it was, he said to Eulenspiegel, "Eulenspiegel, the road is long; I can't find another priest so quickly; and if you should die in the meantime, you and I shall bear the blame before Our Lord God, if you thus miss your chance. Tell me what it is. Your sin cannot be so terrible: I want to absolve you of it. Besides, what good would it do me to get angry? I cannot betray a confession."

Eulenspiegel said, "All right. I'll confess it." It would not be so terrible either, but he was sorry that the priest would become angry — for the sin concerned him. The priest now yearned even more to know what it was, and said to him

95

that whether he had stolen something or done him some damage — no matter what it might be — he should confess it to him. He intended to forgive him for it and never despise him for it.

"Ah, dear Father," said Eulenspiegel, "I know that you'll be very angry about it. But I know and fear that soon I must take my leave of this place. So I'll tell it to you, letting God decide whether you become calm or angry. And, dear Father, it's this: I've slept with your servant girl."

The priest asked how often this had happened.

Eulenspiegel said, "Just five times."

The priest thought, "She ought to get five strokes outside for this." And he quickly absolved him, went to his room, and called the girl to him. Well, he asked her whether she had slept with Eulenspiegel.

The girl, his cook, said, no, it was a lie.

But the priest said Eulenspiegel had confessed it to him — and he believed it.

She said, "No."

He said, "Yes."

And he caught up a stick and beat her black and blue. Eulenspiegel lay laughing in bed, and thought, "This game ought to turn out well now and have a decent result." And he lay there all day.

During the night he became healthy again. And the next day he got up, said he was getting better, and had to leave for another district, so the priest should figure out how much he had eaten there. The priest did the figuring with him, but was so confused he had no idea what he was doing — so he took money but it was no money, for he was happy enough that Eulenspiegel was leaving. The girl felt the same, since it was because of him that she had been beaten.

Well, Eulenspiegel was ready to go. "Sir," he said, "you should be warned that you have revealed my confession. I plan to go to the Bishop of Halberstädt and expose you."

The priest forgot his sin of malice when he heard that Eulenspiegel intended to bring him difficulties and begged him, with great seriousness, to keep silent; it had happened

96

because of rashness; he would give him twenty guilders as long as he did not sue him.

Eulenspiegel said, "No. I wouldn't take a hundred guilders to keep silent about this. I shall go, and prefer charges, as is proper."

With tearful eyes the priest called his servant girl and said she should ask him to tell her what he should give him: she would give it to him. Finally Eulenspiegel said: if he would give him his horse, he would keep silent and it would remain unknown. He would, moreover, take nothing but the horse. The priest liked his horse very much and would rather have given him all his ready cash than lose his horse. But he gave it up against his will, for necessity forced him to; he gave his horse to Eulenspiegel and let him ride off with it.

So Eulenspiegel rode to Wolfenbüttel with the priest's horse. Well, he arrived at the moat. The Duke was standing there, on the drawbridge, and saw Eulenspiegel trotting up with the horse. At once the prince took off the coat he had promised Eulenspiegel, went straight over to him, and said, "Look here, my dear Eulenspiegel. Here is the coat I promised you."

And he got off the horse and said, "Gracious Lord, here's your horse." Well, he was full of thanks for the Duke and had to tell him how he had gotten the horse away from the priest. It made the prince laugh, and he was glad about it — and gave Eulenspiegel another horse in addition to the coat.

But the priest mourned his horse, and beat the girl quite cruelly because of it — so much so that she left him. And thus he lost both.

39. How Eulenspiegel hired himself out to a smith—and how he carried his bellows into the courtyard for him.

Eulenspiegel arrived at Rostock, in the district of Mecklenburg, and hired himself out as a blacksmith's assistant. Now, this blacksmith had a favorite saying, whereby when his assistant was supposed to blow on the bellows, he said, "Ha-ho, follow with the bellows!" Well, Eulenspiegel was standing at the bellows and blowing. And the smith, in a harsh voice, said to Eulenspiegel, "Ha-ho, follow after with the bellows!" And with these words he went into the courtyard, intending to drain off his water.

So Eulenspiegel placed one of the bellows on his shoulder and followed after his master, saying, "Master, I'm bringing one bellows here. Where should I put it? I'll go and bring the other also."

The master looked around and said, "Dear servant boy, I didn't mean it that way. Go put the bellows back."

Eulenspiegel did so, returning it to its place. Now, his master wondered how he might pay him back for this, and decided to get up at midnight every night for five days, wake up his assistant, and have him work. So he woke up both his assistants and let them do some forging.

Eulenspiegel's fellow assistant began to speak: "What can our master mean by waking us up so early? He doesn't usually do so."

So Eulenspiegel said, "If you like, I'll ask him."

The boy said, "All right."

So Eulenspiegel said, "Dear master, why're you waking us up so early? It's just midnight."

His master said, "It's my custom that in the beginning — and for eight days — my boys don't sleep longer than half the night."

Eulenspiegel kept quiet — and his companion dared not speak — till the next night. Then his master woke them up and Eulenspiegel's companion went to work. But Eulenspiegel took his bed and tied it onto his back. Then, when the iron was hot, he came running down from the garret to the anvil, crashing the bed against it so the sparks spewed into the bed.

The blacksmith said to him, "Look here! What're you doing? Have you gone crazy? Can't the bed stay where it's supposed to be?"

Eulenspiegel said, "Master, don't be angry. This is *my* custom — that during the first weeks I lie on the bed for half the night and for the second half of the night the bed lies on me."

His master became furious, telling him to return the bed he had taken. Then he continued rashly, "Now, you maddening fool, get up and out of my house!"

He said, "Yes." So he went up to the garret, putting back the bed he had taken, found a ladder, stuck it against the coping, broke the roof open, went onto the roof with the ladder, pulled the ladder up after him, set it into the street from the roof, climbed down, and so got away.

The blacksmith heard him making loud noises and followed him into the garret with his other assistant. There he saw that he had broken the roof open and climbed out. He now became even more furious and looked for a skewer, throwing it out of the house after him. But his assistant grabbed his master, saying to him, "Master, not like this! Admit he hasn't done anything other than what you told him to. When you told him to get up and out of the house, he did so, as you now see." The smith let himself be pacified.

And what else could he do? Eulenspiegel was gone and his master had to have his roof mended — and had to be satisfied with that.

His assistant said, "Not much to be gained from a fellow-worker like that one. Whoever doesn't know Eulenspiegel — just let him deal with him and he'll get to know him."

40. How Eulenspiegel forged a blacksmith's hammer, tongs, and things together.

When Eulenspiegel left the blacksmith, it was nearing winter. Now, the winter was cold and froze cruelly. And he fell on hard times because of it, for many workers were going without work. Well, Eulenspiegel had no money to waste, so he wandered on and came to a village where a smith was living also, who took him in as a blacksmith's assistant. But Eulenspiegel had no great desire to remain there as a smith's boy — though his hunger and the need of winter forced him to do so — so he thought, "Bear what you can bear, and do what the smith wants — till you can stick your finger into spongy earth again."[1]

But the smith had no intention of hiring him just because times were hard. So Eulenspiegel told the smith that if he would give him work, he would do whatever he wished —

1. *i.e.*, until spring comes.

and eat whatever he gave him. Well, the smith was a wicked man, and he thought, "Take him on for eight days' trial: he won't eat me into poverty that soon."

The next morning they began forging, and the smith drove Eulenspiegel mercilessly, at hammer and bellows, till mealtime when it was getting toward noon. Well, the smith had an outhouse in the courtyard. And as they were preparing to go to table, the smith took Eulenspiegel into the courtyard, led him to the outhouse, and said to him, "Look, you say you're willing to eat whatever I wish, as long as I give you work. Now, nobody'd enjoy what's in here —so you eat it all." And he went into the house, ate something, and left Eulenspiegel standing at the outhouse.

Eulenspiegel kept quiet, but he thought, "You've run the wrong way here, and done such things yourself to many people — to the extent to which it's now being measured out to you. How do you plan to pay him back for this? For it's got to be paid back, though the winter were twice as harsh."

Eulenspiegel worked for him till evening. Then the smith gave Eulenspiegel something to eat, for he had gone hungry all day, and besides it stuck in the smith's head that he had shown him to the outhouse. As Eulenspiegel was getting ready to go to bed, the smith said to him, "Get up tomorrow morning. The girl will work the bellows, and you forge whatever you've got, one thing after the other. And cut horseshoe nails till I get up."

So Eulenspiegel went to sleep. But when he got up, he thought he would now pay him back — even if he had to run through snow up to his knees. He built a fierce fire, took the tongs, melted them in the sand-ladle, and forged them together — doing the same to two hammers, the firing spit and the poker. Then he took the box in which the horseshoe nails lay, poured the horseshoe nails out of it, and cut the heads off them, putting the heads together and the stumps as well. And as he heard the smith getting up, he took his leather apron and got out of there.

The smith entered his workshop and saw that the nails and heads had been cut apart and that his hammer, tongs and other things had been forged together. He now became angry and screamed at the girl to tell him where his assistant had gone. The girl said he had gone out.

The smith said, "He's gone — like a rogue. If I knew where he was, I'd ride after him and give him a fine slapping."

The girl said, "He was writing something over the door as he left. It's a face that looks like an owl's."

Now, Eulenspiegel had this custom whenever he did some mischief where he was not known: he took chalk or coal and drew an owl and a mirror over the door, and underneath wrote, in Latin, *Hic fuit*. And this Eulenspiegel had drawn on the smith's door as well.

When the smith went out of his house that morning, he found it, as the girl had told him. But because the smith could not read the language, he went to the priest and asked him to go with him to read the writing over his door. The priest went with the smith to his door, and saw the writing and the picture.

So he told the smith, "It simply means 'Eulenspiegel was here.'" Now, the priest had heard a great deal about Eulenspiegel — about the sort of fellow he was — and scolded the smith because he had not let him know, for he would greatly have liked to have seen Eulenspiegel.

The smith now grew angry with the priest and said, "How could I let you know about it, when I didn't know myself? But I know now that he was definitely in my house: that you can see well enough by my working tools. But that he never comes back, there isn't much against it." Then he took the coal-brush, whisked off what was above his door, and said, "I don't want any fool's coat of arms over my door."

The priest walked off, leaving the smith standing there. But Eulenspiegel did not appear — and did not return.

41. How Eulenspiegel told something true to a blacksmith, his wife, his assistant, and his servant girl in front of his house.

After he left the smith, Eulenspiegel arrived in Wismar on a holy day. He saw a proper wife and her maid standing in front of the smithy there; and it was the blacksmith's wife. Well, he took lodgings opposite the smithy and during the night broke all four horseshoes off his horse, marching up in front of the smithy the next day. And so he was recognized.

When he came up to the smithy and they realized it was Eulenspiegel, the wife and maid came to an entrance of the house, for they wished to hear and see Eulenspiegel's business. Eulenspiegel asked the smith whether he would shoe his horse.

"Yes," he said. Now, it pleased the smith to be able to converse with him; and after much talk, the smith happened to say to him that if he could tell him one true thing — something that was really true — he would give his horse one horseshoe.

He said, "All right:
"If you've got iron and coals
And wind for your bellows' holes —
You can forge well."

The smith said that, by his soul, that was true, and gave him a horseshoe.

His assistant was putting the irons on the horse and felt compelled to say to Eulenspiegel that if he could also tell him something true concerning him, he would give his horse a horseshoe too.

Eulenspiegel said, "All right:
"If they want to set about something,
A blacksmith and his boy
Must stand to hard employ."

The boy said, "That's true too," and gave him a horseshoe as well.

The wife and maid saw this and pressed closer, to be able to speak with Eulenspiegel too; and they said to him that if he could tell them something true too, they would give him one horseshoe each.

Eulenspiegel said, "Very well." And he said to the wife:
"The wife who stands before her doors
With lots of white in her eye,
If she had the time and were free of chores —
There wouldn't be fish to fry."

The wife said, "By my soul, that's true." And she gave him a horseshoe too.

Then he said to the maid, "When you eat, guard against beef: you won't have to pick your teeth, and your stomach won't bother you."

The maid said, "God protect us, how true that is!" And she gave him an iron also.

So Eulenspiegel rode away, and his horse was well shod for him.

42. How Eulenspiegel worked for a shoemaker and how he asked him what shapes he should cut. His master said, "Large and small—like those the swineherd runs past the gate." So he cut out oxen, cattle, calves, rams, and the like—and ruined the leather.

There was once a shoemaker who much preferred strolling around the market-place to working, and he hired Eulenspiegel for cutting. Eulenspiegel asked what shapes he would like, and the shoemaker said, "Cut both large and small — like those the swineherd runs out of town."

He said, "Yes."

The shoemaker went out, and Eulenspiegel to cutting — and he made pigs, oxen, calves, sheep, goats, rams, and all sorts of beasts out of his leather. In the evening his master returned, intending to see what his assistant had cut — and he found these animals cut out of his leather. He became angry and said to Eulenspiegel, "What've you made out of

106

it? How could you cut up my leather so uselessly for me?"

Eulenspiegel said, "Dear master, I've done it as you wanted it."

The master said, "You're lying. I didn't mean that you should destroy it. I didn't ask you to do that."

Eulenspiegel said, "Master, what's the reason for this anger? You told me I should cut large and small out of the leather — like the swineherd runs past the gate. I did so. That's obvious."

The master said, "I didn't mean it that way. I meant this: they should be large and small shoes, and you should stitch them, one after the other."

Eulenspiegel: "If you'd asked me to do that, I'd gladly have done so. And I'd still be glad to do so."

Well, Eulenspiegel and his master were reconciled, and he forgave him that cutting. For Eulenspiegel promised him he would do it for him as he told him he wanted it done. So the shoemaker cut out leather for soles, put it in front of Eulenspiegel, and said, "Now look: stitch the small with the large, one after the other."

He said, "Yes," and began stitching.

His master delayed in going out, for he wanted to watch Eulenspiegel to see how he planned to do it — since he had realized that he would do exactly what he had told him to do.

Well, he acted according to his master's instructions. Eulenspiegel took one small shoe and one large, put the small into the large, and stitched them together. Well, as his master was going strolling, he became anxious about what he might be doing. Then he saw that he was stitching one shoe through the other.

So he said, "You're my proper assistant: you do everything I tell you to."

Eulenspiegel said, "He who does what he's told doesn't get punished. On the contrary."

His master said, "Yes, my dear helper, that's true. My words ran this way — but my meaning didn't run this way. I meant you should make a pair of small shoes, and *afterwards* a large pair. Or the large first, the small next. You're acting according to the words, not the meaning." And he became angry, took the leather, and said, "Pay attention a little! Look, here's more leather. Cut the shoes out over a last." And he thought no more about it, for he had to go out.

The master was tending to his affairs and had been out almost an hour, when he realized that he had told his assistant to cut the shoes over *a* last. He dropped everything and rushed home. Well, during this time Eulenspiegel had been sitting there, and had taken the leather and cut all of it over a last.

So he said, "Why're you doing the large shoes with the small?"

Eulenspiegel said, "Well, you wanted it that way. I still plan to do everything well. — So now, afterwards, I'll cut the large ones."

The master said, "One can better cut small shoes out of large than large out of small. You're using one last and the other is left for nothing."

Eulenspiegel said, "True enough, master. You told me to cut the shoes out over *a* last."

The master said, "I might go on *telling* you — till I have to run you to the gallows." And he went on to say that he ought to pay for the leather he had ruined for him, since he had to buy more leather.

Eulenspiegel said, "The tanner can fix your leather again." Then he stood up, went to the door, turned around in the house, and said, "If I don't come back to this house — at least I've been here." And he left.

43. How Eulenspiegel sprinkled a soup for a farmer, putting filthy=smelling fish oil on it instead of bread and drippings—and thought that was good enough for the farmer.

Eulenspiegel did a great deal of mischief to shoemakers — not just in one place but in many. When he had done this last bit of mischief, he arrived in Stade. There too he hired himself out to a shoemaker.

On the first day, when he started working, his master went off to the market and bought a cartload of wood. Well, he agreed to give the farmer a soup as well as money and brought the farmer with the wood to his house. There he found no one at home (his wife and maid had gone out) other than Eulenspiegel, who was alone in the house, stitching shoes. Since his master had to return to the market, he told Eulenspiegel to take what he had and make the farmer a soup: he had left him something in the cupboard.

Eulenspiegel said, "All right."

Well, the farmer threw down his wood and came into the

house. Eulenspiegel cut pieces of bread into the bowl for him, but found no melted-down fat in the cupboard. So he went to the tank in which the awful-smelling fish oil was kept, and sprinkled the farmer's soup with that. The farmer began eating and tasted how terrible it was — but he was hungry and ate all the soup.

In the meantime the shoemaker came in and asked the farmer how the soup had tasted. The farmer said, "It tasted very good — and just a little like new shoes." And with that the farmer left the house.

The shoemaker began to laugh and asked Eulenspiegel what he had used to sprinkle the farmer's soup with.

Eulenspiegel said, "You told me to take what I had. Well, I had no fat other than fish fat — for I looked into the cupboard in the kitchen and didn't find any fat. So I took what I had."

The shoemaker said, "Well, that's all right. It's good enough for the farmer."

44. How a bootmaker in Brunswick larded Eulenspiegel's boots—and how Eulenspiegel knocked the windows out of his room.

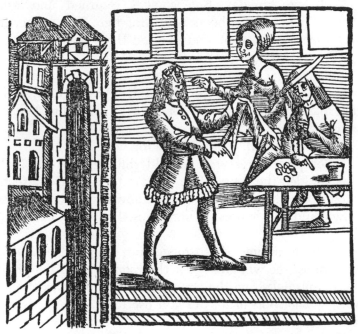

"Christopher" was the name of a bootmaker at the coal market in Brunswick. Eulenspiegel went to him, intending to have his boots oiled. When he came up to the bootmaker, he said, "Master, would you lard[1] these boots for me, so I can have them back by Monday?"

The master said, "Very well."

Eulenspiegel left the house and thought no more about it. When he was gone, the apprentice said to his master, "That's Eulenspiegel, who's too mischievous with everybody." — And that if *he* were to tell him to do "What he told you to do, *he* would do it and not fail to."

The master said, "Well, what did he tell me to do?"

The apprentice said, "He really told you to 'lard' his boots — and he meant to 'oil' them. Now, I wouldn't oil them: I'd lard them, as one bastes a roast."

---

1. "Lard" was evidently a bit of bootmaker's jargon for "oil."

The master said, "That we'll do — just as he told us." So he took bacon, cut it up, and larded the boots with a larding-needle — like a roast.

Well, on Monday Eulenspiegel returned and asked whether they had his boots ready for him. The master had hung them on the wall, and pointed them out to him, saying, "There they hang."

Eulenspiegel saw that his boots had in fact been larded — and he began to laugh, and said, "What a straight-for-ward master you are! You've done it as I told you to. What do you want for it?"

The master said, "One old shilling."

Eulenspiegel presented the old shilling, took his larded boots, and left the house. Well, the master and his apprentice watched, laughing after him; and they said to one another, "How could that happen to him? Now he's been made a fool of."

In the meantime Eulenspiegel ran his head and shoulders against the window — for the room was on the ground floor — pushing from the street, and said to the bootmaker, "Master, what sort of fat did you use for my boots? Is it fat from a sow or from a boar?"

The master and his apprentice were stunned. Finally they realized that Eulenspiegel was lying in the window and knocking the window panes fully half-out — with the result that they were falling toward him into the room. He now became furious and said, "You tricky liar! If you don't stop, I'll beat you over the head with this stick!"

Eulenspiegel said, "Dear master, don't lose your temper. I'd like to know what sort of fat it was that you larded my boots with. Is it from a sow or a boar?"

The master was furious and said he had better leave his windows unbroken.

"If you don't want to tell me what kind of fat it is, I'll have to ask somebody else." And Eulenspiegel jumped out of the window.

Well, the master was quite angry with his apprentice and said to him, "You advised me to do this! Now give me advice on how to have my windows repaired!"

The apprentice was silent. His master was indignant and said, "Who's made a fool of whom? I've always heard whoever's bothered by knaves should cut the traces and let them go. If I'd done so, my windows would still be in one piece."

The apprentice was fired because of this. For his master wanted his windows paid for — since he had given him the idea to lard the boots.

45. How Eulenspiegel sold a shoemaker of Wismar frozen filth for grease.

Eulenspiegel once did a lot of damage in cutting to a shoemaker of Wismar, destroying much of his leather and making the good man quite unhappy. Eulenspiegel realized this, returned to Wismar, and told the shoemaker to whom he had done the damage that he was about to receive a huge load of leather and grease — which ought to yield him great profit —so he might recover his loss.

The shoemaker said, "Well, you're acting fairly, since you've made me a poor man. When you get the goods, let me know."

Then they parted. Well, it was wintertime, and the harnessmakers were cleaning the outhouses. Eulenspiegel went to them and promised them ready money if they would fill twelve barrels for him with the material they were otherwise planning to dispose of in the water. The harnessmakers did so, packing the barrels quite full, so they were four fingers from the top, and left them standing till they had frozen stiff. Then Eulenspiegel hauled them away. Well, he caked six barrels over thickly with grease, beating them tightly shut; smeared six barrels over with cooking fat, beating these all tightly shut; had them brought to his inn, "At the Golden Star," for a Dutch guilder; and sent a messenger to the shoemaker. When he came, they opened the goods on top, and the shoemaker was quite pleased with them. They settled the purchase, with the shoemaker giving Eulenspiegel twenty-four guilders for the load: he was to give him twelve guilders at once, the rest in a year. Eulenspiegel took the money and left — for he was worried about what would happen.

The shoemaker received his goods and was as happy as one who has overcome hopeless injury or debt — and summoned help to be able to oil his leather the next day. The shoemaker's boys came in strength, thinking they would get a good meal, and set about the work, singing loudly, as they usually do. But when they had placed the barrels on the fire and they began to get warm, they regained their natural smell. Everybody said to everybody else, "I think you've been shitting in your pants."

The master said, "If somebody's stepped in some filth, wash your shoes. It stinks terribly everywhere."

They looked all around but found nothing, and began to pour the grease into a kettle and begin oiling. But the deeper they dug with their oiling the more foully it stank. Finally they realized what it was and left the work standing.

The master and his assistants ran to look for Eulenspiegel, to hold him for the damages, but he was gone with the money — and was even supposed to return for the other twelve guilders. So the shoemaker had to take his barrels of grease to the slaughterers' burial place and sustain double his loss.

46. How Eulenspiegel became a brewer's assistant at Eimbeck, and how he boiled a dog called Hops—instead of hops.

Again Eulenspiegel made himself useful in his work.

Once, after people at Eimbeck had forgotten about his shitting on the plums,[1] he returned to Eimbeck and offered his services to a brewer of beer.[2] It happened that the brewer wanted to go to a wedding, so he told Eulenspiegel to brew beer with his servant girl as best he could. He would come back to help him in the evening. Now, above all, he should act industriously and boil the hops well, so the beer would taste strong afterwards and he could sell it. Eulenspiegel said, yes, he would do his best. With that, the brewer and his wife left the house.

Eulenspiegel began boiling enthusiastically. The servant girl instructed him, for she knew more about it than he did.

---

1. Possibly a reference to the eighty-seventh story.
2. Eimbeck was famous for its beer during the Middle Ages. See Lappenberg, p. 255.

Well, when the time came to boil the hops, the girl said, "The boiling of the hops, dear — that you can do very well by yourself. Let me watch the dance for an hour."

Eulenspiegel said, "Yes." And he thought, "If the girl leaves too, you've got a chance for some fun. What sort of joke would you like to play on this brewer?"

Well, the brewer had a large dog called Hops. When the water was very hot, he took it, threw it into the water, and let it boil through till its skin and hair came off and the flesh fell off its legs on all sides. Now, when the servant girl thought it was time to go home — for the hops must have had enough — she went, intending to help Eulenspiegel. And she said, "My dear brother, that's enough now. Drain it off."

But when they moved the straining basket and started to dig into it, one shovelful after the other, the girl said, "Did you put hops in here too? I don't notice any yet on my shovel."

Eulenspiegel said, "You'll find it at the bottom."

The girl fished around and lifted the skeleton on her shovel. She began to scream loudly. "God help me, what did you put in here! The devil drink this beer!"

Eulenspiegel said, "I put into it what our brewer told me to put into it. Why, it's nothing other than Hops, our dog."

At this moment the brewer arrived, quite drunk, and said, "What're you doing, my dear children? Are you being good little things?"

The girl said, "I don't know what the devil we're doing. I went to watch the dance for half an hour, and told our new assistant to boil the hops well in the meantime. And he boiled our dog. You can see its spine here."

Eulenspiegel said, "Yes, sir. You both told me to do so. Isn't it terrible? I do everything that people tell me to — and can never earn any thinks. There may be some brewers somewhere who'll be satisfied if their servants do only half what they're told to do."

So Eulenspiegel quit, and left the place — without earning great thanks.

47. How Eulenspiegel hired himself out to a tailor and sewed under a tub.

When Eulenspiegel arrived in Berlin, he hired himself out as a tailor's boy. When he was sitting in the workshop, his master said, "Boy, when you want to sew, sew well and sew so nobody sees it."

Eulenspiegel said, "Yes." And he took the needle and material with it, crawled under a tub, quilted a seam over one knee, and began to sew it there.

The tailor stood watching this, and he said to him, "What're you doing? This is strange needlework."

Eulenspiegel said, "Master, you said I should sew so nobody sees it. Well, nobody sees it."

The tailor said, "No, my dear assistant. Stop and don't sew that way any more. Start sewing so it can be seen."

This lasted one day or three, when it happened that they worked till nightfall. The tailor was tired and wanted to go to bed. A gray farmer's coat was lying there, half unsewn, which he tossed to Eulenspiegel, saying, "Look, finish the wolf[1] and go to bed too."

Eulenspiegel said, "Yes. You just go ahead. I'll do it properly."

His master went to bed and thought no more about it. Eulenspiegel took the gray coat and cut it up — making a head like a wolf's out of it, with body and legs, and stretching it over separated sticks, so it quite resembled a wolf. Then he went to bed too.

The next morning his master got up, woke Eulenspiegel as well, and found the wolf standing in his workroom. His master was astonished, but he saw that it had been made all right. Eulenspiegel came in just then, and the tailor said, "What the devil did you make out of it?"

He said, "A wolf — as you told me."

The tailor said, "I didn't mean that sort of wolf. I simply called the gray farmer's coat a wolf."

Eulenspiegel said, "Dear master, that I didn't realize. If I'd known your thoughts ran that way, I'd have preferred making the coat to making the wolf."

Well, the tailor was satisfied, since it had happened just once. But it happened after about four days that his master grew tired one evening and wanted to go to sleep early. It seemed to him, however, that it was still too early for his assistant to go to bed. Now, a coat was lying there that had been finished up to its arms. So his master took the coat and its loose arms, threw them to Eulenspiegel and said, "Cast these arms on the coat, and then go to bed."

Eulenspiegel said, "Yes."

His master went to bed — and Eulenspiegel hung the coat on a hook and lit two lamps, one on either side of the coat. He took one arm and threw it at the coat, and went to the other side and threw the other at it also; and when the two lamps burned out, he lit two more — casting the arms on the coat through the night till morning. His master then got up and came into the room. Eulenspiegel did not turn around for his master and kept casting the arms ahead of him.

---

1. A slang term for such coats. See Lappenberg, p. 256.

The tailor stood there, looked at this, and said, "What sort of devilish fraud are you engaged in?"

Eulenspiegel said quite seriously, "This isn't any devilish fraud for me. I've been standing here all night — throwing these crazy arms at this coat, and they won't stay there. It would have been better if you'd told me to go to bed than telling me to 'cast on.' And you knew perfectly well that this was pointless work."

The tailor said, "Is it my fault? Could I know that you would interpret me that way? I didn't mean it that way. I meant that you should sew the arms on the coat."

Eulenspiegel then said, "The devil reward you for it. If you've a fancy to say something other than what you mean, how is one to rhyme the things together? If I'd known your intentions clearly, I'd have sewn the arms on all right — and gotten a few hours of sleep. Well, you sit and sew all day, and I'll lie down and sleep."

His master said, "Oh, no, not that way. I'm not going to keep you as a sleeper."

And they began to quarrel with each other — and so much that during their quarreling the tailor spoke to Eulenspiegel about the lamps: he ought to pay him for those he had burned during this business. At that point Eulenspiegel took up his things and walked away.

48. How Eulenspiegel made three tailor's boys fall off a bench—and told people the wind had blown them off it.

Eulenspiegel stayed at an inn near the market-place in Brandenburg for about fourteen days. Now, hard by the inn lived a tailor who had three boys sitting on a bench and sewing. And whenever Eulenspiegel passed by, they mocked him or threw their remnants at him. Eulenspiegel kept quiet, biding his time. But one day when the market-place was full of people, Eulenspiegel had sawn off the supporting posts of the bench the night before and left them standing on their foundations.

That morning the apprentices placed the bench on its posts, sat down, and sewed. But when the swineherd began his calling — that everybody ought to have his pigs driven out — the tailor's pigs came out of his house, rushed under his window, and began to rub themselves against the bench-posts. The result of their rubbing was that the posts were punched from under the window, and the three boys beneath

121

the window tumbled into the lane. Well, Eulenspiegel took their wares; and as they fell, Eulenspiegel began calling in a loud voice, "Look, look, the wind's blowing three boys out of this window!" — calling it so loudly that it could be heard through the whole market-place. Well, the people ran over and laughed and jeered; but the boys were embarrassed, and had no idea how they had dropped from the window. Finally they realized that the bench-posts had been sawn through — and realized also that Eulenspiegel had done this to them. They pounded new posts into place — and never dared mock him again.

49. How Eulenspiegel called all the tailors of Saxony together to teach them a skill that would help them and their children.

Eulenspiegel announced a convocation and assembly of the tailors of the Wendish towns and of the district of Saxony — also of those in the districts of Holstein, Pomerania, Stettin, and Mecklenburg; also of Lübeck, Hamburg, Sunt, and Wismar. And in his letter he assured them of a grand opportunity — namely that if they would come to him (he was in the city of Rostock) he would teach them a skill that would help them and their children for all time, for as long as the world might last.

The tailors in the cities and country towns and in the villages wrote their opinions of this to one another. They all wrote that they were prepared to come to the city at a certain time and would all assemble there; and each longed more than the next to learn what it might be that Eulenspiegel planned to say or what sort of skill he would teach, since he had written to them so urgently. Well, they came to Rostock at the appointed time — all according to their pledges — with the result that many people wondered what these tailors wanted there.

When Eulenspiegel heard that the tailors had actually arrived at his bidding, he had them come together till they all stood next to one another. The tailors then told Eulenspiegel that they had come there and followed him because of his announcement, in which he had alluded to the fact that he could teach them a skill that would help them and their children. So they asked that he enlighten them, make the skill public, and inform them about it: they would give him a reward.

Eulenspiegel said, "All right. Let's all meet in a meadow, so each of you can hear me."

They all met on a broad plain; and Eulenspiegel climbed up inside a house, peered out of a window, and said, "Honorable men of the craft of tailoring! You should note and understand: if you have a pair of scissors, tape-measure,[1] thread, and a thimble, along with a needle, you have equipment enough for your craft. To acquire these needs no skill for you; rather it follows of itself, if you wish to practice your craft. But this skill you will receive of me, and you'll thank me for it: when you have threaded your needle, do not forget to make a knot at the other end, or you will stitch many stitches for nothing, for the thread will have no reason not to slip out of the needle."

Each tailor looked at the next, and they said to one another, "We all knew this skill well enough before — along with everything he's told us." And they asked him whether he had anything more to say, since they had not planned on traveling ten or twelve miles — and sending messengers to each other — for this nonsense. Tailors had known this skill for a long time — for more than a thousand years.

Eulenspiegel now answered them, saying, "There isn't anybody who remembers what happened a thousand years

---

1. Probably about twenty-seven inches, though the length of the elle, to which Eulenspiegel is here referring, varied a great deal.

ago." He also said that if this were not according to their pleasure and thanks, they might as well take it in displeasure and have no thanks for doing so — and that the crowd could just go back to where it had come from. The tailors, who had come from so far away and who really wanted to be instructed by him, now became angry; but they could not get at him. So the tailors parted from one another again. Some were furious, cursed, and were thoroughly annoyed that they had gone such a great distance for nothing. But those who lived in nearby houses laughed and jeered at the others because they had made such fools of themselves, and said it was their own fault if they believed country rogues and knaves — for they ought to have realized long ago what sort of bird Eulenspiegel was.

50. How Eulenspiegel beat wool on a holy day, because the clothier had forbidden his having Monday off.

When Eulenspiegel arrived in Stendal,[1] he hired himself out to a weaver of wool. Now, this was on a Sunday, so the wool-weaver said to him, "Dear apprentice, you fellows take your days off on Monday[2] — but whoever's accustomed to doing so, him I don't want in my business: a boy's got to work right through the week."

Eulenspiegel said, "Yes, master, I like that best of all."

So the next morning Eulenspiegel got up and beat wool, doing the same on Tuesday; and this quite pleased the wool-

---

1. Stendal was well known for its textiles and wool-weaving during the Middle Ages. See Lappenberg, p. 257.

2. Our colloquialism "blue Monday" apparently has its origin at about this time and may derive from the custom of apprentices' taking their day off on Monday and so making Monday a poor day for business. See Lappenberg, p. 258.

weaver. Now, Wednesday was an Apostle's day, which they had to celebrate; but Eulenspiegel acted as though he did not know about the holy day, got up that morning, and started to clean and beat wool — so it could be heard through the whole street. The wool-weaver at once shot out of his bed, and said to him, "Stop! Stop! This is a holy day."

Eulenspiegel said, "Dear master, you informed me of no holy day on Sunday. On the contrary, you told me to work the whole week through."

The wool-weaver said, "Dear assistant, I didn't mean it that way. Just stop and don't beat any more. I'll gladly give you whatever you might have earned today."

Eulenspiegel was satisfied with that, took the day off, and that evening had a conference with his master. The wool-weaver now told him that he was succeeding quite well with his beating of the wool — only he ought to beat it a little higher.

Eulenspiegel said, "Yes."

He arose early the next morning and stretched the bow over the lath and placed a ladder against it. Then he climbed up, arranging it so the beater could follow him from the basket; took the wool from the basket (which was standing on the ground) up to this platform; and beat the wool so it scattered all over the house. The wool-weaver was lying in bed; and he could hear by the beating that he was not doing it properly, so he got up to watch him.

Eulenspiegel said, "Master, what do you think? Is this high enough?"

His master said, "Ha! True fellow! If you stood on the roof, you'd be even higher. If you want to beat the wool that way, you might as well do it sitting down on the roof instead of standing up here on this ladder." And with that he left the house for church.

Well, Eulenspiegel took his advice. He took the beater, climbed up on the roof, and beat the wool on the roof. His master, outside in the lane, saw this. He quickly ran back, shouting, "What the devil are you doing! Stop! Is it customary to beat wool on the roof?"

Eulenspiegel said, "What're you saying now? You just said it would be better on the roof than on the ladder, because that's higher than its beams."

The wool-weaver said, "If you want to beat wool, beat it; if you want to fool around, fool around: climb off the roof and shit in the wool-basket." With that the wool-weaver went into his house and out into his courtyard. And Eulenspiegel at once climbed off the roof, went into the sitting room of the house, and deposited a huge pile of filth in the wool-basket. The wool-weaver returned from the courtyard, saw him shitting in the parlor, and said, "Oh, may you never have any happiness! You're behaving like a rogue!"

Eulenspiegel said, "Master, I'm doing nothing but what you told me to do. You told me to climb off the roof and shit in the wool-basket. Why are you so angry about it? I'm doing what you told me."

The wool-weaver said, "You'd shit on my head — without being told. Take that filth and put it in a place where no one will have it."

Eulenspiegel said, "Yes," and put the filth on a stone and carried it into the dining room.

The wool-weaver said, "Leave that outside! I don't want that in here!"

Eulenspiegel said, "I know perfectly well that you don't want it in here. Nobody would want it in here. But I'm doing what you told me."

The wool-weaver became angry, and ran to the stable, intending to beat Eulenspiegel over the head with a log. But Eulenspiegel left the house, saying, "Can't I win any thanks anywhere?"

The wool-weaver was in too much of a hurry to grab the piece of wood, and dirtied his fingers utterly. So he let the filthy thing drop and ran to the well to wash his hands again.

In the meantime Eulenspiegel left.

51. How Eulenspiegel hired himself out to a furrier and shat in his workroom for him, because one stink is supposed to drive out another.

Eulenspiegel once arrived in Aschersleben.[1] Now, it was deep winter and a bitter time, and he thought, "What'll you take up now, to bring you through the winter?" There was no one who needed an assistant; but a furrier was living there who wanted to hire an apprentice, if one showed up who belonged to his craft. So Eulenspiegel thought, "What'll you do? It's winter, and hard because of it. You've got to bear what you can bear and bear the winter out." So he hired himself out as an apprentice to the furrier.

When he went into the workshop to sew pelts, he was unused to their stink, and said, "Fie, fie! You may be white as chalk, but you stink like filthy garbage."

The furrier said, "You don't like the smell — and still

1. This city, like Berlin (*cf*. Chapter 53) and Leipzig (*cf*. Chapter 54), first became famous for its fur trade. See Lappenberg, p. 258.

you're sitting here? That it smells is only natural: that's from the wool the sheep has on the outside."

Eulenspiegel kept quiet and thought, "One evil is supposed to drive off another." And he released such a sour fart that both master and wife had to hold their noses.

And the furrier said, "What're you doing? If you like making filthy farts, get out of the room into the courtyard and fart as much as you like."

Eulenspiegel said, "For the health of a human being this is much more natural than the stink of sheepskins."

The furrier said, "Whether it's healthy or not, if you want to fart go into the courtyard.

Eulenspiegel said, "Master, there it'll be lost. No fart enjoys being out in the cold — for they're always where it's warm. And to prove it, release a fart: it'll immediately run back to your nose, to the warmth from which it came."

The furrier kept quiet. He knew perfectly well that he was being made the butt of a joke and thought he would not keep him for long. Eulenspiegel remained sitting there, and sewed and farted and breathed out, and coughed the hairs out of his mouth. The furrier sat and watched him and kept quiet till evening, after they had eaten.

Then his master said to him, "Dear assistant, it seems clear to me that you aren't happy with this trade. I'm convinced you aren't a true furrier's apprentice — that I can see by your attitude. Or you can't have been at it for long, if you aren't used to the work. If you'd merely slept with it for four days, you wouldn't be turning up your nose that way and asking about it. It wouldn't be offensive to you. Therefore, my dear assistant, if you haven't any desire to remain here, tomorrow please go wherever your horse takes you."

Eulenspiegel said, "Dear master, you're speaking the truth when you say I haven't been at this for long. If you'll just let me sleep near the work for four nights, till I'm used to it, then you'll see what I can do."

The furrier was happy with this, since he needed him and he could also sew well.

52. How Eulenspiegel slept among pelts for a furrier—dry and damp, as the furrier told him to.

The furrier and his wife went happily to bed. Eulenspiegel took the prepared hides that were hanging on the frames, the dry hides that had been tanned and the wet ones too. He piled them together on the floor, crawled between them, and slept till morning.

His master now got up and saw that his hides were gone from their frames. He quickly ran over to his workshop to ask Eulenspiegel whether he knew anything about the hides. But he did not find Eulenspiegel, and saw that his pelts, both dry and damp, were lying in a pile on the floor — all mixed up with one another. He now became quite anxious, and in a tearful voice called his maid and wife.

Well, his shouting awakened Eulenspiegel, who peered out of the pelts and said, "Dear master, what's wrong to make you shout so terribly?"

The furrier was astonished, not knowing who was inside the pile of hides and pelts, and said, "Where are you?"

Eulenspiegel said, "Here I am, in here."

His master said, "Ah! May nothing good ever come your way! You've taken my pelts off the frames, the dry hides; and the wet ones out of the limewater — and piled them up together here. You're destroying the one with the other for me. What sort of nonsense is this?"

Eulenspiegel said, "Master, if you're angry about it, and I haven't slept in there more than one night, you'd be much angrier if I slept in there for four nights — as you told me to yesterday evening because I wasn't used to the work."

The furrier said, "You're lying like a knave! I didn't tell you to drag the finished hides across the floor, and the damp ones, and sleep in them." And he looked for a stick to beat him with.

In the meantime, Eulenspiegel went downstairs, intending to run out through the door. The wife and maid were standing at the bottom of the stairs, and they tried to stop him. So he screamed wildly, "Let me go for a doctor! My master's broken his leg!"

So they let him go and ran upstairs. But the master was coming downstairs, running fiercely after Eulenspiegel; and he stumbled, falling on his wife and maid, and all three piled on each other.

Well, Eulenspiegel ran out through the door, and left them in the house together.

53. How Eulenspiegel, in Berlin, made wolves for a furrier, instead of "wolf=pelts."

Swabians are extremely sly people — and this because, first, they avoid employment, and second, they do not realize that slyness destroys one utterly. In reality, they are more fond of the beer mug and of drinking than of working, and for this reason their workshops often stand empty.

A furrier who was a Swabian once lived in Berlin. Now, he was quite skillful in his profession and also careful with his expenditures — so he was also rich and ran a fine work-shop. For he had among his clientele the prince of the dis-trict, the nobility, and many good people and citizens. Well, it happened that the prince decided to hold a great court that winter, with races and tournaments; and he wrote an-nouncements of it to his noblemen and other lords. Since no one wished to be left out, many "wolf-pelts"[1] (or coats) were ordered from the aforementioned furrier at that time. Eulen-

---

1. See Chapter 47, in which this term also appears.

spiegel found out about this, and came to this master to ask for work.

The master, who needed helpers at that time, was happy with his arrival, and asked him whether he also knew how to make "wolves." He said, yes: in the district of Saxony he was by no means the least known for doing so.

The furrier said, "Dear boy, you've come to me at just the right moment. Come on. We'll reach a good understanding between ourselves about your wages."

Eulenspiegel said, "Yes, master. I see that you're honest enough to know very well yourself what they should be, once you see my work. But I don't work with the other workers. I have to be alone, so I can perform my job according to my wishes and without interference."

So he gave him a little room, and placed before him many wolfskins that had been scraped and were prepared as pelts, giving him a mass of various pelts, both large and small. Well, Eulenspiegel began to apply himself to the wolf hides, and cut them up, making wolves out of all of them and stuffing them with hay and shaping legs for them with sticks, to make them lifelike. When he had cut up all the hides and made wolves out of them, he said, "Master, the wolves are ready. Is there anything else to do?"

The master said, "Yes, my dear boy. Sew up as many of them as you can." With that he went up to the room where the wolves, both large and small, were lying on the floor. The master looked at them and said, "What's this supposed to be? May the plague shake you! What a disaster you've brought on me! I'll have you imprisoned and punished!"

Eulenspiegel said, "Master, are these my wages, then? And I've done this according to your own words. You told me to make wolves. If you'd said, 'Make me wolf-coats,' I'd have done that too. And if I'd known I wasn't to earn more gratitude, I wouldn't have used so much energy."

So Eulenspiegel took his leave of Berlin, leaving nowhere a good reputation behind him, and traveled to Leipzig.

54. How Eulenspiegel, in Leipzig, sold the furriers a live cat sewn into a rabbit skin, in a sack, for a live rabbit.

How quickly Eulenspiegel could invent a fine jest — as he proved to the furriers of Leipzig on Shrove-Tuesday Eve, when they held their feast, or drinking bout, together. Now, it happened that they wanted to eat wild game. Eulenspiegel heard of this and thought, "The furrier in Berlin gave you nothing for your work. These furriers ought to pay for it."

So he went to his inn, where his innkeeper had a fine, plump cat — which Eulenspiegel put under his coat. Then he asked the cook for a rabbit skin: he planned to arrange a wonderful trick with it. The cook gave him a skin, into which he sewed the cat. Then he dressed in farmer's clothes and stood before the town hall, keeping his wild game concealed in his jacket until one of the furriers came running past. Eulenspiegel asked him whether he would not like to buy a good hare, and allowed him to look under his jacket.

135

They soon agreed on his giving him four silver guilders for the hare and six pennies for the old sack in which the hare was kept. The furrier carried it to their guildmaster's house, where they all had gathered amid great boisterousness and merriment, and announced that he had purchased the finest hare he had seen in a year. One after another they handled it all over. Then, since they planned to have it on Shrove-Tuesday, they let it run live in an enclosed grass-garden — and got young dogs, because they wanted to hold a rabbit-hunt.

Well, when the furriers got together, they let the hare loose, with the dogs after it. Since the hare could not run well, it jumped into the trees and cried "Mieow!" — and that it would rather be home again. When the furriers saw this, they shouted fiercely, "You good comrades, come on! Come on! Whoever's made fools of us with this cat — we'll beat him to death!"

This might well have happened. But Eulenspiegel had taken off his clothes and changed himself, so they did not recognize him.

55. How Eulenspiegel boiled leather— along with chairs and benches—for a tanner in Brunswick on the Damme.

Shortly after Eulenspiegel left Leipzig, he came to Brunswick, to a tanner who tanned leather for shoemakers. Well, it was wintertime, so he thought, "You'd better put up with this tanner for the winter." And he hired himself out to the tanner.

When he had been with the tanner for eight days, it happened that the tanner was invited out to dinner — and that day Eulenspiegel was to do the leather by himself.

So the tanner said to Eulenspiegel, "Boil a full load of leather in the tub."

Eulenspiegel said, "All right. What should I use as wood for it?"

The tanner said, "What sort of question is that? If I haven't got any wood in the woodshed, I've still got lots of chairs and benches with which you can quite finish the leather."

Eulenspiegel said, "Yes." It would be fine.

The tanner went out to his friends'.

Eulenspiegel hung up a kettle; stuck the leather inside it, one hide after the other; and boiled the leather through till it could be pulled apart with the fingers. Then when Eulenspiegel had boiled the leather through, he broke up chairs and benches — all that were in the house, stuck them under the kettle, and boiled the leather still longer. And when this had been done, he took the leather out of the kettle, laid it out in a heap, left both house and city, and traveled off.

The tanner sensed nothing wrong, drank all day, and went pleasantly to bed that evening. The next morning the tanner wished to see how his assistant had done his leather, so he got up and went into the tanning house. Well, he found the leather utterly boiled through, found neither bench nor chair in either house or courtyard, became quite miserable, and went to his room, to his wife, and said, "Woman, something awful has happened. I have a feeling that our new assistant was Eulenspiegel, because he seems in the habit of doing everything that he's told. He's gone — and he's chopped all our chairs and benches into the fire and boiled the leather far too much."

His wife began to cry, and said, "Get after him, wild and fast, and bring him back!"

The tanner said, "No, I don't want him back. If only he stays away till I send for him."

56. How Eulenspiegel cheated the wine-tapster at Lübeck, by giving him a jug of water instead of a jug of wine.

Eulenspiegel kept wisely on his guard when he arrived in Lübeck, and conducted himself properly, playing no tricks on anyone — for justice in Lübeck is harsh indeed.

Now, at this time there was a wine-tapster in Lübeck, in the Ratskeller; and he was a haughty, proud man. He had managed to convince himself that no one was as wise as he. And he said himself, and had said round about him, that he longed to have a look at the man who could trick him and make a fool of him in his cleverness. Well, because of this, many citizens thoroughly disliked him.

When Eulenspiegel heard about this wine-tapster's presumptuousness, he could conceal his mischievous nature no longer and thought, "You've got to find out what he can do." He took two jugs that had been made exactly alike, putting water into the first jug and leaving the other empty. The jug of water he carried hidden under his coat; and the empty jug he carried in the open. Then he went into the wine cellar with the jugs, had a measure of wine poured out for him, and put the jug with the wine under his coat, setting the water jug in its place. He put it on the little shelf, so he did not see it, and said, "Wine-tapster, what's a measure of wine cost?"

"Ten pennies," he said.

Eulenspiegel said, "That's too expensive. I've got just six pennies. May I have it for that much?"

He became angry and said, "Would you like to put a price on the wine for the gentlemen here? This is a fixed price. If you don't like it, leave the wine in the Gentlemen's Cellar."

Eulenspiegel said, "That's what I wanted to know. I've got these six pennies. If you don't want them, pour the wine back again."

So the wine-tapster grabbed the jug in anger, thinking it was wine when it was water; poured it back into the bung-hole; and said, "What sort of a fool are you — having wine measured out for you, and you can't pay for it?"

Eulenspiegel took his jug and walked away, saying, "I see rather that you're a fool. There's nobody too wise to be tricked by fools — even if he's a wine-tapster."

And with that he left, carrying the jug of wine under his coat; but the empty jug, in which the water had been, he carried in the open.

57. How people tried to hang Eulenspiegel at Lübeck; and how, with clever trickery, he got out of there.

Lambrecht, the wine-tapster, listened to the words Eulenspiegel uttered as he left the cellar. Then he went to get a policeman, ran after Eulenspiegel, and caught up with him in the street. The policeman grabbed him, and they found the two jugs with him, the empty jug and the jug in which the wine was. So they declared him a thief and led him to prison. Now, some offered it as their judgment that he deserved the gallows for this; and some said it was no more than a subtle jest and thought the wine-tapster should have been cautious when he asserted that no one could cheat him. For Eulenspiegel had done so because of his inclination to be so enormously presumptuous. But those who disliked Eulenspiegel said it was theft: he must hang for it. Well, sentence was passed on him — death on the gallows.

Now, when the day of judgment arrived, on which Eulenspiegel was to be led out and hanged, there was an uproar through the whole city, with everyone up on horse or foot — and the Council of Lübeck feared that he might have worked them up or fixed it so he would not be hanged. Some wanted to see how he would take his end, after his having been so wild a fellow. Others declared he knew the black arts and could escape by them. And most would have rejoiced at his escape.

Now, Eulenspiegel kept still on being led out, saying not a word, with the result that everyone was amazed and thought he was in despair. This lasted right up to the gallows. Then he opened his mouth, called the whole Council before him, and asked, with great humility, that they grant him one request. He would ask them for neither life nor limb, nor for either money or property, but for something good to be done afterwards — neither continuous mass nor eternal alms-giving nor everlasting remembrance — but a different thing that would cause no damage in its accomplishment and that it would be easy for the honorable Council of Lübeck to do — without its costing a penny.

The members of the Council gathered and moved to one side to consult; and they were satisfied that they could grant him his request, since he had already stipulated what he would not ask for. Moreover, there were a number of them who very much wanted to know what he intended to request. They told him that whatever he asked for would be done, as long as he did not ask for any of the things he had mentioned earlier. If he wished to have things that way, they would grant him his wish.

Eulenspiegel now said, "I won't ask you for any of the things I told you of before. But if you plan to keep your word with me with respect to what I ask of you, give me your hands on it."

This they did, all together, and promised it to him, by hand and by mouth.

Eulenspiegel then said, "You honorable gentleman of Lübeck: as you've given me your pledge, I'll ask it of you. And this is my request: that after I've been hanged, the wine-tapster come here every morning for three days — the bartender first and the skinner, who'll dig my grave, second

— and that before they eat they kiss me with their mouths on my ass."

Well, they vomited and said this was hardly a civilized request.

Eulenspiegel said, "I consider the esteemed Council of Lübeck honest enough to keep its word with me — that it has pledged me by hand and by mouth."

They all went off to consult about this — with the result that, by permission and for other appropriate reasons, it was decided that they would let him go. Well, Eulenspiegel journeyed from there to Helmstädt, and was never again seen in Lübeck.

58. How Eulenspiegel had a giant purse made at Helmstädt.

Eulenspiegel arranged still another jest, with a purse. For a pursemaker was living at Helmstädt, to whom Eulenspiegel went, asking him whether he would like to make him a large, pretty purse.

The pursemaker said, "Yes. How big should it be?"

Eulenspiegel said that he should make it large enough, for these were times in which one carried large purses that were wide and broad. The pursemaker made Eulenspiegel a large purse. When he came for it and saw the purse, he said, "This purse isn't large enough. It's a mere purselet. If you'll make me one that's large enough, I'll pay you well."

The pursemaker made him a purse out of an entire cowhide, making it so large that one might easily have put a yearling calf into it — a purse that had to be hauled.

When Eulenspiegel came for it this time, he was not pleased with the purse and said the purse was not large enough. If he wanted to make him a purse, he should make

144

one large enough for him: he would give him two guilders for it. The pursemaker took the two guilders and made him a purse. He used three oxhides for it — and the three would have been enough to carry a coffin and into which one might have poured a bushel of corn.

When Eulenspiegel came back, he said, "Master, this purse is large enough, but the large purse I had in mind isn't this purse. So I don't want it either — it's still too small. If you can make me a purse so large that I can take one penny out of it and two are still left inside it — so I'd never be without money and never have to grovel for a living — I'd buy it from you and pay. These purses you've made me are empty. They're useless to me. I've got to have full purses. Otherwise I can't go among people."

And he left, leaving his purses with him, and said, "You keep them in case of a good sale." And he left the two guilders — although he had easily cut leather for him for five guilders.

59. How Eulenspiegel cheated the butchers of Erfurt out of a roast.

Eulenspiegel could not suppress his clownish nature when he arrived in Erfurt, where he was well known among both citizens and students.[1] Once he went to the butchers' because meat was on sale. A butcher now told him that he ought to get something to take home with him.

Eulenspiegel said to him, "What should I take with me?"

The butcher said, "A roast."

Eulenspiegel said, "All right." And he grabbed the roast by its end and left with it.

The butcher ran after him and said, "No, not like this. You've got to pay for the roast."

Eulenspiegel said, "You said nothing to me about paying. You spoke instead about whether I wouldn't like to take something with me" — and that the man had shown him the

---

1. For Eulenspiegel's experience with the students of Erfurt, see Chapter 29.

roast so he might take it home with him. This he could prove with his neighbors, who were standing nearby.

The other butchers came over and said — out of malice — yes, it was true. The other butchers disliked him, for whenever anyone went to them and tried to buy something, he called the people over to him and lured them away. So they declared absolutely that Eulenspiegel should keep the roast. While the butchers were arguing, Eulenspiegel put the roast under his coat and went off with it — leaving them to settle things among themselves as best they could.

60. How Eulenspiegel cheated
the butchers of Erfurt out of another roast.

Eight days later, Eulenspiegel returned to the butchers' stalls. The same butcher now solicited Eulenspiegel again, with flattering words, "Come over and get a roast."

Eulenspiegel said, "Yes," and tried to feel the roast; but the master was quick and at once hugged the roast to himself.

Eulenspiegel said, "Please let the roast lie there. I plan to pay for it."

The butcher laid the roast on his bench again.

So Eulenspiegel continued, "If I tell you a word that will be in your interest, will the roast be mine?"

The butcher said, "Well, you may tell me such words as will be useless to me . . . but you may also tell me words that could indeed be in my interest, and then you could take the roast."

Eulenspiegel said, "I don't plan to touch your roast. My words will please you." And he went on, "I would say this:

'Come on, Mr. Moneybags, and pay the people!' How do you like that? Doesn't it please you?"

The butcher now said, "The words quite please me — and for that reason are much to my liking."

So Eulenspiegel said to those who were standing around them, "Dear friends, you've heard it. Well, the roast is mine."

So Eulenspiegel took the roast and walked off with it, saying sarcastically to the butcher, "Well, I've got another roast — as you promised me."

The butcher stood there, not knowing what he could possibly say to this and, in addition, encountering the ridicule of his neighbors, who were standing there with him. They laughed at him.

61. How Eulenspiegel became a carpenter's boy in Dresden, and did not earn much praise.

Eulenspiegel soon cleared out of the district of Hessen for Dresden by the Bohemian Forest on the Elbe.[1] There he pretended he was a carpenter's boy. A cabinetmaker took him on; he needed helpers, for his assistants had given up the trade and left.

Now, a wedding was being held in the city to which the cabinetmaker was invited. So the carpenter told Eulenspiegel, "Dear boy, I've got to go to the wedding and won't be back during the day. Do well and work hard and put the four planks on that table, in the glue, as tightly as possible."

Eulenspiegel said, "Yes. Which planks belong together?"

The master placed them on top of one another for him — those that belonged together — and went to the wedding with his wife. Eulenspiegel, the trusty helper who always

---

1. This description harks back to a time when the Bohemian Forest was better known than Dresden itself. See Lappenberg, p. 263.

aimed at doing his work more absurdly than properly, started off and bored through the finely milled table planks or counter planks, which his master had stacked there for him, at three or four ends. Then he piled them into plank blocks, wedged them together, boiled glue in a large kettle, stuck the planks in, carried them up inside the house, and shoved them out of the window, so the glue could dry in the sun. Then he took time off.

That evening his master came home, having had a lot to drink, and asked Eulenspiegel how he had worked that day.

Eulenspiegel said, "Master, I've put the four table planks together as tightly as possible in the glue — and had a decent time off as well."

This quite pleased his master, and he said to his wife, "This is a fine assistant. Treat him well. I'd like to keep him a long time." And he went to bed.

But the next morning his master told Eulenspiegel to bring him the table that he had finished. So Eulenspiegel came, dragging his work from the workfloor. When his master saw that the rogue had ruined his planks, he said, "Assistant, have you even learned carpentry?"

Eulenspiegel answered: why was he asking this?

"I'm asking it because you've ruined these fine planks for me."

Eulenspiegel said, "Dear master, I've done as you told me. If it's ruined, that's your fault."

He became angry, and said, "You damned fool! I'll throw you out of my workshop for this! I've no use for your sort of work!"

So Eulenspiegel took his leave of that place and did not earn great thanks — despite his having done all he was told to do.

62. How Eulenspiegel became an optician, and could find no work in any country.

The electors were angry and contentious among themselves, with the result that there was no Roman Kaiser or King. Well, it came about that the Count of Supplenburg[1] was chosen as Roman King by the mass of electors, but there were a number among them who fancied themselves able to take

---

1. Lappenberg (p. 263) rejects the idea that this may have been Lothar III, who was elected Roman King in 1125. However, Lappenberg's argument, which is based on the notions that 1125 is too early a date for Eulenspiegel and that "Supplenburg" is really a degenerate form of "Lützelburg," seems to make little sense. Anachronisms are not infrequent in Eulenspiegel's adventures (*cf.* especially Chapters 27 and 31); moreover, Lothar fits rather well the description given of the newly elected King in this tale, while there is no real evidence to support Lappenberg's theory of "Supplenburg's" mutation. On Lothar III see Paul Fournier, "The Kingdom of Burgundy or Arles from the Eleventh to the Fifteenth Century," *The Cambridge Medieval History*, VIII (Cambridge, 1959), p. 312.

over the empire by force. So this newly elected King had to camp near Frankfurt for six months to see who might try to overthrow him. Since he had assembled so large a crowd, on horse and foot, Eulenspiegel speculated on what it might be possible for him to do there: "Lots of strange Lords are arriving there, who won't think of me as lacking in talent. If I encounter nothing more than their heraldry,[2] I'll do well." And he set out for the place.

Lords were traveling there from all countries. So it happened that the Bishop of Trier[3] and his company found Eulenspiegel in the Wetterau near Friedburg, on the road to Frankfurt. Since he was so oddly dressed, the Bishop asked him what sort of fellow he was.

Eulenspiegel answered, saying, "Gracious One, I am an optician and come from Brabant. There is nothing to do there, so I'm wandering in search of work. But there seems to be absolutely no demand for our craft."

The Bishop said, "I should think your craft would be thriving, better with each day — the reason being that each day the people become more sickly and lose their vision: so many eyeglasses are needed."

Eulenspiegel answered the Bishop, saying, "Yes, gracious Lord, Your Grace speaks the truth. But there's one thing that's ruining our craft."

The Bishop said, "What is it?"

Eulenspiegel said, "If only I might tell Your Grace without Your getting angry!"

"No," said the Bishop. "I'm used to such things from you and your kind. Just speak freely."

"Gracious Lord, it is ruinous to the craft of spectacle-making — so much so that it is to be feared whether it may not vanish — that You and other great Lords, Popes, Cardinals, Bishops, Kaisers, Kings, Princes, Councilors, Governors, Judges of the cities and countries (God save us!) presently just wink at what is right — and this, presently,

---

2. *i.e.*, not their weapons.

3. This would probably have been Archbishop Balduin of Trier, who died in 1354. See Lappenberg, p. 263.

because of gifts of money. But in ancient times, one finds it written, the Lords and Princes, as many of you are, were in the habit of reading and studying after justice, so injustice might befall no one. And for this they needed numerous eyeglasses; so in those days our craft did well. Moreover, Popes studied more at that time than now, so eyeglasses are disappearing. Of course, they are now so well educated from the books they buy that they know their pages by heart — so they don't open their books more than once in four weeks. For this reason our craft is ruined, and I run from one country to the next and can find work nowhere. This evil condition has spread so far that farmers in the country are concerned."

The Bishop understood this text, and said to Eulenspiegel, "Follow after us to Frankfurt. We shall give you our festive regalia and clothes."

This Eulenspiegel did. And he remained with the Lords till the Count was confirmed as Kaiser. Then he traveled with the Kaiser back to Saxony.

63. How Eulenspiegel hired himself out as a cook and house=boy to a merchant in Hildesheim, and behaved quite mischievously.

On the right, in the street that takes one out of the hay-market, there lived a rich merchant. Once he went walking in front of his house, intending to go into his garden. On the way, on a green spot of lawn, he found Eulenspiegel lying down. He greeted him, asked him what sort of fellow he was, and what his trade might be. Eulenspiegel answered him with concealed roguishness and cunning: he was a cook's apprentice and had no employment.

At this the merchant said, "If you can be trusted, I'll take you on myself — and give you new clothes and a nice piece of change. For I have a wife who complains all day long about cooking, and I'd very much like to win her praise."

Eulenspiegel promised him great loyalty and honesty. So the merchant hired him, and asked him his name.

"Sir, my name is Barto-lo-me-us."

155

The merchant said, "That's a long name. It can't easily be said. You'll be called 'Dol.' "

Eulenspiegel said, "Yes, dear Squire. It's all the same to me what I'm called."

"Well, well," said the merchant, "you're the boy for me. Come on, come on. Come into my garden with me. We're going to take some herbs home with us, and young chickens as well. I've invited guests for next Sunday, whom I'd like to treat nicely."

Eulenspiegel went into the garden with him and cut rosemary, with which he was to stuff the chickens in French style — the others with onions, eggs, and other herbs. Then they went home together. When his wife saw her guest's odd clothes, she asked the master of the house what sort of fellow this was and what he planned to do with him — or whether he was just worried that their bread might be molding.[1]

The merchant said, "Woman, be satisfied. He's to be your very own servant. He's a cook."

His wife said, "Yes, dear husband, he looks as if he ought to be able to cook fine things."

"Just be happy," said her husband. "Tomorrow you'll see very well what he can do." And he called Eulenspiegel: "Dol!"

He answered: "Squire!"

"Take a sack and follow me to the butcher's. I want to get meat and a roast."

So he followed him. His Squire bought meat and a roast there, and said to him, "Dol, put the roast to one side tomorrow to let it cool and brown slowly, so it doesn't burn. Put the other meat beside it, so it'll be hot for eating."

Eulenspiegel said yes, got up early, and put the food on the fire. But he put the roast on a spit and placed it between two barrels of Eimbeck beer in the cellar, so it would stay cool and not burn. As the merchant had invited the City Secretary and other guests for dinner, he came to find out whether his guests had arrived and whether the food was ready — and asked his new servant.

---

1. Because there was no one to eat it.

156

He answered, "Everything's ready but the roast."

"Where's the roast?" said the merchant.

"It's lying in the cellar between two barrels. I knew of no cooler place in the house where I could put it, according to your instructions."

"But is it ready?" said the merchant.

"No," said Eulenspiegel. "I didn't know when you wanted to have it."

While this was going on, the guests arrived and he told them about his new servant and how he had put the roast in the cellar. Well, they laughed and made a good joke of it. But the wife was unhappy for her guests' sake, and told the merchant he ought to let the boy go: she could no longer bear him in the house; she could see he was a rogue.

The merchant said, "Dear wife, be calm. I'd like to use him for a trip to the City of Goslar; and when I get back, I'll have him take off." He could barely persuade his wife to be satisfied with this.

When they had eaten and drunk and there had been good cheer all evening, the merchant said, "Dol, prepare the carriage and grease it. Tomorrow we're going to Goslar. There's a priest called Father Heinrich Hamenstede;[2] the man is here and will travel back with us."

Eulenspiegel said yes, and asked what he ought to use for this. The merchant threw him a shilling and said, "Go and buy wagon grease and have my wife put old fat under it."

This he did; and when everyone was asleep, Eulenspiegel greased the carriage inside and out, and especially where one was supposed to sit. The merchant arose early the next morning with the priest, and told Eulenspiegel to hitch up the horses. He did so. They seated themselves and drove off. But the priest began to heave around, and said, "What, by the gallows, is so fatty here? I'd like to stop, so this car-

---

2. A Father Heinrich Hamenstede, who was Chaplain at Volkers-heim near Bockenem and at Saint Aegidien in Goslar, was actually alive toward the end of the fifteenth century. Lappenberg (p. 266) suggests that N.'s intention, in mentioning him here and in having him driven under the gallows later in the story, was obviously satirical.

riage stops throwing me around and making my hands so shitty everywhere."

They ordered Eulenspiegel to stop and told him they were both being smeared with grease, front and back. Then they began to get angry with Eulenspiegel. In the meantime a farmer who was driving to market came by with a load of straw. They bought several bundles from him, wiped off the carriage, and seated themselves inside once more.

The merchant now said angrily to Eulenspiegel, "You damned fool! May nothing good ever come your way! Drive to beat the gallows!"

Eulenspiegel did so. When he arrived under the gallows, he stopped short and unhitched the horses.

The merchant said to him, "What're you trying to do — or what do you mean by this — you fool!"

Eulenspiegel said, "You told me to drive under the gallows. Here we are. I thought we were going to rest here."

At this the merchant saw by looking out of the carriage that they were stopped under the gallows. What could they do? They began to laugh at the joke, and the merchant said, "Hitch up, you fool, and drive straight on and don't look to either side!"

Eulenspiegel now removed the coupling pins from the traveling carriage; and when he had driven an acre's length further, the carriage separated, and the rear portion of it, with the roof, remained standing still. But Eulenspiegel went on by himself. They screamed after him, and had to run till their tongues were hanging out of their mouths before they caught up with him. The merchant tried to beat him to death; the priest helped him, as best he could.

Well, they completed their journey and returned home. His wife now asked how it had gone.

"Strangely enough," said the merchant, "but at least we're back." And with that he called Eulenspiegel and said, "Fellow, stay here tonight. Eat and drink what you like. But tomorrow clear out of my house. I won't have you here any more. You're a tricky fool — wherever you come from."

Eulenspiegel said, "Dear God, I do everything I'm told — and still earn no thanks. But if you're not pleased with my service, I'll clear out of your house and leave tomorrow, according to your words."

"Yes, do that," said the merchant.

The next day the merchant got up and said to Eulenspiegel, "Eat and drink yourself full and get yourself out of here. I'm going to church. Don't let yourself be found here again."

Eulenspiegel kept quiet. As soon as the merchant was out of the house, he began clearing out — chairs, tables, benches. And whatever he could carry and haul he brought into the lane — copper and pewter pots and candles — so the neighbors began to wonder what was going on there, with all these things being lugged into the street.

The merchant found out about it. He came puffing up and said to Eulenspiegel, "You trusty servant — what're you doing here! Do I still find you here?"

"Yes, Squire. I wanted first to obey your words — since you told me to clear out the house, and then leave." And he went on, "Grab here with your hands: this load is too heavy for me. I can't manage it alone."

"Leave it lying!" said the merchant. "And go to the devil! These things cost too much to be thrown into filth like this!"

"Dear Lord God," said Eulenspiegel, "isn't it a great wonder? I do everything I'm told — and still earn thanks nowhere! I'm not fooled: I was born in an unlucky hour."

So Eulenspiegel took his leave of that place, letting the merchant take back what he had cleared out. His neighbors laughed at him, to his face and behind his back.

64. How Eulenspiegel became a horsedealer in Paris, and removed the tail from a Frenchman's horse.

Eulenspiegel played an amusing trick on a horse-dealer by the lake at Wismar. For a horse-dealer always came there who would purchase no horse unless, during the bargaining, he pulled the horse by its tail. This he did even to horses that he did not buy — for he discovered by this pulling his indication whether the horse would live long. And his sign was this. If a horse had a long tail, he pulled it by the tail: if the long hair in its tail were curly, he did not buy it, since he was of the opinion that it would not live long. If the hair in the tail were straight, he bought it — and had a strong feeling that it would live long and had a hardy constitution. Well, this had become so common an idea at Wismar that everyone swore by it.

As this tale has to do neither with Paris nor with a Frenchman, it may be assumed that some sort of (perhaps typographical) error has taken place here.

Eulenspiegel found out about this, and at once thought, "You ought to play some trick on him, be it what it may, to free these people of this superstition." Well, Eulenspiegel was now able to help himself with black magic. For he obtained a horse, practiced black magic on it according to his purposes, and rode to the market with it. And he asked so high a price for the horse that they refused to buy it from him — until the very merchant arrived who pulled horses by their tails. He asked a good price of him for his horse.

The merchant could see very well that the horse was a fine one, and fine for its money. So he went over to it, planning to pull hard on its tail. Now, Eulenspiegel had so arranged things that as soon as he pulled on the horse's tail it came off in his hand — while the horse was made to look as if he had removed the horse's tail.

The merchant stood there, getting worried. But Eulenspiegel began to shout, "Curses on this villain! Look, dear citizens, how he's insulted and ruined my horse!"

The citizens came over and saw that the merchant had the horse's tail in his hand and that it no longer had its tail. Well, the merchant was quite afraid for himself. But the citizens intervened and arranged it that the merchant gave Eulenspiegel ten guilders — and that he kept his horse. So Eulenspiegel rode off on his horse, and replaced its tail.

But after that experience, the merchant never again pulled a horse by the tail.

65. How Eulenspiegel played a huge joke on a pipemaker at Lüneburg.

At Lüneburg lived a pipemaker who had been a country tramp and had been run out of the country with other lazy logs.[1] He was sitting at his beer. Well, Eulenspiegel arrived at these festivities and found much company there. So the pipemaker invited Eulenspiegel to dinner — but with this purpose, to make a fool of him — and told him, "Come by tomorrow at noon and eat with me, if you can."

Eulenspiegel said yes, not understanding his words right away, and arrived the next day, intending to go to dinner at the pipemaker's. When he came up to his door, the door was bolted above and below and all the windows were closed. Eulenspiegel walked back and forth before the house two or

---

1. Lappenberg (p. 267) suggests that this description of the "Pfeifendreher" is facetious — that he is to be thought of less as an actual pipemaker than as a "piper," or wandering musician, who has transformed himself from "piper" into "pipe-turner."

three times, till it was after midday; but the house remained shut. He now realized that he had been tricked. He left the place and kept quiet till the next day.

Eulenspiegel now approached the pipemaker in the market-place and said to him, "Look, you worthy fellow, are you in the habit of doing things like this — of inviting people for dinner, then going out yourself and shutting the doors above and below?"

The pipemaker said, "Didn't you hear how I invited you? I said, 'Come by tomorrow at noon and eat something with me — if you can.' Well, you found the doors locked, so you couldn't come."

Eulenspiegel said, "Thanks very much. I didn't realize that. I'm learning something every day."

The pipemaker laughed and said, "I don't want to annoy you. Go there now. My door's open. You'll find cooked and baked things on the fire. Go on ahead. I'll come after you: you should eat by yourself. I don't want any guests but you."

Eulenspiegel thought, "That'll be fine." So he went at once to the pipemaker's house, and found it as he had told him. The maid was turning the roast, and his wife was moving about arranging things. So Eulenspiegel went into the house and told the wife that she and her maid were to come at once: the master of the house had just been presented with a large fish, a sturgeon, which they were to help him carry home. He would turn the roast in the meantime.

The woman said, "Of course, dear Eulenspiegel. I'll go with the girl and be back in a flash."

He said, "Go, quickly!"

The woman and her maid went off toward the market. But the pipemaker met them on the way and asked them why they were rushing so much. She said Eulenspiegel had come to the house and told them that he had been presented with a huge sturgeon which they were to help him carry home.

The pipemaker became angry and told his wife, "Couldn't you have stayed home? He hasn't done this for no reason. There's some trick here."

Now, in the meantime Eulenspiegel had shut up the

163

house above and below; so when the pipemaker, together with his wife and maid, arrived at the house, they found the door closed.

He then said to his wife, "Now you see the sort of sturgeon you were supposed to get."

And they knocked on the door.

Eulenspiegel came to the door and said, "Stop your knocking. I'm not letting anyone in. The master of the house ordered and definitely said I was to be in here alone. He wants no guests but me. Go away and come back after dinner."

The pipemaker said, "That's true. I said that. But I didn't mean it. Well, let him eat. I'll play another trick on him for this." And he went, with wife and maid, to a neighbor's house to wait till Eulenspiegel was finished.

Well, Eulenspiegel prepared the food thoroughly, sat down at the table, stuffed himself, and put what was left back — for as long as seemed to him to be appropriate. Then he opened the door and left it open.

The pipemaker now came in and said, "Fine people don't do the sorts of things you've done, Eulenspiegel."

But Eulenspiegel said, "Should I have done with another what I was supposed to do by myself? If I'm invited to dinner, and the master of the house wants nobody but me — and I bring more guests — he certainly won't be happy." And with these words he left the house.

The pipemaker looked after him: "I'll pay you back for this, rogue that you are."

Eulenspiegel said, "Whoever can do so best is master."

Well, the pipemaker went that very hour to the horse-slaughterer and told him, "There's a good man at the inn, Eulenspiegel by name, whose horse has died." He ought to pick it up. And he showed him the house. The horse-slaughterer recognized the pipemaker at once, and said, yes, he would do it. So he drove his slaughterer's cart up to the inn the pipemaker had shown him and asked for Eulenspiegel. Eulenspiegel came to the door and asked what he wanted. The horse-slaughterer said the pipemaker had come to him and told him that his horse had died, that he ought to pick it up: but was he indeed Eulenspiegel and was this true?

164

Eulenspiegel turned around, pulled down his pants, and stuck up his ass. "Look here, and tell this to the pipemaker: if Eulenspiegel hasn't been sitting in this alleyway, then I don't know what street he's sitting in."

The slaughterer became angry, drove his slaughterer's cart to the pipemaker's house, left the cart standing there, and complained to him so strongly that the pipemaker had to give the horse-slaughterer ten guilders.

And Eulenspiegel saddled his horse and rode out of the city.

A long time ago, at Gerdau in the district of Lüneburg, there lived an old couple who had been married to each other for about fifty years and who had grown children whom they had well provided for and established. Now, there was a most greedy priest living in that parish at the same time — a man who always enjoyed being wherever people might be feasting or carousing. So this priest arranged things among his parishioners as follows — that every farmer had to invite him to dinner at least once a year and take care of him and his maid for one or two days, and do so in the best of spirits. But for many years the two old people had had no wake, baptism or banquet that the priest might have turned into a wild party. This annoyed him, so he thought of a scheme to force the farmer to give him a feast. He sent him a messenger to ask him how long he and his wife had been established in the state of matrimony.

The farmer answered the priest, "Dear Father, it's been so long that I've forgotten."

The priest answered him, "This could be a dangerous situation for your holy soul. If you've been together fifty years, the vows of matrimony expire, like a monk's in a cloister. So talk to your wife, come back to me, and let me know about this, so I may recommend help for your blessed souls, as I am required to do for you and all my parish children."

The farmer did so and discussed it with his wife, but was unable to give the priest an accurate account of the years of his marriage. And full of worry, they returned to the priest, so he might offer them sound counsel in the matter of their unworthiness.

The priest said, "Because you do not know the exact number of years, and out of concern for your souls, I shall, next Sunday, unite you anew — so in case you are not in a state of matrimony you shall arrive in it. Slaughter a fine ox for the event, and sheep and pigs; invite your children and good friends to your banquet; and enjoy yourselves — for I'll be there too."

"Ah, dear Father, just do so. For me this won't be a matter of just a pile of chickens. Could we have lived so long with one another — and now for the first time be out of wedlock — that would not be good." With that they went home to make preparations.

The priest invited various prelates and priests with whom he was acquainted to the affair. Among these was the Prior of Ebsdorf, who always had a decent horse or two and also greatly enjoyed eating. Eulenspiegel had been staying with him for some time. The Prior said to him, "Take my young stallion and come along. You'll be welcome."

Eulenspiegel did so. When they arrived there — and were eating and drinking and growing merry — the old woman, who was supposed to be the bride, was sitting on the table, as brides are supposed to do. But as she was tired and felt weak, she was allowed to go outside. So she went behind the house, to the River Gerdau, and put her feet in the water. At the same time, the Prior and Eulenspiegel came by, riding home to Ebsdorf. Well, Eulenspiegel honored the bride with some fine jumping of the young stallion — but did so too much, with the result that his belt-purse, which was carried on one's side in those days, fell off. When the good woman saw this, she got up, took the purse, and went to sit by the river. Well, when Eulenspiegel had ridden an acre's length further, he missed his purse for the first time, and raced quickly back to the Gerdau to ask the good old farmer's wife whether she had not picked up or found an old, rough purse.

The old woman said, "Yes, friend. For my wedding I received a rough purse indeed. I still have it and am sitting on it. Is that the one?"

"Ha," said Eulenspiegel. "If you've had it since your wedding, it must be quite a rusty purse by now. I've no desire for your old purse."

Thus was Eulenspiegel — roguish and crafty as he was — nonetheless tricked by the old farmer's wife and forced into losing his purse. The women of Gerdau still have that same rough bride's-purse. I believe that the old widows there are even protecting it. Whoever is interested ought to ask about it.

67. How Eulenspiegel tricked a farmer at Ueltzen out of some green fabric from London by convincing him it was blue.

Eulenspiegel always preferred eating cooked and baked things, so he was always alert to where he might get them. Once he went to the fair at Ueltzen, for many Wends and other country people were coming to it. He strolled here and there, observing everywhere what there was to do. Among other things, he saw that a country fellow was purchasing a green fabric from London[1] and planning to go home with it. Eulenspiegel thought, at last, that he might like to trick this farmer out of his fabric. He asked after the village where the farmer lived, picked up a Scottish priest[2] and a tramp, and went out of the city with them to the road by which the farmer had to travel. Then he made his plans for

---

1. Exports of English fabrics were well known in Germany, even earlier than the fourteenth century. See Lappenberg, p. 269.
2. The "Scottish priest" was probably a Benedictine and originally Irish. See Lappenberg, p. 269.

how they would handle him, so the farmer with the green fabric would be persuaded it was blue: each of them was to station himself an acre's length away from the other, out of the city.

When the farmer came out of the city with his fabric, intending to carry it home, Eulenspiegel asked him where he had bought that fine, blue material. The farmer answered that it was green, not blue. Eulenspiegel said it was blue: he would bet twenty guilders on it — and the first person to come up to them, who knew green from blue, would tell him so well enough, so they could be satisfied. Eulenspiegel now gave a signal to the first fellow to come over.

The farmer said to him, "Friend, we two have just bet twenty pennies on the color of this fabric. Tell the truth, whether it's green or blue, and as you say it, so we'll let it be."

He lifted it and said, "It's a fine blue fabric."

The farmer said, "No! You're both rogues — and probably set this up with each other to trick me."

Eulenspiegel now said, "Hold on! To let you see I'm right, I'll let this go, and let the matter be settled by this pious priest who's just coming over. What he says will make or break me." The farmer agreed to this also.

When the priest got closer to them, Eulenspiegel said, "Father, tell the truth: what's the color of this fabric?"

The priest said, "Friends, that you can see well enough yourselves."

The farmer said, "Yes, Father, that's true. But these two are trying to convince me of something I know must be a lie."

The priest said, "What do I care about your quarrel? What do I care whether it's black or white?"

"Ah, dear Father," said the farmer, "settle it for us. I beg you to do so."

"If you want it that way," said the priest. "Well, I can't say anything other than — the fabric is blue."

"Do you hear that?" said Eulenspiegel. "The fabric is mine."

The farmer said, "Indeed, Father, if you weren't an ordained priest, I'd think you were lying and that all three of you were rogues. But as you're a priest, I have to believe it."

So he gave Eulenspiegel and his companions the fabric, with which they dressed themselves against the winter — while the farmer had to go about in his torn coat.

68. How Eulenspiegel shat in the baths at Hanover, thinking the place was a House of Cleansing.

The bathkeeper at the baths in Hanover, near the Lein Gate, did not wish to have the place called "Bathhouse" but "House of Cleansing." Eulenspiegel found out about this, and when he got to Hanover, went to the baths, undressed, and said, as he stepped into the bathing room, "God bless you, sir, and your house servants, and everyone whom I find in this clean house."

The bathkeeper was pleased with this, told him he was welcome, and said, "Dear guest, you're speaking the truth. This is a clean house and also a house of cleansing — and not a bathhouse. For the tub is in the sun, and is also in earth, ashes and sand."[1]

---

1. This sentence has no intelligible meaning – as Lappenberg (p. 270) himself admits. Lappenberg suggests that something has perhaps been omitted here.

Eulenspiegel said, "That this is a house of cleansing is obvious, for we come into it unclean and come out of it clean." With these words Eulenspiegel deposited a great pile in the water trough in the middle of the bathing room, creating a stink through the whole place.

The bathkeeper then said, "It seems clear to me that your words aren't appropriate to your deeds. Your words pleased me, but your deeds don't suit me. For your words were fine, but your deeds stink terribly. Is this how one behaves in a house of cleansing?"

Eulenspiegel said, "Isn't this a house of cleansing? I need cleansing more inside than outside — otherwise I wouldn't have come in here."

The bathkeeper said, "One usually does that sort of cleansing in the lavatory.[2] This is a house of cleansing-by-sweating — and you're turning it into a shithouse."

Eulenspiegel said, "Doesn't this filth come from the human body? If one wants to cleanse oneself, one must cleanse oneself inside as well as outside."

The bathkeeper became angry and said, "One cleanses oneself of this sort of stuff in the shithouse, and the horse-slaughterer takes it out to the slaughterer's burial place. But I'm not in the habit of washing and scouring it." And with these words the bathkeeper ordered Eulenspiegel out of the baths.

Eulenspiegel said, "Mr. Keeper, let me bathe for my money: you'd like having a lot of money, and I'd like a good bath."

The bathkeeper said he should simply get out of his place; he had no interest in his money. If he refused to leave, he would show him the door at once.

Eulenspiegel reflected, "This would be dirty fighting — naked with razors." So he started out through the door, and said, "How nicely I've bathed for a bit of filth." Then he went out and got dressed in a room in which the bathkeeper and his employees usually took their meals.

The bathkeeper tried to keep him in there and frighten

---

2. A pun? "Sprachhuss" also means "city hall."

173

him by pretending to hold him prisoner, so he could threaten him. But in the meantime Eulenspiegel noticed that he had not cleansed himself enough in the bathing room. He saw a folded table, opened it, shat some filth on it, and closed it again. Well, the bathkeeper soon let him out, and they settled their quarrel.

Eulenspiegel then told him, "Dear master, in this room I cleansed myself thoroughly for the first time. You'll be thinking about me a great deal before noon. I'm leaving this place."

69. How Eulenspiegel bought milk from the countrywomen in Bremen, and poured it together.

Eulenspiegel did strange and amusing things in Bremen. Once he went to the market there and saw that the farmers' wives brought a great deal of milk to sell. So he waited for a market-day on which much milk was arriving, acquired a large vat, set it up in the market-place, purchased all the milk that was brought for selling, and had it all poured into the vat. Now, for each woman he marked a ring around the vat — she had this much, the next had that much, and so on; and he told the women to wait till he had all the milk together: then he would pay each woman for her milk.

The women sat in a circle in the market-place, and Eulenspiegel kept buying milk till no more women were arriving with it, and the vat was nearly full.

Eulenspiegel now turned, making a joke of the thing, and said, "I haven't any money at the moment. Whoever doesn't want to wait fourteen days may take her milk out of the vat." And with that he left.

The women created an uproar and riot: one had this much, the other that much, the third the same, and so on — till they were beating and smashing one another over the head with their pails, little casks and bottles, and pouring milk into their eyes and over their clothes and on the ground, and it looked as though it had rained milk.

The farmers, and all who saw this, laughed at this absurdity — that women would go to market in such a fashion — and Eulenspiegel was much praised for his roguishness.

70. How Eulenspiegel gave twelve blind men twelve guilders—how they took them, how they spent them, and how at last they lived miserably because of them.

Since Eulenspiegel was always wandering from one district to the next, a time came when he arrived in Hanover again and engaged in many curious exploits. Once he went riding an acre's length on the road by the gate and ran into twelve blind men.

When Eulenspiegel came up to them, he said, "You blind men — where are you coming from?"

The blind men stopped, for they could hear very well that he was seated on a horse. They thought he must be a high-ranking personage, and doffed their hats and caps and said, "Dear Squire, we've been to the city. A rich man died there, for whom a funeral was held, and alms were given out. But it was horribly cold."

Eulenspiegel said to the blind men, "It's cold indeed. I'm

afraid you may freeze to death. Look here, here are twelve guilders for you. Go back to the city, to the inn from which I've just come" — and he told them which house it was — "and spend these twelve guilders, for my sake, till winter is over and you can go on your way again before frost-time."

The blind men stood there, bowing and thanking him profusely; and each blind man thought the next had the money, and the next thought the third had the money, and the third thought the fourth had the money, and so on, till the last thought the first had it. Well, they went into the city, to the inn that Eulenspiegel had told them of. When they arrived at the inn, the blind men all said that a good man had ridden up behind them and given them, by the grace of God, twelve guilders which they were to spend, for his sake, till winter was over. The innkeeper was eager for the money and took them in for twelve guilders. He did not reflect that he ought to have asked them which blind man had the twelve guilders, but said, "Yes, my dear brothers, I'll treat you nicely." He slaughtered and chopped and cooked for the blind men, and let them eat, till it seemed to him that they had exhausted the twelve guilders. Then he said, "Dear brothers, if we do a reckoning, the twelve guilders are just about spent."

The blind men said yes, and each asked the next which of them had the twelve guilders, so he might pay the inn-keeper. The first did not have the guilders; the second did not have them either; the third also did not; the fourth the same; and the last had the twelve guilders no more than the first. The blind men said so, and scratched their heads, for they had been tricked.

So had the innkeeper. He sat down to think. "If you lose them now, your food won't be paid for. But if you keep them on, they'll stuff themselves and eat even more — and still have nothing — till you have twice the loss." So he led them out to his pigsty, locked them in, and put straw and hay in front of them.

Eulenspiegel was thinking that the blind men must have used up that money by now, so he disguised himself and rode into the city, to the innkeeper at the inn. When he came into the courtyard, intending to tie up his horse in the stall, he saw the blind men lying in the pigsty. He then went into the house and said to the innkeeper, "Mr. Innkeeper, what reason can you have for keeping poor blind men in your pigsty? Don't you have any pity on them, that they've got to eat stuff that must be doing harm to life and limb?"

The innkeeper said, "I wish they were where all rivers meet[1] — and I had my food paid for." And he told him everything about how he and the blind men had been tricked.

Eulenspiegel said, "What, Mr. Innkeeper, can't they offer any security?"

The innkeeper thought, "Oh, if I just had some!" And he said, "Friend, if I could get definite security, I'd take it and let those unhappy blind men go."

Eulenspiegel said, "All right then. I'll inquire through the city, and see that I find you a pledge."

Eulenspiegel now went to the priest and said, "My dear Lord Priest, wouldn't you like to act like a good friend? My innkeeper was possessed of the evil spirit last night, and he wants to ask you whether you'll exorcise it for him."

The priest said, "Of course. But he'll have to wait patiently for one or two days. One can't be in too much of a hurry about such things."

Eulenspiegel quickly said to him, "I'll get his wife, so you can tell her that yourself."

The priest said, "Yes, have her come."

So Eulenspiegel returned to the innkeeper and said, "I've found you a pledge. The man's your priest, who will promise it to you and give you what you want. Just let your wife go to him with me. He'll tell her about it."

The innkeeper was agreeable, and delighted, and sent his wife to the priest with him.

Eulenspiegel now began, "Dear Father, here's his wife. Just tell her yourself what you told me and what you promised me."

The priest said, "Certainly. My dear woman, just wait one or two days, and I'll help him with this."

---

1. *i.e.*, in the sea. See Lappenberg, p. 271.

The woman said, "All right." Then she returned home with Eulenspiegel and told the master of the house about it. The innkeeper was happy, and let the blind men go and dismissed her. And Eulenspiegel got ready too, and sneaked out of there.

On the third day the wife went back and asked the priest for the twelve guilders the blind men had spent.

The priest said, "Dear woman, is this what your husband told you to do?"

The woman said, "Yes."

The priest said, "I was told that your husband was possessed by the evil spirit. Bring him to me, so I can help him free of it, with God's help."

The wife said, "Charlatans, who are liars, act this way when they're supposed to pay up. You'll find out right away whether my husband has been captured by the evil spirit." And she ran home and told her husband what the priest had said.

The innkeeper readied himself — with pikes and halberds — and raced back to the priest's house. The priest took note of this, and called his neighbors to help. He blessed himself and said, "Come help me, my dear neighbors! Look — this man is possessed of the evil spirit!"

The innkeeper said, "Priest! Reflect — and pay me!"

The priest stood there and blessed himself.

The innkeeper tried to attack the priest. His neighbors got between them, but only after great efforts could they separate them. And as long as that innkeeper and the priest lived, he demanded payment for his expenses. But the priest said he owed him nothing — rather that he was possessed of the evil spirit. He wished only to free him of it. This lasted for as long as they both lived.

After Eulenspiegel played that joke[1] in Bremen, he became quite well known. It was like this in the city of Bremen — that all the citizens enjoyed having him around and wanted him to play all sorts of pranks. So Eulenspiegel spent a long time in that city.

Once there was a convocation of citizens and inhabitants as well as merchants. They had an agreement among themselves that one of them would prepare a roast, with cheese and bread — and whoever did not come would have to pay the host for the entire meal. When Eulenspiegel arrived at these festivities in the Bremen market-place, they took him for a clown, since he wanted to join their assembly. Well, as the question of the banquet went around, it came to Eulenspiegel too; so he invited his companions to his inn, pur-

---

1. *Cf.* other Bremen stories, such as Chapter 69. This one is perhaps out of place.

chased a roast, and placed it on the fire. As feasting time was approaching, the company gathered in the market-place and debated among themselves whether they wanted to go to Eulenspiegel's to eat. And each asked the next if nobody knew whether he had cooked something or not — so they would not go there for nothing. Well, they came to an agreement that they would go there together: better that everybody discover the trick than one person alone.

Well, when the company arrived at the inn where Eulenspiegel was staying, he took a piece of butter, stuck it into the groove of his behind, turned his ass backwards to the fire, over the roast, and basted the roast that way, with the butter from his groove. And as his guests arrived at the door, stopped, and tried to see whether he had cooked anything, they saw him standing that way near the fire and basting the roast.

So they said things like this: "The devil be his guest! I won't eat that roast."

But Eulenspiegel demanded payment from them for the food — which they all cheerfully offered as long as they did not have to eat the roast.

72. How Eulenspiegel sowed stones in a city in Saxony; and how, when he was asked about it, he said he was sowing rogues.

Soon after this, Eulenspiegel arrived at a city on the Weser. There he observed the great commerce of the people and what their transactions were like, till he was familiar with all their ways and how their business was handled.

Since he had fourteen inns there, what he owed in one place he found in the next, and heard and saw what he had not known. But they grew tired of him, and he likewise grew tired of them. So he collected little stones near the river, walked back and forth through the lanes near the city hall, and sowed his seeds on either side.

Strangers came up to him and asked him what he was sowing.

Eulenspiegel said, "I'm sowing rogues."

The merchants said, "There's no need for you to sow them here. There are more than enough of them here already."

Eulenspiegel said, "That's true. But they're living in the houses. They ought to be running around outside."

They said, "Why don't you also sow honest people?"

Eulenspiegel said, "Honest people? They wouldn't grow here."

Words like these came to the attention of the Council. Eulenspiegel was sent for and ordered to collect his seeds and get himself out of the city. He did so — and arrived, ten miles from there, in another city, planning to sow his seeds in Ditmarschen. But the news had preceded him to the city. So if he wanted to enter the city, he had to promise to travel through it, with his seeds, without eating or drinking. Since nothing else seemed possible, he rented a little boat, planning to have his seeds and goods lifted into the boat. As it was being taken up from the ground, the sack tore open in the middle, leaving both seeds and sack behind.

Well, Eulenspiegel ran off, and is still supposed to return.

73. How Eulenspiegel hired himself out to a barber in Hamburg, and entered his shop through his windows.

Eulenspiegel once arrived in Hamburg and went to the hops-market.[1] As he was standing there looking around, a beard-shearer came by who asked him where he was from.

Eulenspiegel said, "I come from here and there."

The master asked him, "What craft are you apprenticed to?"

Eulenspiegel said, "I'm a barber, to be brief about it."

The master hired him.

Now, this barber lived at the hops-market, just across from where they were standing; and his house had high windows facing the street, where his shop was located. So the master said to Eulenspiegel, "See that house over there,

---

1. Such a market is reliably reported to have existed in Hamburg in 1353. See Lappenberg, p. 275.

where those high windows are? Go in there, and I'll follow you presently."

Eulenspiegel said yes, went straight into the house through the high windows, and said, "God, Almighty God, bless this craft."

The beard-shearer's wife was sitting in the shop and spinning. She became quite frightened and said, "See if the devil isn't leading you! You're coming through the windows! Isn't the door wide enough?"

Eulenspiegel said, "Dear woman, don't be angry. Your husband told me to do this, and hired me as an apprentice."

The woman said, "It's a trusty servant indeed who does his master harm."

Eulenspiegel said, "Dear woman, shouldn't a servant do what he's told?"

At this his master came in and heard and saw the argument Eulenspiegel had started. His master then said, "Boy, what's this? Couldn't you have gone through the door and left my windows in one piece? What reason could you have for entering my house through the windows?"

"Dear master, you told me to go in where the high windows were; you were to follow me. Well, I did what you told me — but you didn't follow, though you said I should go first."

His master kept quiet, for he needed him, and thought, "If I want to recoup my loss here, I'd better accept what he's done — and deduct it from his wages."

So the master let Eulenspiegel work for one or three days. Then his master told Eulenspiegel to sharpen the shearing knives.

Eulenspiegel said, "Yes, gladly."

His master said, "Make them even on the back, like the blade."

Eulenspiegel said yes, and started sharpening the shearing knives, making the reverse edges like the blades. His master came over to see what he was doing, and saw that he was sharpening the knives, reverse edges and blades alike, and that he was also about to sharpen the knives he had lying on the grindstone.

His master then said, "What're you doing! This is getting to be awful."

Eulenspiegel said, "How's it getting to be awful? I'm not hurting you, since I'm doing what you told me to."

His master became angry and said, "I'm telling you that you're an awful, damned fool! Stop! Just give up your sharpening! And go back where you came from!"

Eulenspiegel said yes, went into the shop, and jumped back out through the windows — where he had come from. The beard-shearer now became even angrier, and raced after him with the bailiff to catch him, so he would pay for the windows he had broken.

But Eulenspiegel was quick. He got on a ship and out of the country.

74. How a woman who had snot hanging out of her nose invited Eulenspiegel for a meal.

Once it happened that a court was to be held, and Eulen-spiegel wanted to ride to it. But his horse was lame, so he went to it on foot.

Now, it was quite hot and he began to get hungry — and there was a small village on the way. There was no inn in the small village; but it was noontime, so he went into the village, since he was well known there. He went into a house where the wife was sitting and making cheese and had a lump of whey in her hands. Since she was sitting over the whey, neither of her hands was free — and a huge piece of snot was hanging out of her nose. Eulenspiegel wished her good day, and saw the snot. She noticed it but could not wipe her nose with her arms; nor could she suck it back in.

So she said to him, "Dear Eulenspiegel, go sit down and wait. I'm going to give you good, fresh butter."

But Eulenspiegel turned and went out.

188

The woman called after him, "Wait and eat something first."

Eulenspiegel said, "Dear woman, after that falls off." And he went into another house, thinking, "You wouldn't like that butter. Whoever's got a little dough doesn't need to throw eggs into it: it'll get fatty enough from her snot."

75. How Eulenspiegel ate the white jam by himself, because he let a lump fall out of his nose into it.

Eulenspiegel played quite a trick on a farmer's wife, so he could eat her white jam all by himself. He came into a house and was hungry. Well, he found the wife alone, sitting by the fire and cooling a white jam. It tasted so good to Eulenspiegel's eyes that he became greedy to eat it, so he asked the woman whether she would give him her white jam.

The woman said, "Yes, my dear Eulenspiegel, gladly. If I could do without it myself, I'd give it to you to eat all by yourself."

Eulenspiegel said, "My dear woman, that may indeed happen, according to your words."

The woman gave him all the white jam, putting the bowl of white jam on the table with bread as well. Eulenspiegel was hungry and began to eat; but the woman came over, intending to eat with him, as farmers usually do.

Eulenspiegel now thought, "If she joins in, there won't be

anything here before long." So he coughed up a big ball and threw it into the bowl of white jam.

The woman became angry and said, "Fie on you! Now, you rogue, you'll have to eat up that white jam by yourself!"

Eulenspiegel said, "My dear woman, your first words were thus: you would like to do without it yourself, and I could then eat the white jam by myself. Just now, though, you were coming over to eat with me — and you'd have eaten this bowlful of white jam in three gulps."

The woman said, "May nothing good ever come your way! If you won't allow me to have my own food, how could you ever allow me to have yours?"

Eulenspiegel said, "Woman, I'm acting according to your words."

So he ate up all the white jam, washed out his mouth, and left.

76. How Eulenspiegel shat in a house and blew the stink through a wall to a host who disliked him.

Eulenspiegel traveled fast. Well, he arrived in Nürnberg and was there for fourteen days. Now, a pious man was living at the inn[1] where he was presently staying — one who was rich and liked going to church and had no liking for musicians. If they were or came to wherever he was, he left. This man had a custom — that once a year he invited his neighbors to dinner, and treated them handsomely, with food and wine and the best of drinks. And if the neighbors whom he usually invited had a stranger staying with them — business people, two or three — he always invited them too and welcomed them. Well, the time came around when everybody was offering invitations, and Eulenspiegel was in the house neigh-

---

1. Logically, as the story subsequently shows, he cannot have been living at, but next door to, the inn. Some error, perhaps in the re-telling, has taken place here.

192

boring that in which he was staying. Well, the man offered an invitation to the neighbors, as was his custom, and to the guests they had, who were strangers; but he did not invite Eulenspiegel, who looked like a clown and musician — like people whom he was not in the habit of inviting.

Now, when the neighbors went to dinner at the house of this pious man, along with the respectable strangers whom he had also invited and who were staying with them, Eulenspiegel's innkeeper (with whom he was staying) went along too, with his own guests who had also been invited to dinner. And his innkeeper told Eulenspiegel that the rich man had taken him for a clown and had therefore not invited him.

Eulenspiegel was content with that, but he thought, "If I'm a clown, I ought to show him some clowning." Of course, it annoyed him that the man scorned him so.

Well, it was just after Saint Martin's Day, when parties like this usually took place;[2] and the host was sitting in an expensive room with his guests, where he was serving them their meal. Now, the room was hard by the wall of the inn where Eulenspiegel was staying. When they were seated and were truly enjoying themselves, Eulenspiegel bored a hole through the wall into the room in which the guests were sitting, took a bellows, made a great pile of his filth, and blew it with the bellows into the hole he had bored into the room. Now, this stank so terribly that nobody had the least desire to remain in that room. Everybody looked at the person next to him: the first thought the second was making the stink; the second thought the third was making the stink. Well, Eulenspiegel did not stop his bellows till the guests had to get up and could no longer remain there because of the stink. They searched under the benches; they looked in every corner — but to no avail. Nobody knew where it was coming from, and everybody went home.

Eulenspiegel's innkeeper now came by — and he was so sick with the stink that he brought up everything he had in

---

2. Saint Martin's Day (see Chapter 5, n.), which falls on November 12, was commonly followed by parties, dinners, and celebrations.

his stomach. He told him how terribly the room had stunk with human filth.

Eulenspiegel began to laugh and said, "If that rich fellow didn't want to invite me to dinner and be generous to me with his food, at least I've been much more generous and true to him than he was to me: I've been generous to him with my food anyhow. If I'd been there, the place wouldn't have stunk so badly." And within the hour he paid his innkeeper and rode off, for he was worried about what might happen.

Well, his inkeeper listened carefully to what he said — that he knew something about the smell — but he still could not understand how he could have done it: it puzzled him greatly. When Eulenspiegel was out of the city, the innkeeper went looking around the house and found the bellows, which was quite coated with shit, and found the hole as well, which he had bored through the wall of his neighbor's house. He found them within the hour, brought his neighbors over, and told them about it — how Eulenspiegel had done it and what he had said.

The rich man said, "Dear neighbor, nobody's improved by rogues and musicians. That's why I never want them in my house again. If this nonsense emerged from your house, I can't do anything about it: I knew your guest was a clown. I could read it in his appearance. Better that this happened in your house than in mine: he might have done worse things to me."

Eulenspiegel's innkeeper said, "Dear host, you've noticed something all right, and that's the way it is: you've got to set up two lights for a clown.[3] And that's something I'll certainly have to do, since I've got to take in all kinds of people. I've got to take in clowns along with the best of people, just so someone comes."

With that they parted. Eulenspiegel was gone, and he did not come back.

---

3. *i.e.*, keep both eyes open.

77. How Eulenspiegel frightened an innkeeper at Eisleben with a wolf he had promised to catch.

At Eisleben there lived an innkeeper who was haughty, who considered himself clever, and who fancied himself an important householder.

Well, during the days of winter, after a great snow had fallen, Eulenspiegel arrived at his inn. Three merchants then arrived from Saxony, traveling toward Nürnberg,[1] and they came to the inn in the dead of night.

Well, the innkeeper was quite sharp-tongued and short in welcoming the three merchants. He said, "By the devil, where are you coming from?" — because they had been so long in getting there and had arrived at his inn so late.

The merchants said, "Mr. Innkeeper, you shouldn't be so angry with us. We had quite an adventure along the way. A

---

1. Grieninger has "Nünrberg."

wolf gave us a lot of trouble. He attacked us, so we had to fight him off — and that's what kept us so long."

When the innkeeper heard this, he was quite scornful of them and said it was a disgrace that they had allowed a wolf to hold them up. If he were in open country and two wolves met him on the moor, he would beat them and drive them off — they would not frighten him. But they had been three, and had let themselves be terrified by one wolf. This lasted all evening, till the innkeeper showed them to their beds; and Eulenspiegel sat nearby and listened to his jeering.

When they went to bed, the merchants and Eulenspiegel were placed in one room; and the merchants began to discuss among themselves how they could pay the innkeeper back for this.

Eulenspiegel than said, "Dear friends, it's clear to me that the innkeeper's a pompous boaster. If you'll listen to me, I'll pay him back so he'll never speak to you about that wolf again."

This delighted the merchants, and they promised him money.

Eulenspiegel now told them to continue with their business trip, and when they returned, to stop at the inn again. He would also be there, and then they would pay him back. And so it happened. The merchants got ready for their journey, paid their bill, paid Eulenspiegel's as well, and rode off.

But the innkeeper called sarcastically after the merchants, "You merchants, be careful that no wolf meets you in the meadow!"

The merchants said, "Mr. Innkeeper, thank you for warning us. If wolves eat us, we won't be back. And if wolves eat you, we won't find you here again." And with that they rode away.

Eulenspiegel now rode into the Harz Mountains to set traps for wolves. And God gave him the good luck to catch one. He killed it and let it freeze stiff, waiting for the merchants to return to the inn at Eisleben, and met the three merchants there, as they had agreed. But Eulenspiegel had brought the dead wolf without anybody's knowing about it.

During dinner that evening the innkeeper kept teasing

the merchants about the wolf. They said that so, indeed, it had gone with them and the wolf: now, if it happened that he met two wolves in the meadow, would he really ward off one of them while he killed the other? The innkeeper boasted greatly how he would cut both wolves to pieces — and this lasted all evening, till they went to bed.

Well, Eulenspiegel kept quiet till he approached the merchants in their room. Then Eulenspiegel said, "Good friends, be silent and watch. What I'm going to do you're going to like too. Keep a light burning for me."

Well, when the innkeeper and all his servants were in bed, Eulenspiegel crept softly out of the room. He took the dead wolf, which was frozen stiff, carried it to the hearth, and planted it on sticks so it stood up properly. Then he pried open its mouth and stuck two children's shoes in its mouth. He now returned to the merchants in their room and called, "Mr. Innkeeper!" The innkeeper, who was not yet asleep, heard this and called back, asking what they wanted — whether a wolf was perhaps biting them.

They now called, "Ah, dear Innkeeper, send your maid or boy to bring us something to drink! We can't stand this thirst!"

The innkeeper became angry and said, "That's the Saxon way all right: they drink day and night." And he called to his maid to get up and bring something to drink to their room.

The maid got up and went to the fire, intending to light a lamp. She looked up — and looked the wolf right in the mouth. She was terrified, let the lamp fall, and ran out into the courtyard, thinking only that the wolf had already devoured the children.

Eulenspiegel and the merchants called again for something to drink. The innkeeper thought his maid was asleep, so he called his servant boy. The boy got up and also tried to light a lamp. He too saw the wolf standing there. He at once thought it had eaten the maid whole — so he dropped the lamp and ran into the cellar.

Eulenspiegel and the merchants heard these things, and he said, "Be still now. This game's about to get interesting." Eulenspiegel and the merchants then called for the third time: where were the maid and boy? — They weren't bringing anything to drink. He should come himself, and bring a light; they could not leave their rooms.

The innkeeper thought only that his boy must also have fallen asleep. He got up, getting angry, and said, "The devil serve these Saxons their drinks!" He, too, lit a lamp at the fire. But when he saw the wolf standing before him on the hearth and saw that it had the shoes in its mouth, he began to scream, and he cried, "Murder! Save me, dear friends!" And he ran to the merchants in their room and said, "Dear friends, come help me! A terrible animal is standing at the fire — and it's eaten my children, my maid, and my boy!"

The merchants were soon ready, and Eulenspiegel too, and they went to the fire with the innkeeper. The boy emerged from the cellar; the maid came in from the garden; his wife brought his children out of their rooms: they were indeed all very alive. Eulenspiegel then went over and poked the wolf with his foot: it lay there and lifted not a paw.

Eulenspiegel said, "This is a dead wolf. Were you doing all that screaming over this? What sort of a weak fellow are you? Can a dead wolf bite you in your own house and chase you and all your servants into corners? And it isn't long since you were going to kill two living wolves in open country. But you've only got words where some have courage."

The innkeeper listened and realized he had been fooled. He went into his room, to bed, feeling ashamed of his vain words and that a dead wolf had so humiliated him and all his servants. The merchants laughed. Then they paid what they and Eulenspiegel had spent and rode off.

But after that, the innkeeper no longer talked so much about his bravery.

78. How Eulenspiegel shat on an innkeeper's table in Cologne, and told him he would come and find it.

Just after this, Eulenspiegel arrived at an inn in Cologne. Well, he kept to himself for two or three days and so went unrecognized; but during those days he noticed that his innkeeper was a rogue.

He now thought, "Guests don't have it so good where their innkeeper's a rogue. You'd better look for another hotel."

That evening his innkeeper revealed to Eulenspiegel that he already had another hotel: for he showed the other guests to bed, but not him.

Eulenspiegel then said, "What's this, Mr. Innkeeper? I pay as much for my food as those whom you've shown to bed — and I'm supposed to sleep on this bench?"

The innkeeper said, "Look, here are a couple of sheets for you." Then he loosed a fart, with another on top of it, and said, "Look, here's a pillow." And he loosed a third fart, and really began to stink, saying, "See? There's a whole bed for you. Get by somehow till morning, and then pile these together for me again."

Eulenspiegel kept quiet, but he thought, "See? Of course you see: you've got to pay this rogue with a trick." And he stretched out on the bench for the night.

Well, the innkeeper had a pretty folding dinner-table. Eulenspiegel opened it, shat on it, and closed it again. The next morning he got up early, went up to the innkeeper's room, and said "Mr. Innkeeper, I thank you for my overnight stay," and with that let fall a huge shit, and said to him, "Those are the bed-feathers; the pillows, sheets, and blankets I've put together in a pile."

The innkeeper said, "Mr. Guest, that's fine. I'll look for it when I get up."

Eulenspiegel said, "Just look around. You'll find it." And with that he left the house.

The innkeeper was to have many guests for lunch, and he said, "My guests shall eat at my pretty table." But when he opened the table, a terrible stink overwhelmed him; he found the filth inside and said, "He pays according to one's labor all right: a fart paid for with a shit." And he asked that he be brought back, planning to try him further. Eulenspiegel returned, and they settled their fooling, so from then on he got into a good bed.

79. How Eulenspiegel paid the innkeeper with the sound of his money.

Eulenspiegel stayed a long time at that inn in Cologne. Then it happened that the food was brought to the fire too late, so it was high noon before the food was ready. Eulenspiegel was annoyed that he had to go hungry so long. Well, the innkeeper could see that this annoyed him, so he told him that whoever could not wait till the food was ready could just eat whatever he had. Eulenspiegel went to eat a roll and then went to sit by the hearth. Well, when it struck twelve, the table was laid, the food was served, and the innkeeper and his guests took their places — but Eulenspiegel remained in the kitchen.

The innkeeper said, "What's this? Don't you want to sit at the table?"

"No," he said. "I don't want to eat. I got full from the smell of your roast."

The innkeeper said nothing and ate with his guests. After the meal was over, they paid the innkeeper; then one left, another stayed behind — but Eulenspiegel remained sitting by the fire. The innkecper now came over to him with his counting board. He was angry and told Eulenspiegel to give him two Cologne white-pennies for the meal.

Eulenspiegel said, "Mr. Innkeeper, are you the sort of man who takes money from someone who hasn't eaten his food?"

The innkeeper said toughly that he had better just give him the money. Even if he had eaten nothing, he had still gotten full from the smell; he had been sitting near the roast and that was the same as if he had sat at the table and eaten the roast. So he would count that as a meal.

Eulenspiegel took out a Cologne white-penny and threw it on the bench. "Mr. Innkeeper, do you hear that sound?"

The innkeeper said, "I hear the sound all right."

Eulenspiegel was quick with his penny and stuck it back in his purse. Then he said, "The sound of that penny helps

201

you exactly as much as the smell of your roast helped my stomach."

The innkeeper was peeved, for he wanted the white-penny; but Eulenspiegel would not give it to him and wanted to bring the matter to court. The innkeeper gave in. He had no desire to go to court: he was afraid he might pay him back as he had with the table. So he let him go.

Well, Eulenspiegel left that place — leaving the innkeeper to honor his own bill — and left the Rhine. Then he traveled back to the district of Saxony.

After he played that trick, Eulenspiegel rode out of Rostock[1] with purpose, and arrived at an inn in a country town.

Now, there was little to eat in the house, for there was nothing but poverty there and the innkeeper had many children — whom Eulenspiegel did not enjoy being around.[2] Well, Eulenspiegel tied up his horse in the stable, went into the house, and walked over to the fire. But he found a cold hearth and a bare house. He at once saw there was nothing but poverty in the place.

So he said, "Mr. Innkeeper, you've got terrible neighbors."

The innkeeper said, "Yes, Mr. Guest, so I do. They steal everything I've got in the house."

Eulenspiegel now began to laugh, and he thought, "The innkeeper here is like a guest." He wanted to stay there, de-

---

1. This tale ought perhaps to follow other chapters having to do with Rostock, such as 39 or 49.

2. *Cf.* Chapter 21.

spite the children whom he did not like — for he saw that they went to do their business behind the door of the house, one child after the other.

So Eulenspiegel asked the innkeeper, "Why are your children so unclean? Don't you have some place other than behind your front door for them to do their business?"

The innkeeper said, "Mr. Guest, why get angry about it? I'm not unhappy about it: I'm leaving tomorrow."

Eulenspiegel kept quiet. Later, when he needed to shit, he shat a huge pile of filth in the fireplace.

Well, the innkeeper came in while Eulenspiegel was at this business and said, "The plague on you! Shitting in the fireplace? Isn't the courtyard big enough?"

Eulenspiegel said, "Mr. Innkeeper, why get angry about it? It doesn't bother me either: I'm leaving today." And he mounted his horse and rode out through the door.

The innkeeper called after him to stop and clean the filth out of his hearth.

Eulenspiegel said, "Whoever's last sweeps the house. That way my filth and your filth will be cleared out together."

81. How Eulenspiegel destroyed a dog and paid an innkeeper with its skin, because it had eaten with him.

Now, it happened that Eulenspiegel came to stay at a house in a village[1] and found the innkeeper's wife alone. Well, she had a shaggy little dog that she loved very much and that was always lying in her lap when it had nothing to do.

Eulenspiegel was sitting by the fire and drinking beer from a jug. The woman had accustomed her dog to getting a bowlful of beer whenever she was drinking, so it could drink too. Well, while Eulenspiegel sat and drank, the dog got up, rubbed itself against Eulenspiegel, and jumped on his neck.

The innkeeper saw this and said, "Oh, give him a bit to drink in the bowl. That's what he wants."

Eulenspiegel said, "Certainly."

---

1. According to Chapter 82, this must be near Stassfurt.

The innkeeper went about her business, and Eulenspiegel drank and gave the dog some to drink in the bowl, sticking in a bit of meat too. Well, the dog became quite full, lay down by the fire, and stretched out there.

Eulenspiegel now told the woman, "Let's figure out how much I owe you." And he continued, "Dear Innkeeper, if a guest ate your food, drank your beer, and had no money, would you still give the guest credit?"

It did not occur to the woman that he meant her dog, and she thought, "He must mean himself." So she said to him, "Mr. Guest, there's no credit here. People give either money or a pledge."

Eulenspiegel said, "Then for my part, I'm happy. Anybody else takes care of his own bill."

The innkeeper went out. Then, as soon as he could manage it, Eulenspiegel took the dog under his coat to the stable. There he skinned it, put the skin under his coat, and went back to the house to the fire.

Eulenspiegel then called the woman to him and said, "Let's settle up."

The innkeeper totaled what he had spent, but Eulenspiegel paid for only half his meal. So she asked who was supposed to pay for the other half: he had, after all, drunk his beer by himself.

Eulenspiegel said, "No, I didn't drink it by myself. I had a guest who drank with me and who had no money — but he had a good pledge. He's going to pay the other half."

The woman said, "What guest? What sort of pledge have you got?"

Eulenspiegel said, "It's his very best coat, which he was wearing." And he pulled out the dog's skin and coat for her, saying, "Here, dear Innkeeper. This is the coat of the guest who drank with me."

The woman was shocked. She saw at once that it was her dog's skin, became angry, and said, "Oh, that nothing good ever comes your way! How could you skin my dog!" And she flew into a rage.

Eulenspiegel said, "Innkeeper, it's your own fault. Rage all you like. You told me yourself to take care of your dog, and

I said, 'The guest has no money.' You didn't want to give him credit; you wanted money or a pledge. Well, he had no money, and the beer had to be paid for. So he had to leave his coat as a pledge. Take it, please, for the beer he drank."

The innkeeper became even angrier and told him to walk straight out of her house and never come back.

Eulenspiegel said, "I'm not going to walk out of your house: I'm going to ride out of it." And he saddled his horse, rode out through the door, and said, "Innkeeper, keep that pledge till I get your money. For I'm planning to come back, uninvited. If it then happens that I don't drink at your house, I won't have to pay for any beer."

82. How Eulenspiegel convinced the same innkeeper that Eulenspiegel was lying on the wheel.

Now listen to what Eulenspiegel did near Stassfurt.[1]

There is a village nearby, and he took lodgings there. He dressed differently, went to his inn, and noticed there was a wheel standing in the house. He stretched out on it and wished the lady-innkeeper good day. Then he asked her whether she had heard anything about Eulenspiegel. She said that what she had heard about that rogue she would not like to hear repeated.

Eulenspiegel said, "Woman, what's he done to you to turn you against him? Because wherever he goes he doesn't leave without some trick."

She said, "I found that out all right. He was here and skinned my dog — and offered me its skin for the beer he drank."

---

1. Actually, "at Stassfurt." This, however, cannot be, according to the previous tale.

Eulenspiegel said, "Woman, that wasn't nice."

The woman said, "He'll have his own surprises, I'm sure."

He said, "Woman, that's happening already: he's stretched on the wheel."[2]

The innkeeper said, "God be praised for it."

Eulenspiegel said, "I'm him! Adieu! I'm leaving!"

---

2. The medieval punishment of strapping prisoners to a revolving wheel was commonly reserved for serious criminals, such as arsonists, thieves, and highwaymen; mere murderers were simply stabbed to death with a sword. See Lappenberg, pp. 278–279.

83. How Eulenspiegel seated a lady=innkeeper in hot ashes on her bare ass.

Nasty, angry gossip brings nasty rewards.

When Eulenspiegel left Rome[1], he arrived at a village with a large inn where the innkeeper was not at home. Well Eulenspiegel asked his wife whether she had met Eulenspiegel.

The woman said, "No, I don't know him. But I've heard this about him: that he's a perfect scoundrel."

Eulenspiegel said, "Dear Innkeeper, why do you say he's a scoundrel when you don't know him?"

The woman said, "What's it matter that I don't know him? There's nothing against the idea. People say he's a wicked fellow."

Eulenspiegel said, "Dear woman, has he done anything wicked to you? You've just heard gossip that he's a scoundrel."

---

1. See Chapter 34, which this tale ought perhaps to follow.

The woman said, "I'm just telling you what I've heard from the people who come and go here."

Eulenspiegel kept quiet. But the next morning he got up early, raked aside the hot ashes, returned to her bed, lifted the lady-innkeeper out of her sleep, set her bare ass into the hot ashes, and quite scorched her ass. Then he said, "How's that woman? Now you've got the right to say that Eulenspiegel's a scoundrel. You've experienced him now and even seen him: you'll remember him by this."

The woman began to scream with pain. But Eulenspiegel left the house, laughed, and said, "That's how to finish one's trip to Rome."

84. How Eulenspiegel shat in his bed and convinced his innkeeper that a priest had done it.

Eulenspiegel played a wicked trick at Frankfurt-on-the-Oder. He arrived there with a priest and they both stayed at the same inn. That evening the innkeeper's wife treated them handsomely, offering them fish and venison.

When they were ready to sit down at the table, the woman seated the priest near the head of it. She also served the priest the best of what was in the serving-bowl, saying, "Father, eat this for my sake."

Eulenspiegel sat far down the table and looked the innkeeper and his wife firmly in the eye — but no one served him anything or asked him to eat. He had to pay just as much anyway, though.

When the meal was over and it was time to go to bed, Eulenspiegel and the priest were placed in one room, and each found a fine bed ready for him to sleep on. Well, the next morning the priest was up early. He said his prayers, paid the innkeeper, and traveled on. Eulenspiegel remained lying there till it was about to strike nine; then he shat in the bed in which the priest had lain.

The innkeeper's wife now asked her house-boy whether the priest or the other guest was up yet, or whether they had already reckoned up and paid.

The boy said, "Yes. The priest was up at a good hour. He prayed, paid, and left. But I haven't seen the other fellow today."

The woman was worried he might be ill, so she went into the room and asked Eulenspiegel whether he did not want to get up.

He said, "Yes, Mrs. Innkeeper. I wasn't feeling quite well."

In the meantime the woman tried to take the sheets off the priest's bed. As she uncovered it, there was a huge pile of filth lying in the middle of the bed.

"God save me," she said. "What's lying here!"

"Yes, Mrs. Innkeeper, that doesn't surprise me a bit,"

said Eulenspiegel. "Because last night that priest was served everything good and the very best that came to the table. There wasn't anything said all evening except, 'Father, eat this.' It surprises me that so much of what the priest ate stayed in him — that he didn't shit all over the room as well."

The woman was furious with the innocent priest and said that if he came back, he would be sent on his way. But Eulenspiegel — that honest boy — she would gladly let stay with her.

85. How a Dutchman ate Eulenspiegel's baked apple, into which he had put saffron, from his plate.

Eulenspiegel paid back a Dutchman, fairly and honestly. For it happened that merchants from Holland were once staying at an inn in Antwerp. And Eulenspiegel, who was also there, was a little sick — so he did not want meat but cooked soft-boiled eggs for himself.

When the guests were sitting at the table, Eulenspiegel came to the table too, bringing his soft-boiled eggs with him. One of the Dutchmen took Eulenspiegel for a farmer and said, "What's this, farmer? Don't you like the innkeeper's food? Do you have to have eggs cooked for you?" And with that he took both eggs, broke them open, poured them out, one after the other, on his neck, placed the shells in front of Eulenspiegel, and said, "There — lick the barrel; the yolk's gone." The other guests laughed, and Eulenspiegel with them.

That evening Eulenspiegel bought a fine apple which he hollowed out and filled with flies or gnats. Then he baked the apple slowly, peeled it, and sprinkled it with ginger on the outside. When they were sitting at the table that evening, Eulenspiegel brought his baked apple out on a plate and turned away, as if he were going to get more. When he turned his back, the Dutchman snatched the baked apple, taking it from the plate, and gulped it down. Within an hour the Dutchman began to vomit, bringing up everything he had in his stomach and feeling terrible, so the innkeeper and the other guests thought he must have poisoned himself with the apple.

Eulenspiegel said, "That's no poisoning. It's a cleansing of his stomach. For a cleansed stomach receives its food easily. If he'd told me he was so greedy to gulp down my apple, I'd have warned him. For there weren't any gnats in my soft-boiled eggs, but there were plenty in my baked apple. He'll have to vomit them up again."

With that the Dutchman came to himself and no longer felt worried. But he said to Eulenspiegel, "Eat and bake! I wouldn't eat with you again, even if you had fieldfares!"

86. How Eulenspiegel made a woman break all her pots at the market in Bremen.

After Eulenspiegel played that trick, he traveled back to Bremen, to the Bishop.[1] He had a lot of fun with Eulenspiegel and liked him too, since he was always engaged in some roguish adventure — which both made the Bishop laugh and keep his horse free of charge.

Eulenspiegel then acted as if he were sick of clowning and wanted to go to church. The Bishop really scoffed at him for this, but he refused to be dissuaded and went and prayed, till the Bishop became exceedingly annoyed.

Well, Eulenspiegel secretly made an arrangement with a woman, a potter's wife, who sat selling pots in the market-

1. See Chapter 69 for a related story. Lappenberg (p. 280) suggests that the Bishop may have been Archbishop Burchard Grelle, who died in 1344, and whose character might indeed have led him to play the sort of trick described in this tale. The trick, at any rate, is, as Lappenberg suggests, quite in accord with the spirit of the times.

place. He bought up all her pots, and agreed with her on something she was to do when he waved or gave a signal.

Eulenspiegel then returned to the Bishop and pretended that he had just been to church. The Bishop began to jeer at him again, till at last Eulenspiegel said to the Bishop, "Gracious Lord, come to the market-place with me. There's a potter's wife there with clay pots. I'll make a bet with you: I won't speak to her or wink at her — but with silent words I'll make her get up, grab a stick, and smash those clay pots to pieces herself."

The Bishop said, "That I'd like to see." But first he wanted to bet thirty guilders with him that the woman would not do it. The bet was made, and the Bishop went to the market-place with Eulenspiegel.

Eulenspiegel pointed the woman out to him, and they went into the city hall. Well, Eulenspiegel kept close to the Bishop, but made signs to the woman, with words and gestures, as if he wanted her to do it. Finally he gave the woman the sign they had agreed on. She at once got up, took a stick, and smashed her clay pots to pieces — and everybody in the market-place laughed.

When the Bishop got home again, he took Eulenspiegel aside and asked him to tell him how he had made the woman break her own pots: then he would give him the thirty guilders, according to their bet.

Eulenspiegel said, "Of course, Gracious Lord, with pleasure." And he told him how he had first paid for the pots and afterwards arranged it with the woman. He had not used black magic. Well, when he told him everything, the Bishop laughed and gave him the thirty guilders. But Eulenspiegel had to promise him to tell nobody about it: he would get him a fat ox if he kept his word. Eulenspiegel said, yes, he would be happy to keep quiet about it; then he got ready, got up, and traveled off.

As soon as Eulenspiegel was gone, the Bishop sat down at the table with his knights and servants, and told them he knew the trick by which he could also make the woman break all her pots. His knights and servants had no interest in seeing pots smashed — but they did want to learn the trick of it.

The Bishop said, "If each of you gives me a good, fat ox for my kitchen, I'll teach the trick to all of you."

Now, it was just autumn, when oxen are fattest, so each of them thought, "You can risk a few oxen to learn this trick — that can't do you any harm." So each knight and servant sent the Bishop a fat ox, bringing them together, and the Bishop received sixteen oxen. Well, each ox was worth four guilders, so the thirty guilders he had given Eulenspiegel were paid back twice over.[2]

As the oxen were standing there together, Eulenspiegel came riding up and said, "Half this loot belongs to me."

The Bishop told Eulenspiegel, "Stick to what you've promised me: I'll treat you as I promised you. Just let your Lords keep their bread, too." And he gave him a fat ox. Eulenspiegel took it and thanked the Bishop.

The Bishop then took his servants, drew himself up, and told them to listen to him: he would tell them all about this trick. And he told them everything — how Eulenspiegel had arranged the thing beforehand with the woman and how he had paid for the pots. As the Bishop told them this,[3] all his servants sat there looking betrayed, but not one of them dared say a word to the others. One scratched his head; the next scratched the nape of his neck; and they all felt miserable about this business, for they were all angry about their oxen. In the end they had to accept things, and they consoled themselves with the idea that he was after all a Noble Lord. If they had been forced to give him the oxen first, well, the oxen were still there, and it had all been just a joke. Actually, they were less annoyed about the oxen than about having been such fools as to give their oxen for this trick — which had been just a trick — and that Eulenspiegel had gotten an ox.

---

2. Grieninger has "thrice."

3. Grieninger has "As he told this to the Bishop," a probable error since it makes no sense.

87. How a farmer who was taking plums to the market in Eimbeck gave Eulenspiegel a ride in his cart, and how Eulenspiegel shat on them.

The Most Serene and High-Born Princes of Brunswick once held racing, jousting, and tilting matches with many foreign Princes and Lords, knights and servants, and their tenants as well, in the city of Eimbeck.[1]

Now, this was during summer, when plums and other fruits were getting ripe. Well, an honest, simple peasant was living at Oldenburg near Eimbeck,[2] who had an orchard of plum trees. He had a cartful of his plums picked, intending to drive it to Eimbeck; for lots of people were there and he thought he could get rid of his plums better now than at other times.

When he got near the city, Eulenspiegel was lying there in the shade, under a green tree. Well, he had drunk so much at the Lord's court that he could neither eat nor drink — and looked more dead than alive. As the honest man was driving past him, Eulenspiegel called out to him as feebly as he could, saying, "Ah, good friend, look, I've been lying here sick like this and without any help for three days and nights — and if I lie here this way for one day more, I'm sure I'll die of hunger and thirst. So for the sake of God, drive me up to the city."

The good man said, "Ah, good friend, I'd be happy to do so, but I've got plums in my cart. If I put you on top of them, you'll ruin them all for me."

---

1. Grieninger has Lübeck in the title, but Eimbeck in the story. Chapter 46, which also takes place in Eimbeck, ought probably to follow this one.

2. No such place exists near Eimbeck. Three villages: Stadtoldendorf, Markoldendorf, and Klein Oldendorf, are close to Eimbeck, however. Lappenberg (p. 281) suggests that N. may have had one of these in mind.

Eulenspiegel said, "Take me along. I'll manage in the front of the cart."

The man was old. He strained life and limb in getting the rogue (who made himself as heavy as possible) into his cart. Then, on account of the sick man, he drove more slowly.

When Eulenspiegel had been traveling a while, he pulled the straw off the plums, secretly lifted his behind, shat on the poor man's plums, and pulled the straw back over them. When the farmer reached the city, Eulenspiegel cried, "Stop! Stop! Help me out of the cart! I want to stay outside here, at the gate."

The good man helped the evil rogue out of his cart and drove to the market by the shortest route possible. When he got there, he unhitched his horse and rode it to his inn. In the meantime, many citizens were coming into the market-place, and among them was one who was always first when-ever something was brought for selling but who rarely bought anything. He now came over, pulled the straw half off, and made his hands shitty. The man now returned from his inn. Eulenspiegel had changed his clothes and arrived there too, by another way, and said to the farmer, "What've you brought to sell?"

"Plums," said the farmer.

Eulenspiegel said, "You've brought them like a rogue! These plums are shitty! You ought to be kept out of the country with these plums!"

The man looked at him, realized who it was, and said, "There was a sick man lying outside the city — a man who looked just like this man standing here, except he had differ-ent clothes on. I drove him — for the sake of God — up to the gate. And that very rogue did this disgraceful thing to me."

Eulenspiegel said, "That rogue definitely deserves a beating."

Well, the honest man had to drive his plums off to the slaughterers' graveyard, and could sell them nowhere.

88. How Eulenspiegel counted the monks into matins at Marienthal.

Now, the time came when Eulenspiegel had run around through every country. He was old and fed up and began to feel worried about dying. So he thought he ought to commit himself to a cloister, in his poverty, end his days well, and serve God for the rest of his life, because of his sins. If God took charge of him, he would not be lost.

So for this reason he went to the Abbot of Marienthal[1] and asked him whether he would take him in as a brother: he would leave the cloister his entire estate. Knaves were acceptable to the Abbot too, and he said, "You're still strong. I'll be happy to take you in, as you've asked. But you'll have to do something and have a job. For as you see, my brothers and I all have things to do, and each of us is assigned something."

---

1. Marienthal, not far from Halberstädt, is the site of a Cistercian Abbey. See Lappenberg, p. 287.

Eulenspiegel said, "Yes, Father, that's fine."

"All right then! Now — God knows — you don't like working. You'll be our porter. That way you can continue your easy life and have nothing to worry about — just getting food and beer from the cellar and opening and closing the gate."

Eulenspiegel said, "Worthy Lord, may God reward you for thinking so well of me, an old, sick man. I'll do everything you tell me and not do anything you forbid me."

The Abbot said, "Look, here's the key. You mustn't let everyone in. Let every third or fourth person in. For if lots of people are let in, they'll eat the cloister into poverty."

Eulenspiegel said, "Worthy Lord, I'll handle it properly."

Well, of all who arrived there, whether they belonged to the cloister or not, he always admitted only every fourth person — and no more. Complaints about this reached the Abbot, who said to Eulenspiegel, "You're a perfect scoundrel! Can't you let in those who are surrendered to the cloister and belong here?"

"Father," said Eulenspiegel, "I've been letting in every fourth person and no more, as you told me; and I've obeyed your order."

"You've done it like a rogue," said the Abbot, who would have been glad to get rid of him. And he appointed another gatekeeper, for it was clear to him that Eulenspiegel had no intention of giving up his old tricks. Then he assigned him another job, saying, "Look, you're to count the monks into matins at night — and if you miss even one, you can just go on your way."

Eulenspiegel said, "Father, that's a hard job for me. But if it can't be any other way, I'll have to do it as best I can."

And that night he ripped a number of steps out of the staircase.

Now, the Prior was a God-fearing old monk who was always first at matins. He came quietly to the staircase; but as he tried to walk downstairs, he fell through and broke a leg. Well, he screamed horribly, so the other brothers ran over to see what was wrong with him — and they fell downstairs, one after the other.

Eulenspiegel now said to the Abbot, "Worthy Lord, have I done my duty? I've counted all the monks." And he handed him the tally-board, on which he had notched them off as they fell one after the other.

The Abbot said, "You've counted like a damned rogue! Get out of my cloister and go to the devil where you please!"

So he went toward Mölln. There he was stricken with illness, and a short time afterwards he died.

89. How Eulenspiegel became ill at Mölln, how he shat in the pharmacist's medical book, how he was brought to "The Holy Ghost," and how he said a sweet word to his mother.

Eulenspiegel became weak and quite ill as he went from Marienthal to Mölln. There he stayed with a pharmacist to get medicine. Now, the pharmacist was rather malicious and tricky, so he gave Eulenspiegel a strong laxative. When morning came, the laxative began to work, and Eulenspiegel got up to purge himself of it. But the house was locked up everywhere. He was full of worry and need, so he went into the pharmacy, shat into one of the books, and said, "The medicine came from here. It ought to be returned here. That way the pharmacist doesn't lose anything. I can't pay for it anyway."

When the pharmacist found out about this, he was furious with Eulenspiegel and no longer wanted him in his house. So he had him brought to the hospital (called "The Holy Ghost"[1]). He now said to the people who were taking him there, "I've struggled hard and always prayed to God to let the Holy Ghost come into me. So he sends me the opposite — that I come into the Holy Ghost. And He stays outside of me, and I enter Him." The people laughed at him and left him. Indeed, a man dies as he has lived.

It became known to his mother that he was ill. She got ready in a hurry and came to him, thinking to get money from him, for she was an old, poor woman. When she came to him, she began to cry and said, "My dear son, where are you sick?"

Eulenspiegel said, "Dear Mother, here between the bedbox and the wall."

"Ah, dear son, say a sweet word to me."

Eulenspiegel said, "Dear Mother, 'honey' — that's a sweet plant."

---

1. Such a hospital actually existed at Mölln in the thirteenth century. See Lappenberg, p. 287.

His mother said, "Ah, dear son, give me some sweet advice to remember you by."

Eulenspiegel said, "Yes, dear Mother. When you want to do your business, turn your ass away from the wind. Then the stink won't get into your nose."

His mother said, "Dear son, give me some of your belongings."

Eulenspiegel said, "Dear Mother, one should give to him who has nothing and take from him who has something. My goods are hidden — where, nobody knows. If you find something that's mine, you may take it, for of my goods I leave you all that's crooked and straight."

In the meantime Eulenspiegel was getting very ill, so the people urged him to confess and take communion. Eulenspiegel did so, for he knew very well that he would never get up from his sick bed.

90. How Eulenspiegel was told to repent of his sins—so he repented of three sorts of tricks he had not played.

Eulenspiegel should feel repentance and sorrow for his sins during his illness; then communion would let him die more sweetly — or so an old beguine[1] told him.

Eulenspiegel said to her, "It won't happen that I'll die sweetly, for death is bitter. Also, why should I confess in secret what I've done during my life? Lots of countries and people know what I've done. The man I've treated well will speak well of me, and the man to whom I've done something won't keep quiet because I'm repentant. I'm repentant about only three sorts of things; and I'm sorry that I didn't, and couldn't, do them."

The beguine said, "Dear God, just be happy if it's something awful you didn't do; and just be sorry for your sins."

Eulenspiegel said, "All I'm sorry for are those three things I didn't do — and could never get to do."

The beguine said, "What are those things? Are they good or bad?"

Eulenspiegel said, "There are three things. The first is this. In the days of my youth, whenever I saw a man walking

1. The origin of this term is unknown. Dayton Phillips, in his interesting study, *Beguines in Medieval Strassburg* (Stanford University Press, 1941), p. 2, suggests that the word is derived "from the Old French word *beige* or *bege*, referring to the gray-brown color of the penitent robe of undyed wool worn by 'beguines.'" Phillips believes that "a person wearing such a robe came to be called *beguinus*, through the addition of the Latin diminutive suffix *-inus* to the adjective *bege*, and that the use of this combination in Germanic-speaking provinces gave the *g* its hard sound." Beguines, in any case, is the name for certain laymen and laywomen who were first organized in Belgium and France during the twelfth century. While they devoted themselves primarily to charitable and religious lives, they were nonetheless free to marry. For a good history of the beguines in the Middle Ages, see Ernest W. McDonnell, *The Beguines and Beghards in Medieval Culture* (Rutgers University Press, 1954). Lappenberg (p. 287) believes that beguines were undoubtedly at work in Germany before 1350, the year of Eulenspiegel's death.

in the street, whose coat was falling down below his cloak, I followed him, thinking his coat would trip him, because I wanted to lift it up. But whenever I got up to him, I saw his coat really was that long — so I got angry and would gladly have snipped his coat off, as much of it as hung below his cloak. And I'm just sorry I could never do so. — The second thing is: whenever I saw somebody sitting or walking, who was picking his teeth with a knife, that I couldn't stick the knife through his throat. That also makes me sorry. — The third thing is: that I can't stitch up the asses of all the old women who are past their prime. That makes me sorry too, since they're of no use to anybody on earth and just make the ground shitty where fruit grows."

The beguine said, "Oh, God save us! What're you saying! — I hear you all right. If you were strong and had the power, you'd sew up my hole for me too — for I'm a woman of easily sixty."

Eulenspiegel said, "I'm sorry that hasn't been done."

The beguine then said, "Well, the devil protect you!" And she walked away from him and left him lying there.

Eulenspiegel said, "There's no beguine who's really devout when she's angry. Then she's more spiteful than the devil."

91. How Eulenspiegel made his will—in which the priest covered his hands with shit.

Be careful, all you religious and worldly people, that you do not dirty your hands on wills, as happened with Eulenspiegel's will.

A priest was brought to Eulenspiegel to confess him. When the priest came to him, the priest thought, "He's been an extraordinary person, so he must have gotten a lot of money together. It can't be otherwise; he must have a remarkable amount of money. You ought to lure it out of him now, at his final end. Maybe there'll be some for you, too."

Well, when Eulenspiegel began to confess to the priest and they began to talk, the priest said to him, in the middle of other things, "Eulenspiegel, my dear son, reflect on your soul's holiness at your end. You've been an amazing fellow and have committed many sins for which you should be sorry. But if you have a bit of money — I would give it to honor God and poor priests, such as I am. Thus would I advise you, for that money was strangely come by. And should you decide to do such a thing — to reveal it to me and give me that money — I shall arrange it that you arrive in God's grace. And should you wish to give me some too, I would thank you all the days of my life and read vigils and masses for you."

Eulenspiegel said, "Yes, my dear fellow, I'll think of you all right. Just come back this afternoon. I'll put a piece of silver right into your hand: that way you'll be certain of it."

The priest was delighted and came running back that afternoon. Well, while he was gone, Eulenspiegel got a jug, filled it half-full with human filth, and strewed a bit of money on top of it, so the money covered the filth.

When the priest returned, he said, "My dear Eulenspiegel, here I am. If you would like to give me something now, as you promised me, I shall receive it."

Eulenspiegel said, "Yes, dear Father. If you'll just grab modestly and not be greedy, I'll let you make a grab into this jug, so you'll remember me."

The priest said, "I'll do it as you wish and take as little as I can."

So Eulenspiegel opened the jug and said, "Look, dear Father, the jug's rather full of money. Well, reach in and pull out a handful. But don't reach too far."

The priest said, "Yes." But he became rather eager — being driven by greed — so he plunged right into the jug, thinking he would pull out a good handful, and shoved his hand far into it. He now discovered something damp and soft under the money. He pulled his hand out again. His knuckles were covered with the filth. The priest then said to him, "Ah, what a terrible rogue you are! If you can trick me now, at the very end, when you're lying on your death-bed, those you tricked in the days of your youth have every right to complain."

Eulenspiegel said, "Dear Father, I warned you not to dig too deep. If your greed betrayed you and you ignored my warning, that's not my fault."

The priest said, "You're a rogue to end all rogues! If you could talk yourself out of the gallows at Lübeck, you'll be able to answer me all right." And he walked away, leaving Eulenspiegel lying there.

Eulenspiegel called after him to wait and take his money. The priest refused to listen.

92. How Eulenspiegel divided his wealth into three parts—one for his friends, one for the Council of Mölln, and one for the priest there.

As Eulenspiegel became more seriously ill, he made his last will and testament, dividing his wealth into three parts — one for his friends, one for the Council of Mölln, and one for the Church Father there — but with this stipulation: that when God should take him and he went his way to death, that his corpse be buried in hallowed ground and his soul dispatched with vigils and masses according to Christian practice and custom. Then, after four weeks, they might together unlock the fine chest, well secured with expensive locks, that he showed them — if it were still locked — and divide among themselves what was in it and come to an agreement about his property.

The three parties took this cheerfully, and Eulenspiegel died. When all had been done according to his will, and the four weeks had slipped by, the Council, the Church Father, and Eulenspiegel's friends came over and opened the chest to divide the treasure he had left. But when it was opened, there was nothing there but a stone. Everybody looked at everybody else — and they began to get angry. The priest thought that since the Council had been keeping the chest, they had secretly removed the treasure and locked the box again. The Council thought his friends had taken the treasure during his illness and filled the chest with stones. His friends thought the priest must have secretly carried off the treasure when everybody left to let him confess Eulenspiegel. Well, they parted unpleasantly.

The priest and the Council now decided to dig Eulenspiegel up again. But when they began to dig, it stank so badly that no one could stay there. So they closed the grave again.

Well, he remained in his grave, and in his memory a stone was placed on it — which can still be seen there.

93. How Eulenspiegel died and how pigs knocked over his bier during the vigils, so he took a tumble.

After Eulenspiegel had given up the ghost, people came to the hospital to mourn him. Well, they placed him on a bier on wooden planks. The priests came to sing vigils and started singing.

The hospital sow now came in with her piglets, walked under the bier, and began to rub herself, so Eulenspiegel tumbled off it. The women and priests rushed over to chase the sow and piglets outside — but the sow became angry and refused to let herself be driven off. Well, the sow and piglets ran madly through the hospital, leaping and racing over the priests, over the beguines, over the sick, over the healthy, over the coffin in which Eulenspiegel was lying — causing the old beguines to scream and yell so much that the priests gave up their vigils and ran outside, letting the others finally chase the sow and piglets away.

The beguines now set about placing the tree of the dead[1] back on the bier. But it got placed incorrectly — with Eulenspiegel's belly facing the ground while his rear was turned upwards. Well, when the priests left, the beguines said they would bury him. The priests were happy to let them do so, but they would not come back. So the beguines picked up Eulenspiegel and carried him the wrong way around, lying on his belly because the tree was turned over, to the churchyard. There they set him down beside the grave.

The priests now came back and asked what advice they would give on how to bury him — he could not simply lie down in his grave, like other Christians. Then they noticed that the tree was turned over and that he was lying on his belly. Well, they began to laugh and said, "He's showing us himself that he wants to lie turned over. Well, that's how we'll do it."

---

1. This was an actual tree trunk, which had been dug out and to which the body was firmly strapped, that served as the coffin. See Lappenberg, p. 289.

94. How Eulenspiegel was buried—for he was to be buried not by religious or lay people but by beguines.

Things went strangely at Eulenspiegel's burial. For when they were all gathered in the churchyard, around the tree of the dead in which Eulenspiegel was lying, and they set it on the two ropes and tried to lower it into the grave, the rope at his feet snapped and the tree shot into the grave — leaving Eulenspiegel standing upright in his coffin.

Everybody who was standing there now said, "Let him stand. As he was strange while he lived, he wants to be strange in death too."

So they filled in the grave and left him standing up that way, properly on his feet.[1] Then they placed a stone over the grave and on half of it carved an owl, with a mirror which the owl held in its claws; and over that they wrote on the stone:

> Don't move this stone: let that be clear —
> Eulenspiegel's buried here.
> Anno domini MCCCL.

---

1. Curiously enough, Ben Jonson, at his own request, was buried standing on his feet in Westminster Abbey. The parallel, as Lappenberg (p. 289) suggests, may not be accidental, as Jonson mentions an "Howleglass" in his *Masque of the Fortunate Isles* (1626). On Jonson's posture in death see Marchette Chute, *Ben Jonson of Westminster* (New York, 1953), p. 347.

95. How Eulenspiegel's epitaph and inscription were carved over his grave at Lüneburg.

EPITAPH

Don't move this stone: let that be clear —
Eulenspiegel's buried here.

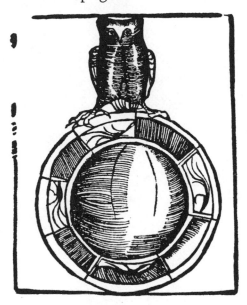

Printed by Johannes Grieninger in the
free city of Strassburg, on Saint
Adolph's Day, in the year
MCCCCCXV.

According to Chapter 93, Eulenspiegel was buried at Mölln; the announcement here that Lüneburg was his burial site is consequently mystifying. Lappenberg (p. 289) reports that a Senator Albers of Lüneburg remembered (as recently as 1846) having seen a gravestone, in the cemetery of the Church of Saint Mary at Lüneburg, on which was carved an owl — but no mirror. As this cemetery has since been torn up, no confirmation of Albers' childhood memory is possible. Lappenberg himself believes that the confusion between Mölln and Lüneburg is either a deliberate final joke of the author's or a mistranslation (of the sort to be found perhaps in Chapter 64, in which the title gives us a location for the tale that is at variance with the location given in the tale itself) of one of the author's successors.

Appendix

The earliest known version of the famous German *Volksbuch* of Till Eulenspiegel is a printed quarto published by Johannes Grieninger in Strassburg on Saint Adolph's Day (August 29), 1515. This volume, which is here translated, measures 31.5 by 20.5 centimeters; contains 261 pages, or according to Grieninger himself, 130 leaves; 86 different woodcuts; and 95 (instead of Grieninger's announced 96) tales of Till Eulenspiegel. Exactly one copy of Grieninger's quarto survives, and this is in the North Library of The British Museum, where, according to what I have been told by the Museum's staff, it has been located for the past one hundred fifty to two hundred years. The staff's confidence in this is based on a Museum stamp, affixed to the title page of the book, which has not been used for the past one hundred fifty years. Nobody knows precisely how the book was acquired. In fact Grieninger's book is no longer a volume by itself, but is bound rather carelessly with *Der schelmen zunft Anzeigung alles Weltleüffigen/mŭtwils/Schalckheite ūn Pribereyen diser Zeyt/Durch doctor Thomas Murner von Strassburg/schympflichenn erdichtet/unnd zu Franckfurt an dem Meyn geprediget.* Murner's book was printed in Strassburg by Grieninger's colleague Johannes Knobloch in 1516.

Grieninger's volume is, despite its casual treatment, in good condition. It is only slightly more faded than the excellent photographic facsimile made of it by Edward Schröder in 1911. Schröder's facsimile, *Ein kurzweilig lesen von Dyl/ Ulenspiegel geborē uss dem land zu Brunsswick. Wie/er sein leben volbracht hatt. xcvi. seiner geschichten,*[1] is the text I

---

1. Photographic reproduction by Emery G. Walker, London; paper reproduced to match the original by J. Batchelor & Son, Ford Mill, Little Chart; zinc plates and printing by Graphische Kunstanstalt, F. Bruckmann, A.-G., Munich; Leipzig im Inselverlag, 1911.

have used for translation. Schröder's "Gleitwort" (referred to hereafter as "Gleitwort") has, moreover, provided important evidence that this is indeed the earliest known version of the German *Volksbuch*.

Grieninger himself published at least two versions of Eulenspiegel's tales, this of 1515 and another of 1519. However, his version of 1519 cannot correctly be described as simply a second printing: it contains a number of alterations which seek to clarify ambiguities in his text of 1515.[2] The versions are nonetheless quite similar. Both are written in Alemannic Middle High German,[3] modified by inconsistencies of spelling,[4] syntax, punctuation, and grammar, together with certain stylistic eccentricities of the writer. There are also a number of typographical errors, the more important of which I have commented on in my footnotes to the tales and which suggest that Grieninger may have put the book together rather quickly.[5]

Little is known about Johannes Grieninger — except that

---

2. These are too numerous, and too trivial, to list here. One example may therefore suffice. In Chapter 1 of the edition of 1519, Eulenspiegel's godfather (the one from whom he gets his name) is identified as "Thyl von Vtzen." In the edition of 1515, he is referred to simply as someone whose first name is "Dyl." This discrepancy, and others like it, have, as will be seen later in this study, some relevance to the question whether both texts are not related to an earlier, common text.

3. The phrase is ambiguous. A more correct description might be: the dialect of German spoken in an area bounded roughly by Strassburg, Zürich, Augsburg, Nürnberg, and Würzburg at this time. Obviously, the German here is to be differentiated from, say, that of *Parzival*. See Hermann Paul, *Mittelhochdeutsche Grammatik* (Tübingen, 1963), pp. 17–48.

4. Sometimes of the same word within a single tale. Such inconsistencies suggest to me that the author may have been writing out loud in a way that we do not yet understand.

5. As it seemed less instructive than clerical to include Grieninger's minor errors, as well as at least one of his eccentricities of style, in the present translation, I have tried, where possible, to avoid doing so. This may be a good place, however, to list these oddities for those who may be interested. Grieninger introduces the titles of most chapters with the phrase "The [blank] chapter tells" — with the "blank" replaced by a Roman numeral. I have eliminated this phrase.

he was clearly a master printer among the earliest European printers who followed Gutenberg, that he worked under various names, and that, like many early printers, he displayed none of the prejudices of some modern publishers against doing obscene, vulgar, popular, and entertaining books as well as religious and classical ones. E. Voulliéme, in *Die deutschen Drucker des fünfzehnten Jahrhunderts* (Berlin, 1922; pp. 153–154) supplies the best account of his life, together with some good discussion of his typography — though his grasp of Grieninger's growth into an eminent publisher is superficial. His father's name was "Reinhard," a name which, with variations such as "Reinhardi de Grüningen," he signed to a number of his books. He himself was born in Grüningen in Württemberg (hence the signatures, in others of his books, of "Grüninger," "Greyninger," and "Grieninger"). By 1480 he was living in Basel, at the house of a goldsmith named Erhart, whose widow later sued him for ten guilders for his keep. In the record of the law suit he is already referred to as a "Meister" — from which Voulliéme concludes that he must by now have established himself as a printer and that he probably went to Basel in the first place simply to learn printing. On October 2, 1482, he became a citizen of Strassburg. He now set up shop in earnest, forming a partnership with a "Meister Heinrich von Ingweiler" — about whom nothing is known except that the partnership must have dissolved almost immediately: von Ingweiler's name appears on only a few of the extant copies of their first book, the *Petrus Comestor Historia scholastica,* published on August 28, 1483. Grieninger now worked on alone, his reputation and success increasing rapidly. Paul Kristeller's fine study of Grieninger's professional career, in his *Die Strassburger Bücher-Illustration im XV. und im Anfange des*

It seemed not only clumsy and superfluous, but also confusing: Grieninger's numerals are frequently wrong, probably because either he or his typographer was working in haste. Thus his original title page tells us that we are about to read ninety-six tales of Till Eulenspiegel, when in fact there are ninety-five; Chapter 20 is called Chapter XXI; Chapter 31 is called Chapter XXVIII; and Chapter 42 is called Chapter XLIII, with this error running through the rest of the book.

XVI. Jahrhunderts (Leipzig, 1888), reveals that between 1494 and 1530 Grieninger published 139 books, in Latin, German, and Italian.[6] Among them were Brant's *Das nüv schiff vô Nar* (*Ship of Fools,* 1494; this went through a number of editions); editions of Horace, Virgil, and Boccaccio; various religious missals, diurnals, and breviaries; and volumes on Roman history, alchemy, medicine, folk history, liquormaking, and literature — all of these, of course, in addition to the two versions of the *Till Eulenspiegel.* His last known publication bears the date of March 10, 1529, though another book, by Amandus Farkal and dated 1530, is described as having been made "in Kosten Grüningers."[7] The date of his death has not been established with certainty.

The date of his earliest known — and the earliest known — German edition of the tales of Till Eulenspiegel is, however, another matter. Schröder's "Gleitwort" (p. 5 ff.) offers the following arguments, which have already been partially summarized here:

> The *A* copy, Strassburg, Joh. Grieninger, 1515, is reproduced so exactly by our edition — aside only from the positions of the folio sheets, which are irregular in the original but made clearly evident through the signatures of our facsimile — that a description seems superfluous. The only specimen is in the library of the British Museum. . . . There it was bound together with the Strassburg edition of Murner's *Schelmenzunft* of 1516, not right away, but early; since 1883, the whole has had a new binding which exhibits *Ulenspiegel* (as earlier) as its only title.[8]

> *D,* the undated Antwerp copy of Michiel van Hoochstraten.[9] . . . For the age of *D* we establish the year 1519 as the *terminus ante quem non,* on three grounds: in that year Michiel van Hoochstraten moved into the house "At the New Grape"; Johannes Grieninger released the *B* copy [of 1519], which was the chief written copy for the Antwerp editor; and finally, Servais Kruffter[10] was settled in Basel until 1519, and only thereafter emigrated to Cologne.

6. Kristeller, pp. 87–106. For Kristeller's discussion of Grieninger see pp. 24–50.

7. Kristeller, p. 105.

Schröder thus dates the only competing text — that of van Hoochstraten, which Nijhoff believed to have been published in 1512 — as actually having been published in 1525. This argument is based in two additional pieces of evidence: first, that van Hoochstraten uses woodcuts obviously taken from Grieninger's book; and second, that van Hoochstraten borrows phrases from Chapters 13 and 28 of Grieninger's book.[11] It therefore seems correct to suggest that the present translation is from the earliest available text of the tales.

The woodcuts of this edition appear also to be originals, designed specifically for the book — with one exception, the woodcut for Chapter 20, which, as Kristeller notes, had apparently been used by Grieninger in his volume of Horace (1498).[12] Kristeller believes that the woodcuts were made by Urs Graf.[13] This notion strikes me as unsupportable. Graf worked in Strassburg only from 1503 to 1507, where indeed he appears to have known publishers of books — among them Johannes Knobloch, for whom he completed one of his masterpieces, the Ringmann *Passion*, illustrated with twenty-five woodcuts, in 1506.[14] However, in 1507 Graf moved to Zürich, and by 1509 he had returned to Basel, the city of his apprenticeship. There is no evidence that he either ever returned to Strassburg or ever collaborated with Grieninger

---

8. Translation mine — as are all translations through this study.

9. As Schröder points out, Martinus Nijhoff, who published a photographic facsimile of this text in 1898, believed that it might have appeared as early as 1512. See Schröder, "Gleitwort," p. 10.

10. Krufter's edition of Eulenspiegel's tales was published between 1519 and 1532. Krufter's work probably influenced van Hoochstraten's. See Schröder, "Gleitwort," p. 10; and below, p. 246.

11. Schröder, "Gleitwort," pp. 10–11.

12. Kristeller, p. 99.

13. Kristeller, p. 9.

14. Kristeller, p. 120. For a good study of Graf's life and fickle but passionate character see Emil Major, *Urs Graf, ein Beitrag zur Geschichte der Goldschmiedekunst im 16. Jahrhundert* (Strassburg, 1907). Excellent reproductions of his woodcuts may be found in H. Th. Musper's *Der Holzschnitt in fünf Jahrhunderten* (Stuttgart, 1964), pp. 218–220, and especially in Emil Major and Erwin Gradmann, *Vrs Graf* (Basel, 1943) — though Major's romantic introduction here is nearly unreadable.

on any of his books. In fact, in 1515, the year in which Grieninger issued his first version of Eulenspiegel's tales, Graf was
having nothing to do with either books or art: he was in
Italy, fighting at the battle of Marignano against French and
German mercenaries. Actually, Kristeller's own analysis of
Grieninger's career may easily indicate something quite different: that Grieninger may have had the woodcuts done by
some younger artist, or artists, as yet unknown.[15]

The originality of the woodcuts will in any case quickly
be admitted by anyone who compares them to the tales with
which they obviously correspond. Schröder believes that at
least four, and perhaps five, artists worked on the pictures.[16]
Again, this seems to be questionable. The figure of Eulenspiegel himself is strikingly consistent throughout the book
(with the possible exception of the woodcut for Chapter 26,
which is repeated in Chapter 66); the appearances of Eulenspiegel in disguise (which are frequent; see, for example,
Chapter 82) prove nothing one way or the other; neither do
the facts that some woodcuts are obviously superior to others
and that some are more detailed than others. If Grieninger
repeats a number of his woodcuts in this book, it must be
admitted that he also does so in many of his other books (see
Kristeller, pp. 87-106) and that it was not, and is not, an
uncommon practice of printers to repeat illustrations which
they have once used successfully. The woodcuts are, moreover, not only often successful but also often excellent and
beautiful. The figures which accompany Eulenspiegel, and
the compositions of the pictures, exhibit care, insight, and cultural understanding: like the tales which they illustrate,
they are full of adult frankness, scatology, and humor. There
is also interesting evidence that Grieninger valued highly the
aesthetic impact of his works. In 1525, in a letter to Pirck-
heimer, one of his artists, he writes, "Albrecht Dürer knows
me well. He also knows well that I love art, even though I

---

15. Kristeller (p. 47) writes that after 1500 a change came about
in Grieninger's operations. Instead of retaining artists indefinitely,
regardless of how much work may have been at hand, he now began
to hire them by the book.

16. "Gleitwort," p. 8 ff.

can't understand it that he so scorns my little thing: I didn't give it out as art."[17] It is thus impossible to agree with Schröder's rather illogical statement ("Gleitwort," p. 6), "I know, however, of no work of the Grieninger House that was as carelessly printed as the *Eulenspiegel*." To judge from the appearance of the book, as well as the obvious meticulousness with which he selected his illustrations for it, it seems absurd to suggest that his tales of Till Eulenspiegel are a careless product. The book may have been done in a hurry — and this perhaps due to popular demand. But quite clearly it was done with respect.

II. THE AUTHOR

In the "Foreword" to the tales, which is written in the first person singular, the author tells us these facts about himself: that his initial is "N."; that he is writing in the year 1500; that he has been asked to put these tales together by people who have promised him "favor and esteem"; that he is a person of "small understanding"; that he believes (or says he does) in God; and that he does not know how to write Latin. He also makes his ambition quite clear: "to create a happy feeling in hard times, so my readers and listeners may experience good, pleasant entertainment and fun." His work will, if successful, give the greatest pleasure to people lonely in winter, "when the hours grow short." This information is skimpy enough — and while reading his tales tells a great deal about the author personally, it tells nearly nothing about him biographically. The peculiar quarrels among scholars over the identity of the author have likewise added nearly nothing to the information about him.

Scholarly investigation of the tales begins properly with the monumental and generally superb work of J. M. Lappenberg, whose *Dr. Thomas Murners Ulenspiegel* (Leipzig, 1854) is the first critical edition of Grieninger's text of 1519.[18]

---

17. Kristeller, p. 47 n.
18. Lappenberg did not know of the existence of Grieninger's earlier edition.

I have relied extensively on Lappenberg's notes to the tales in my own notes: succeeding scholars have scarcely improved on his observations and have in fact often used them as the basis for their own. As his title indicates, Lappenberg believes that the tales were written by Dr. Thomas Murner — but his evidence for believing this consists of a mere coincidence between what was probably a joke and Murner's literary interests. The probable joke, which Lappenberg wishes to take seriously, runs this way:

> In a text presumably appearing in 1521 — *Ain schöner Dialogus und gesprech zwischen aim Pfarrer und aim Schulthaysz, betreffend allen übel Stand der gaystlichen*, o. J. u. O., 4 — it is said: "Murner has so far produced those high flying voids, namely *die narrenpschwerung, die schelmenzunfft, der grethmillerin jartag*, also the *Ulenspyegel*, and other nice little books." If this reference is also the sole contemporary one that speaks of Murner's rôle in the *Ulenspiegel*, its truth is at least in general not to be doubted.[19]

Lappenberg points out that Murner is the provable author of the first two works mentioned here, *Die Narrenbeschwörung* (published by Johannes Knobloch in 1518) and *Die Schelmenzunft* (which, as mentioned above, was published by Knobloch in 1516), while the third, *Greth Müllerin Jahrzeit*, is mentioned by Murner himself as being one of his books. Lappenberg argues further, with some truth, that Grieninger was Murner's "usual" publisher. Grieninger actually published at least four books by Murner: *Logica/memoratiua/ Chartiludiū Logice* (1509); *Ein andechtig geistliche/Badenfart/des hochgelertē Herrē Thomas Murner* (1514); *Murner Der Keiserl. stat rechen ein ingāg* (1521); and *Murner. Von dem grossen/Lutherschen Narren wie in doctor Murner beschworen hat* (1522).[20] Nonetheless, there seem to be good reasons to doubt Lappenberg's argument. The best of these are summarized by Schröder:

> Despite all this, the man [the author of the *Eulenspiegel*] was a humorist with occasional satirical impulses — but whoever

---

19. Lappenberg, p. 385.
20. Kristeller, pp. 87–106.

took the whole as uniform and where possible as an original product could easily have placed it in a line of descent with the satirical rhymed works of Murner, which came out in the second decade of the sixteenth century and were in part printed by Grieninger. This was already done by the author of an anonymously printed (probably 1521) "Dialogus zwischen einem Pfarrer und einem Schultheiss," on which Lappenberg, like others before him, solely relied: he polemicizes against Murner (whom he does not explicitly name) as an opponent of Luther's, and attributes to him, along with authentic works — der Narrenbeschwörung, Schelmenzunft, Greth Müllerin Jahrzeit — "also the ulenspyegel and other nice little books." ... But this is in fact a matter of a hasty guess here, not of definite knowledge. Right into the Zusatzgeschichten [the tales added in subsequent editions] not a trace of Murner's highly characteristic style is to be found; where Murner refers to the Ulenspiegel, or where he himself treats the same or related tales in his rhymed poems, he stands out so clearly against the phrasing and tenor of the Volksbuch that all thought of his "authorship," which we today, apart from this, would have really to confine to Lappenberg, is to be rejected.[21]

But if Murner did not write the tales, who did? Two questions arise here. The first is whether Grieninger's edition of 1515 is not really a translation from an earlier, Low German text; the second is whether the author, in his "Foreword," is not simply following literary conventions in what he tells us about himself — or, to put the matter more succinctly, whether he is not telling some pleasant lies.

The argument in favor of an earlier text, of which this one is somehow a translation, is strong. In Chapter 1 of Grieninger's text of 1515, a reference is made to the destruction of the "wicked thieves' castle" at Ambleben "by Magdeburg, with the help of other states, somewhat more than fifty years ago." Servais Krufter's edition of the tales, Ayn kurtz wylich/lesen van Tyel vlenspiegel: geboren/vysz dem land Brunzwyck. Wat he seltzamer boitzen be/dreuen hait

---

21. "Gleitwort," pp. 37–38. Further, philological arguments against Murner's authorship may be found in H. Lemcke, Der hochdeutsche Eulenspiegel (Freiburg, 1908).

syn dage, lüstich tzo lesen (date uncertain; published in either Basel or Cologne between 1519 and 1530, but certainly after Grieninger's edition of 1519),[22] puts this event at sixty years or so prior to the actual writing. The destruction of the castle, at any rate, took place in 1425[23] — a fact which would place the composition of the tales somewhere in the 1480s. Lappenberg (p. 348) offers additional evidence, which is corroborated by Grieninger's edition of 1515:

> There are also to be found some, if even only very few, traces in the tales — which formed the original foundation of the *Ulenspiegel* — to point to a Low German text. Among these, the most important is Ulenspiegel's epitaph, where our High German text saw itself forced to make do with a form of "erhaben" in place of the verb "erheben," solely in order to rhyme with "begraben." Other traces are to be found in the erroneous naming of the place "Koldingen," Chapter XVI [16], perhaps also in the obliterated rhymes of Chapter XLI [41].

If indeed, as seems likely, Grieninger's edition of 1515 is really a translation into Middle High German of an earlier Low German text which has been lost, the question of authorship is hardly resolved. Schröder draws attention to a number of Low German "elements," which together with the many errors of content, continuity, and place names shared by both Grieninger's editions of 1515 and 1519, suggest that some earlier version must have existed — probably in Low German and probably written by someone from Brunswick.[24] It is impossible that the edition of 1519 simply reproduced that of 1515:

> That B cannot be copied from A is made quite clear even in the first chapter, in which only B presents the historical family name of the godfather "Dyl" von [Vtzen].[25]

It is certainly unlikely that the identity of the author will be established from such evidence.

Indeed, it is a question whether there ever was a single

---

22. See Lappenberg, pp. 148–152.
23. See my note to Chapter 1, p. 5.
24. "Gleitwort," p. 5.
25. Schröder, "Gleitwort," p. 5.

author — whether several writers did not, at separate times, have a hand in creating the tales before they were translated into the edition of 1515. This, at any rate, is the position of Eduard Kadlec, whose "Unterzuchungen zum Volksbuch von Ulenspiegel,"[26] remains the best study to date of the sources of the tales. Kadlec (pp. 183-184) treats N.'s protest that he does not know how to write Latin, along with his refusal to tell us his name, as indicating first that he knew perfectly well how to write Latin, and second that he was too ashamed of having written a mere "popular" book to make his identity public. This reading is rather obscure. It is undoubtedly the case that N. knew some Latin — though how much nobody can judge, and Kadlec's own evidence to this effect is quite weak. It amounts to a mere listing of ordinary Latin phrases and certain nouns derived from Latin. An equivalent argument might be that any speaker of English who knew some French words which have come into English, such as "perfume," could write in French. Was not the knowledge of some Latin, but not necessarily enough to write in Latin, commonplace in any event in medieval Germany? Shakespeare who knew "small Latine, and lesse Greeke," undoubtedly knew a great deal more Latin than what passes for Latin-learning through Caesar today — and yet he probably could not have written his plays in Latin. There is also no evidence that N. was "ashamed" of his work: indeed the evidence, including that of his giving us only his initial, may easily be read in the opposite direction. We have, first, N.'s quite obvious enthusiasm for his work, something which certainly must qualify as much as evidence in such an argument as Kadlec's lists of words. For the tone throughout the tales is interested, committed, gossipy, pleasurable, and sometimes witty. This is hardly the tone of a writer who does not care or who is ashamed. What is remarkable, moreover, is not that N. gives us only his initial, but that he gives us even that much. For at no point does N. describe himself as the author — in the usual sense of that word — of the tales. What he says (and it seems to me that not enough

26. *Prager Deutsche Studien* (Prague, 1916), xxvi.

247

attention has been paid to what he says) is that various persons have asked him to "bring together . . . these accounts and tales." Such a statement suggests a very different idea from what is suggested by our notion of "author." Might N. not be a writer and compiler? The word "tales," in addition, implies that these are stories which have not only been told before, but which have gained popular acceptance and which may have even become parts of a legend. Certainly the idea that N. has been asked to bring together "accounts and tales" must point to the conclusion that these accounts and tales were both already in existence and somehow well known. That this was actually the case will be discussed more fully below.[27]

In trying to decide, therefore, what we mean by our use of the word "author" here we must perhaps be open-minded. We will also have to answer, if possible, the following questions. Are there distinguishing and consistent qualities of language, ideas, and techniques of narration in these tales which might suggest, if not prove, that one man wrote them? Does the book have any distinguishing and consistent organization, either literary or psychological, that might suggest the presence of a single guiding mind? If the answer to both of these questions is "yes," then it follows that N. — whoever he is — must either be the writer of the Low German text, the translator of it, or its transcriber. At any rate, the

---

27. See Section IV, The Sources. It is perhaps worth adding that N.'s "Foreword" exhibits a number of the principles for ending compositions advocated in Matthieu de Vendôme's *Ars Versificatoria*, an influential work on the art of rhetoric in poetry (written in the late twelfth century; to be found in Edmond Faral's *Les arts poétiques du XIIe et du XIIIe siècle*, Paris, 1924; iv). Vendôme suggests, among other things, that an author beg to be excused for his failures (*veniae petitionem*) and that he ask someone else to improve his work — both of which N. does. It is possible that N.'s "Foreword" is simply a gentle parody of more serious forewords in more serious books; indeed, his rather lighthearted tone seems to suggest this. At any rate, the fact that he uses standard conventions of rhetoric in his foreword and that he tells us nothing really personal about himself makes it an act of uninspired daring to draw any large conclusions about him from what he says.

book, in its original form, is probably then the work of one man.

Mere examinations of the book's attitudes, in a search for personal commitments of the author or authors, do not prove helpful. Kadlec (pp. 187–188), who wishes to discover a series of such commitments, points out that the first paragraph of Chapter 28, in which both John Huss and the students of the University of Prague are treated with disdain, reflects profound opposition to both the Hussites and Protestantism. But Kadlec's conclusion — that we find here introduced into the tales a new voice, whose sophistication jars against the simpler, disinterested attitudes of the earlier tales — does not follow. For all the tales are shot through with attitudes — and whether these are "simple," "sophisticated," or simply honest remains in the end a matter of opinion. The very real consistency of these attitudes, however, far from being a matter of opinion, is quite clear — and also quite usual for any number of contemporary *Schwankbücher* and satires, these ranging from Chaucer's *Canterbury Tales* to the tales of Hans Sachs. If, for example, we make a classification of the book's attitudes, we discover at least these six categories: contempt for dishonest Catholicism and other religions; contempt for dishonest scholars; contempt for dishonest tradesmen, hotel-keepers, and farmers; contempt for dishonest officials and nobles; contempt for dishonest citizens and politicians; and contempt for dishonest doctors.[28] The target of this enormous and often fascinating contempt is most often the emerging middle class: corrupt but comercially successful priests, scholars, merchants, nobles, innkeepers, minor landowners, politicians, and tradesmen. The tone clearly reflects greater bitterness toward those who are taking power than toward those who have either always been

---

28. See, respectively, Chapters 11, 12, 13, 31, 34, 36, 37, 38, 62, 66, 86, 90, 91, 92, 93; Chapters 28, 29; Chapters 19, 20, 33, 39, 40, 41, 42, 43, 44, 45, 46, 47, 48, 49, 50, 51, 52, 53, 54, 55, 56, 58, 59, 60, 61, 63, 64, 65, 67, 68, 69, 70, 73, 74, 75, 76, 77, 78, 79, 80, 81, 82, 83, 84, 85; Chapters 10, 22, 23, 24, 25, 26, 27; Chapters 14, 32, 57, 71, 72, 92; and Chapters 15, 16, 17, 89. For a division of the tales along strictly occupational lines see Kadlec, pp. v–vi.

deprived of it or whose interest in power has always been satisfied. The intention in Chapter 34, for example, cannot be to ridicule the Pope, but to demonstrate the hypocrisy of the Catholicism of Eulenspiegel's innkeeper. The Pope — clearly a figure of power — appears here without blemish and even as extraordinarily generous. If the author's attitude is "popular" or even primitively socialistic,[29] therefore, it is of a socialism intermixed with a rather caustic view of mankind's capacity for goodness.

But is this unusual? If such "commitments" or "attitudes" can also be discovered in numerous other contemporary works — as indeed they can[30] — is it reasonable to consider them evidence of any purely personal style of mind or individual presence? Obviously, proofs of the existence of one or more authors become exceedingly difficult, if not impossible, to establish by such means. Indeed, it is only when we begin to examine Eulenspiegel's adventures on textual and thematic grounds, and to compare their uses of language and their ideas with those of their probable literary sources, that the originality of N.'s accomplishment begins to become clear. For, examined on these grounds, the book reveals at least seven areas of novel, and perhaps even profound, enterprise.

First, an obvious but distinguishing feature of the tales is their organization around the birth, life, and death of a single hero. Of the eight likely literary sources of many of the tales only three — *Les repues franches,* the tales of Pfaffe Amis and the tales of Pfaffe vom Kalenberg — deal exclusively with one hero;[31] and of these only the latter two

---

29. Glimmerings of such an attitude may be seen in many of the tales, in which it is clear that Eulenspiegel's and perhaps N.'s sympathies lie more with those who own no productive property (and the economics of whose lives must therefore be precarious) than with anybody else. See, for example, Chapter 60, in which Eulenspiegel, after promising a butcher to tell him "a word" that will be in his interest, remarks shrewdly, "Come on, Mr. Moneybags, and pay the people!"

30. The nearly contemporaneous medieval German drama, in addition to Chaucer's *Canterbury Tales,* exhibits, of course, attitudes nearly parallel to those that may be found in Eulenspiegel's tales.

31. These sources are discussed in Section IV, The Sources, below. They are referred to here only by way of comparison with Eulenspiegel.

can be described as having had any extensive influence on the tales of Till Eulenspiegel.[32] The comments of Wilhelm Henning, in his introduction to his translation into modern German of *Die Geschicht des Pfarrers vom Kalenberg, Hans Clawerts werkliche Historien, Das Lalebuch: Drei altdeutsche Schwankbücher*, speak interestingly to this point:

> One can thus divide the *Schwankbücher* into two large groups: the *Schwankzyklen* [jest-cycles], which group themselves around a central figure; and the collections of single jests.... [The *Schwankzyklen* find] their prototype in the *Pfaffe Amis*, a satirical jest-poem of around the middle of the thirteenth century, written by Der Stricker. The Middle High German poet here fastened on to the form of the French *fabliaux*. Except that with the *fabliaux* it is a matter of single, unconnected jests; what is new in the *Pfaffe Amis* is precisely the form of the *Schwankzyklus*.[33]

As Henning points out, *Till Eulenspiegel* belongs clearly among the *Schwankzyklen* — a fact which in itself significantly separates N.'s work from all those extra-German *Schwankbücher* which probably had some literary influence on it.

Second, the narrative or descriptive language of the tales, from one end of *Eulenspiegel* to the other, is, in contrast to all the sources, strikingly and astonishingly lacking in nearly all conventional figures of speech and rhetoric.[34] There is in fact scarcely an instance of metaphor, simile,[35] hyperbole, personification, metonomy, alliteration, anaphora, *suggestio falsi*, zeugma, syllepsis, anticlimax, apostrophe, pleonasm, litotes, meiosis, hypallage, histeron proteron, asyndeton, and euphemism to be found in any narrative passage in the

---

32. Five tales probably derive from *Les repues franches*. See page 286, below. A further and more important distinction is that Eulenspiegel, in contrast to all his sources, is a fictional hero. This is dealt with in Section III, The Hero.

33. Wilhelm Henning, *Die Geschicht des Pfarrers vom Kalenberg, Hans Clawerts werkliche Historien, Das Lalebuch: Drei altdeutsche Schwankbücher* (Munich, 1962), p. 5.

34. N.'s "Foreword," as has been suggested above, is an exception here.

35. Two similes do occur in Chapters 2 and 7; similes may also — but most rarely — be found in a number of other chapters.

original — and I have attempted to preserve this consistency in my translation. The absence of these quite usual devices of the usual writer, moreover, becomes fascinating once it is noticed that while N. may have eliminated them from his narrative passages, he has not eliminated them from his passages of conversation. Here, in fact, metaphors and similes abound, while other rhetorical instruments, such as hyperbole, appear with some frequency. What is more fascinating is that the speech of Eulenspiegel himself, and his behavior, often glosses, interprets, and attempts to satirize the metaphors, similes, and hyperboles addressed to him by other characters in the tales. He even appears, in many of his adventures, to be acting as a rather clever linguist and psychologist for people who either cannot speak precisely or cannot speak intelligibly — who, in other words, constantly speak in metaphors, similes, and hyperboles whose actual meanings they ignore. In Chapter 23, for example, Eulenspiegel is told by the King of Denmark, who enjoys his company and wishes to reward him for it, to have his horse shod with the "best" horseshoes — and that the royal treasury will pay the cost. The King, as Eulenspiegel at once realizes, is exaggerating: he does not mean "best" at all — the term is an obvious hyperbole — but "good, new, and conventional." Eulenspiegel takes the King at his word, however, and has his horse shod with gold shoes and silver nails. When the King finds out about this (he seems to have been an unusualy pleasant king), he is amused; he even acknowledges his exaggerated language by saying to Eulenspiegel, "You do exactly what I tell you!" But the point here is that the King appears to have learned a lesson of speech and fact: once he admits his mistake, Eulenspiegel has the gold shoes removed and remains with the King "to the end of his days." This is not the case, however, with the hero of the probable literary source of this tale, Pfaffe vom Kalenberg, in a somewhat earlier *Volksbuch*.[36] Here Pfaffe vom Kalenberg is told by a prince to buy himself, at the Prince's

---

36. See pp. 280–283, for a fuller discussion of the influences of this *Volksbuch* on *Eulenspiegel*.

cost, a new pair of shoes, as his own look too shabby to be worn by a priest. Pfaffe vom Kalenberg refuses. It is, he explains, immodest and unwise to spend much money on mere physical decoration; he would prefer simply to have his old shoes repaired. The Prince compliments him on his piety. But Pfaffe vom Kalenberg has really been lying; for when he has his old shoes repaired, he has the work done by a goldsmith who covers them with gold enamelling. Pfaffe vom Kalenberg's purpose, as the tale makes plain, is to deceive somebody: he is perfectly willing to allow the Prince to pay for the gold on his shoes and makes no offer, once his mischief is revealed, to have the gold replaced. The contrast with Eulenspiegel's tale could not be clearer: where Pfaffe vom Kalenberg delights in simply cheating somebody, Eulenspiegel seems to care, in this adventure at least, about the language people speak — and the relations between that language and the world in which people live. The same may be said of more than half of Eulenspiegel's tales — in which, quite clearly, he spends his time either in reacting to the metaphors and hyperboles of others (and as often as not making no money in the process) or in showing others, through rhetorical devices of his own, how language deceives as well as reveals. In Chapter 49, for instance, he calls together a convocation of tailors to tell them, as he puts it, something that will "help them and their children for all time, for as long as the world might last." The tailors assume, quite naturally, that he plans to divulge some novel skill, and crowd into a meadow to hear what Eulenspiegel has to say. But all Eulenspiegel does, during a somewhat elaborate speech, is to tell them to be careful, when threading their needles, that the thread does not slip out. The tailors are understandably furious, but Eulenspiegel has kept his word: what he has told them is indeed something that will help them and their children — even if they knew it beforehand. N.'s idea, again, seems to be that figures of speech and rhetoric often confuse men's notions of reality. But this idea suggests two further, more interesting questions. First, how is humanity to speak without such devices? And second, is linguistic deception unavoidable between human beings?

These questions seem also to be parts of N.'s idea — and they are almost never, and certainly never as consistently, the themes of the tales in any of the literary sources of Eulenspiegel's adventures. For the distinguishing mark of N.'s tales — in contrast to other, similar ones — is that N. sets up two worlds, a world of metaphor or trickery in conversation, and a world of spare, simple language in his paragraphs of description. The one comments on the other, and both contribute to the literary and perhaps philosophical meanings he has in mind.[37] For while word-plays, puns, and figures of speech abound in all of the literary sources of Eulenspiegel's tales — from Poggio's *Facetiae* to Heinrich Bebel's *Schwänke* to *Les repues franches* to *Il novellino* and the *Schwankbücher* of Pfaffe Amis and Pfaffe vom Kalenberg — the heroes of these tales invariably use their victories in games of words for purely personal profit and almost never for linguistic and psychological illumination. N.'s two clearly separate worlds, of unadorned language in his narrative passages, and of figurative speech in his conversational passages, not only do not appear in these other tales: it is possible that they may be rather unusual in literature.

The third distinguishing feature of the text of *Till Eulenspiegel* is its emphasis, throughout, on the word "truth" and on Eulenspiegel's either telling the "truth" or on his having done what various employers have "told him to do," thereby literally or "truthfully" carrying out their instructions. Thus, in Chapter 30, he describes himself as one who practices "telling the truth;" in Chapter 14, a crowd of onlookers says of him that he is "a charlatan, but still he spoke the truth;" in Chapter 46, he says, "Isn't it terrible? I do everything that people tell me to — and can never earn any thanks;" in Chapter 50, he tells a wool-weaver who is furious with him, "I'm doing what you told me;" in Chapter 63, he says, "Isn't it a great wonder? I do everything I'm told — and still earn thanks nowhere;" and so on, through more than sixty per cent of the tales. The persistent emphasis here on the word

---

37. What meanings these may be are discussed more fully in Section III.

"truth" and on the literal or "truthful" interpretation of instructions does not appear in the sources of Eulenspiegel's tales; nor is there any evidence, in the sources, of the obvious fascination with simply the word "truth" to be found here. For in the sources, again, the emphasis appears to be on the success of deception, as a sport to be enjoyed in itself, rather than on its possibly more serious implications.[38] Thus the source of Chapter 14, *Die Geschicht des Pfaffe vom Kalenberg,* presents its hero as having a quantity of surplus wine with which he wishes to make some extra money. He announces that he intends to fly from the tower of his church, and naturally attracts a considerable crowd. He appears in the tower, dressed as an angel with wings, and struts back and forth, shaking his feathers, as if about to fly. But instead of flying, or doing anything at all, he simply continues to strut back and forth — and his audience, feeling the heat of the afternoon, begins to get thirsty. He then sells the surplus wine to the crowd, and that is all. The humor of the story, if indeed there is much, lies in its demonstration of the silliness of human gullibility. But the author of Eulenspiegel's tales carries his exploration of this silliness one step further, into an exposition of its relation to "truth" or "reality." In Chapter 14, after announcing that he too plans a flight (from the roof of the City Hall this time), Eulenspiegel steps out before an audience of the citizens of Magdeburg who have come to see his performance, and surprises them by ridiculing his own proposal — while also ridiculing the people who have gathered to watch him. "I thought," he says, "there was no greater fool or buffoon in the world than I. But I see very well that this whole city's utterly full of fools. . . . So you see very well it's all been a lie." And it is the crowd, in this tale, that is left with the last word: "There goes a charlatan; but still he spoke the truth." N. thus shifts our attention from the merely childish aspects of the deception to the more interesting questions of the nature of truth and the nature of Eulenspiegel's character as a charlatan. It ought also to be

---

38. These implications, which concern language and its relations to thought, are discussed in Section III, The Hero.

remembered that this episode is merely one of many similar ones — that, in other words, (a) the book contains, again in contrast to its sources, dozens of events in which the word "truth" becomes the fulcrum for the meaning of what occurs; and (b) the book's final effect, or meaning, results from feeling these dozens of events, with their seemingly endless questionings of "truth," in concatenation.

The fourth indication that *Till Eulenspiegel* is to be thought of as a somehow serious and unique book — and that its author has been remodeling his predecessors' works to suit his own more interesting purposes — appears when it is realized that *Eulenspiegel,* alone among comparable *Schwankbücher* and *Volksbücher,* contains, of all things, no sexual experiences. At least it contains none in which Eulenspiegel himself clearly participates. In Chapter 38 he cheats the Priest of Küssenbrück out of his horse by telling him that he has slept with his maid — but the maid denies it, and we get the feeling that Eulenspiegel has probably invented the story simply to deceive the priest.[39] In any event, this is the only episode in the book which refers even mildly to Eulenspiegel's sexual life. But does he, indeed, have a sexual life? Or is he to be thought of, like Gulliver, as a hero with a massively and satirically anal experience of the world, and with — perhaps as a result of this — no experience of either sex or love?[40] For both *Die Geschicht des Pfarrers vom*

---

39. The title of the story (but not the story itself) describes Eulenspiegel's confession here as "false." This is actually one of the saddest tales in the book: the suspected maid is beaten; and the Priest, who loves her, loses both his maid and his horse.

40. Norman O. Brown's well-known study of Jonathan Swift, "The Excremental Vision," in *Life Against Death* (Middletown, 1959) argues fascinatingly that Swift anticipates Freudian theories of anal eroticism in a number of his satirical poems as well as in *Gulliver's Travels.* Brown writes (p. 190): "But above all the Yahoos are distinguished from other animals by their attitude towards their own excrement. Excrement to the Yahoos is no mere waste product but a magic instrument for self-expression and aggression." The same may be said of Gulliver himself (who, for example, puts out a fire in the palace of the Lilliputian Queen by urinating on it) and of Eulenspiegel (who in Chapters 80, 87, and 91, for example, uses his excrement as an obvious means of aggression). The point, which I discuss below, is, however, that while both Gulliver and Eulenspiegel have a

Kalenberg and *Die Geschicht des Pfaffe Amis* contain not only tales in which the hero seduces women and exhibits a clear interest in sex, but also (in the *Pfaffe vom Kalenberg*) woodcuts in which the hero appears in bed with the women he seduces. No equivalent representations are to be found in *Eulenspiegel* — and this despite the facts that all of the other sources of the tales contain many stories whose theme is sex and that they constantly present sexual experiences in, to say the least, a positive manner. Of course, the elimination of sexual experiences might not in itself be of much importance, were it not for the constant, contrasting appearances, throughout the book, of anal experiences of all types. The word "shit" is liberally used — it may be found in more than fifteen tales; and in many other tales equivalent expressions, such as "excrement," often appear. To be sure, "shit" shows up in many of the sources as well: the tales of Pfaffe Amis and Pfaffe vom Kalenberg and the *Facecie* of Gonella, offer ample impressions of the anal possibilities of the *cinquecento*. But these sources seem to balance, as it were, their anal episodes with sexual episodes: their emphasis does not lie, as it seems to in *Eulenspiegel*, on the one to the exclusion of the other, but on the conceivable meanings of both. Is it not then likely that N. was deliberately omitting the delights of sex precisely to emphasize a particular and unusual "excremental vision" of humanity?

The fifth point is simple but perhaps crucial to what has just been said. This is that more than sixty per cent of the tales in Grieninger's 1515 edition of *Eulenspiegel* have no clear antecedents and must therefore be considered original. The notion becomes more interesting once it is noticed that most of N.'s excremental tales (such as Chapters 10, 12, and 15) are probably original: it is perhaps possible by now to suggest that part of N.'s accomplishment in *Eulenspiegel* lies in his creation of his own "excremental" hypothesis of the human experience, prior to Swift's.[41]

---

great many anal experiences, neither appears to have any sexual experiences.

41. Many of the woodcuts are, of course, similarly "excremental," a fact which suggests that the artist who made them may have read Eulenspiegel's tales along the lines proposed here.

The sixth distinguishing quality of *Eulenspiegel* is that, in contrast to its sources, it frequently presents us with episodes rather than anecdotes. These terms, as I wish to use them here, need some clarification. By "anecdote" I mean any brief, narrated event, whose point lies not so much in its exploration of character — though it may superficially explore the eccentricities of a particular character during its telling — as in its effort to move its listeners quickly to either sadness, delight, or laughter. Most conversation contains anecdotes, as indeed do most of the *Schwankbücher* that serve as sources for Eulenspiegel's adventures (Poggio's *Facetiae* is a good example here); but the fact that we speak of conversation as anecdotal rather than episodic (unless we are being unpleasant to someone) indicates the sort of distinction involved. For by "episode" I wish to mean not simply an expanded anecdote, but an anecdote whose conclusion contains both a pungent point and, more important, a set of complex themes. Thus an episode, which does not exist solely for the sake of its point or climax, may contain many anecdotes. It may be remarked that a further distinction, between "episode" and "story," lies, quite simply, in their rival emphases on character: in a story we expect, and get, a rather full illumination of character, while in an episode we expect no such thing: the events and themes are what count. Thus Chaucer's "Miller's Tale" may be described as an anecdote which has been expanded into an episode and then into a story: while we are left at the end with an episode's complexity of themes — the explorations of the Christian myth of the flood as well as notions of adultery and lechery, to mention just a few — we are held to the tale as much by its delightful conflicts between personalities as anything else. This is not the case with episodes pure and simple — as in Eulenspiegel's adventures with the tailors, the citizens of Lübeck, the furriers, various priests, the carpenters, and others. For all of these adventures become episodes both because they include many chapters involving a particular profession or class of people and because, by confronting a similar experience again and again, they raise questions, which become themes, about these classes. This is why it is possible to describe Eulenspiegel's meeting with the furrier, in Chapter 52, as a mere anecdote: its pleasure lies in Eulenspiegel's making a fool of his employer. But Eulenspiegel more or less repeats his behavior in Chapter 53; and in Chapter 54, in which he sells some furriers a live cat sewn into a rabbit's skin, he even succeeds in making fun of the talents of furriers in general, by raising the question whether they can really tell the difference between one sort of pelt and another. By this time anecdote, or trivial event, has become episode: the humor of these three tales, taken together, may charm us, but we find ourselves more interested in their collective force — and in the sort of humorous indictment suggested by their collective force. By Chapter 54, in fact, we are probably ready to admit that N. has succeeded in laughing a whole class of people out of court. And this sort of literary behavior may be discovered throughout the book: it extends, in fact, not only to various groups, but eventually — and seriously as well as charmingly — to humanity as a whole; and this happens precisely because of the author's consistent procedure of elaborating mere anecdotes into episodes, through numerous and related chapters, until their humor becomes an heuristic weapon — until mere anecdote, or observation, becomes a series of digressive explorations of society. Again, no similar process is to be found in the sources of N.'s work. Books such as the tales of Pfaffe Amis or the tales of Pfaffe vom Kalenberg are simply too short to permit the sort of impressive elaboration which is here meant by "episode;"[42] and most of the related *Schwankbücher*, such as *Il novellino*, *Les repues franches*, the *Facetiae* of Poggio, and Heinrich Bebel's *Schwänke*, stress the opposite, or anecdotal, quality, exhibiting virtually no interest in more abstract implications.

The seventh piece of evidence that *Eulenspiegel* is to be thought of as the largely original creation of one unique

---

42. Ironically, N. condenses those tales which he borrows from *Pfaffe Amis* and *Pfaffe vom Kalenberg*, eliminating or cutting sharply the long speeches in verse to be found in them. It is, moreover, precisely the tales which N. borrows from these two sources that he does not elaborate into episodes.

imagination is to be found in its organization. First, it must be noted that none of the sources possesses anything other than a sequential organization: one story, or chapter, simply follows the next, and the order in which it follows the next makes virtually no difference to its meaning. This is not the case with *Eulenspiegel*. Chapters here — far from piling on each other in some random fashion — are frequently (though not always) grouped both according to subject[43] and to their possible psychological effects on the reader. For example, N. has evidently taken great pains to insure that we sympathize with Eulenspiegel. Unlike the heroes, such as Pfaffe Amis, of the sources of his tales, Eulenspiegel is presented to us as by no means invincible — as by no means the constant victor of his exploits. He becomes in fact not only a sympathetic character but also a more interesting one precisely because of his carefully timed defeats. These occur throughout the book, and they seem to be spaced in such a manner as to guarantee that we think of him as both successful and human in the vast majority of those other tales in which he obviously triumphs. He is ridiculed in Chapters 2 and 3 (and the ridicule seems to create our sympathy for his rather sadistic behavior in Chapters 4 and 5), and utterly defeated in Chapters 7, 18, 66, and 74. In a large number of the other stories, moreover, he is cast as an avenger, as a righter of wrongs inflicted on him; and this fact, again, permits us to sympathize with a behavior whose sadism we would normally find repulsive.[44] In Chapter 37, for instance, he makes a priest nauseous because the priest has stolen his sausage; in Chapter 39 he wrecks the bed and roof of the house of a smith who tries to overwork him; in Chapter 40 he ruins a smith's tools because the man has offered him excrement to eat — and so on. To be sure, many of the other tales exhibit a sheer sadism which has no basis in any injustice; but the point is that N. seems to be trying, through a deliberately timed series of misadventures, to organize our understanding

43. One of many possible sets of classifications of the tales may be found on p. 249, above.

44. The question of his repulsive behavior is taken up again on pp. 269–270, below.

ch we have here been trying to listen to, will have to
ow us whatever is important about him.

III. THE HERO

ill Eulenspiegel is one of the most famous and entertaining
characters — and one of the queerest fish — in the history
of German fiction. Even his name, which in modern German
of course means "owl glass" or "owl mirror" or "wise mirror,"
or, metaphorically, "wise reflection," has been subjected to
the silliest disputes by various scholars who are convinced
that he did not know what his name meant. Eulenspiegel
died, or so this volume of his tales tells us, in 1350; but it is
a question whether he ever lived. Eulenspiegel practices, or
so he says in Chapter 30, "the telling of the truth;" yet his
definition of "truth" is odd, and by any usual standards he
must be judged a liar. His incessant need to reveal human
reality as clearly and absurdly as possible — this, if anything, is the theme of his life — has so horrified translators
and adaptors of his tales that they have consistently mis-
translated, misadapted, misrepresented, and mistreated them,
subjecting the tales to a prudishness that would no doubt
have made Eulenspiegel and his sixteenth-century audience
laugh with derision.[48] In fact it is safe to say that while

---

48. It would be superfluous and pointless to list here all the
efforts, by well-intentioned translators, adaptors, and scholars, to turn
Eulenspiegel's often vigorous scatology and satire, like Gulliver's, into
a series of bland anecdotes mildly amusing to children. Suffice it that
the tendency continues. Johannes Aickol's *Till Eulenspiegel's Streiche*
(Düsseldorf, 1903), Otto von Schacking's *Till Eulenspiegel* (Regensburg, 1914), and Friedrich Albert Meyer's *Lustige Streiche Till Eulenspiegel's* (Wolfenbüttel, 1921) are but three early twentieth-century
examples of an unending attempt to make Eulenspicgel a sentimental
and somehow childish figure. Charles Theodore Henry de Coster's
Ulenspiegel (Brussels, 1867) is even more ambitious: de Coster sees
Eulenspiegel as not only sentimental but conventionally moral. Need-
less to say, his work has nearly no relationship to the original. For a
fine though melancholy account of Eulenspiegel's career in England
see Friedrich W. D. Brie's *Eulenspiegel in England* (Berlin, 1903),
p. 69 ff. Brie attributes Eulenspiegel's failure to catch the imagination
of English-speaking peoples to diplomatic versions and adaptations
which do not really echo the spontaneity of the original.

for his hero's usual behavior. Again, it is worth noticing that
the volume, as a whole, reveals an apparently well devel-
oped symmetry: Eulenspiegel's mother, who disappears in
Chapter 9, reappears in Chapter 89; Eulenspiegel's youth,
during which he seems often to be made the butt of the cruel
jokes of others (as in Chapters 1, 2, 3, and 7), seems to be
complemented by his old age, during which his victories over
various hypocrites follow without interruption (in Chapters
89 through 94); and the sole episode of what we might call
his "false death," two chapters during which the citizens of
Lübeck try to hang him, appears in almost the exact middle
of the book (Chapters 56 and 57), becoming in a real sense
the centerpiece of his life: the Priest who confesses him on
his death-bed, in Chapter 91, refers to this episode as typical
of Eulenspiegel's cleverness. The book is, in other words,
more than a compilation and is much better organized, and
with a higher degree of psychological sensitivity, than one
might at first suspect.

What I have been trying to suggest through these paragraphs is twofold: first, that *Eulenspiegel's* internal evidence
strongly indicates — though it does not, because it cannot,
absolutely prove — the presence of a single author here, with
an original imagination; and second, that this author seems
to have been torn, though not always to his disadvantage,
between conflicting desires to write both a "pure" *Schwank-
buch* and a "pure" satire. For N.'s sensibility seems constantly
to vacillate between the sort of pure jest or *Schwank* that,
finally, lacks the moral and philosophical perceptions of
conscience, and serious mockery, of the sort to be found in
high satires such as *Gulliver's Travels*. This is perhaps why
the book strikes us as so ambivalent: it is neither pure
Schwankliteratur nor pure satire; yet it is clearly both — and
perhaps unique as *Volksliteratur* precisely because it is both.
For if *Eulenspiegel* does not fit neatly into classifications
such as "*Schwankliteratur*" or "satire," it also does not fit
neatly into other classifications, such as "picaresque novel"
or "novella" or "novel." With the exception of the hero himself there is nearly no effort to delineate characters in Eulenspiegel's tales — something we would expect in these other

forms (as indeed we expect it in Chaucer's *Canterbury Tales* and *The Decameron* of Boccaccio). And yet *Eulenspiegel* is not, in the end, a ragged book. To read all the tales at one sitting, and to examine the pieces of evidence cited above, not singly but as a collection, is, perhaps, to receive an impression of genuine coherence. For the final effect of *Eulenspiegel* is the delight of coherence: we feel in the end that we have read a unified, dramatic work of some sort, rather than simply a set of unconnected adventures. If the book defies any strict and conventional classification,[45] and if the author sometimes appears to be leaning in two directions at once (a fact which has no doubt caused the scholarly confusion over whether one man wrote the book), we are undisturbed: we enjoy ourselves, and enjoyment of the work must remain the supreme test of the correctness of critical terms applied to it. I have remarked earlier that in trying to decide what we mean by our use of the word "author" here we ought perhaps to be open-minded; it may not now be amiss to add that we must mean by "author," among other things, that *Eulenspiegel's* maker is both medieval, in his building of his own work out of the works of others, and modern, in the freedoms he grants his own voice in these tales. C. S. Lewis distinguishes rather beautifully between these generally acknowledged medieval and moden conceptions of "author":

> One is tempted to say that almost the typical activity of the medieval author consists in touching up something that was already there; as Chaucer touched up Boccaccio, as Malory touched up French prose romances which themselves touched up earlier romances in verse, as Laȝamon works over Wace, who works over Geoffrey, who works over no one knows what. We are inclined to wonder how men could be at once so original that they handled no predecessor without pouring

---

45. The term *"Volksbuch"* is, of course, commonly applied to works such as *Eulenspiegel, Die Geschicht des Pfaffe Amis,* and *Die Geschicht des Pfaffe vom Kalenberg.* This term has, however, suffered from what must be considered its unacceptable definition as meaning a book which somehow springs from the "soul" of its society, and is thus even today less a critical description than a social one. A re-definition of *"Volksbuch"* is attempted in Section IV, The Sources.

new life into him, and so unoriginal tha[...] thing completely new. The predecessor [...] than a 'source' in the sense in which an [...] the source of a Shakespearian play. Shake[...] bones from the novel's plot and flings the res[...] oblivion. Round those bones he builds a n[...] purport, atmosphere, and language have rea[...] common with his original. Chaucer's *Troilus* sta[...] different relation to the *Filostrato*.[46]

And N.'s sources (as will be more fully seen in S[...] The Sources, below) stand in a very different re[...] *Eulenspiegel.* In many instances the author has accep[...] assimilated materials that are certainly not his own; [...] has nonetheless succeeded in projecting his own voice[...] *Weltanschauung* through the book. And the result (as I h[...] to demonstrate more completely in Section III, The Her[...] is far from a child's *Weltanschauung* in a child's book: it i[...] the *Weltanschauung* of a mature, perhaps brilliant, but[...] definitely original mind.

These rather odd conclusions therefore seem possible: that we are dealing here with the earliest known translation into Middle High German of a Low German text written in the 1480s by someone from Brunswick; that the translation may or may not have been made in or around the year 1500; that the original author may or may not have been a sincere Catholic and may or may not have been a priest;[47] but that he was one man. In the end, of course, his biographical identity is of little importance: his literary identity or voice,

---

46. C. S. Lewis, *The Discarded Image* (Cambridge, 1964), p. 209.

47. One of Lappenberg's reasons for assigning the authorship of the tales to Murner was that the apparent devoutness of the author's Catholicism, together with his obvious opposition to Protestantism (as reflected, for example, in Chapter 28) and his evidently intimate acquaintanceship with the Catholic Church, suggested that he could have been a priest. But "suggested" is all. What is most interesting about N. is his absolute intellectual independence (which, not surprisingly, coincides with the questioning spirit of the Reformation and Renaissance): he is perfectly willing to shatter the dishonest smugness of anybody, no matter what his religion.

almost every German believes he knows who Eulenspiegel
is and has read his adventures, he probably does not know
him at all and has, on the contrary, read some puerile adaptation. Two cultural disasters have accompanied this betrayal
of fact. The first is that not only have we been prevented
from enjoying the book but have also been denied what is
probably one of the fullest and most interesting pictures of
life as it was lived in the Middle Ages. The second is that
Eulenspiegel's import, as a living character with clever ideas
about the world, has been largely distorted. Far from being
simply a fool, clown, rogue, and example of the medieval
literary type of the buffoon or rascal, he is, as I hope to show,
an early and interesting linguistic philosopher.

W. Krogmann's excellent essay "Ulenspiegel"[49] has finally
laid to rest the often fantastic ideas concerning his name.[50]
These ideas had sprung from two facts: first, that "Eulenspiegel" is obviously a modern rendering of the earlier Low
German "Ulenspiegel," whose meaning and origins were un-
clear; and second, that the book itself (or so it was thought)
makes no mention of the meaning of his name — this leading
to the conclusion that it might have meant something other
than "Eulenspiegel." Thus Schröder, who observes that the
family name "Ulenspeygel" was not unknown in Brunswick
as early as 1337, is led to say that "the author of the *Volksbuch* also nowhere makes a connection between the name
and the character of the hero: whether he did not concern
himself with its meaning, or whether he took it as self-
evident for his Low German readers, we do not know."[51]
But this reading is at best quite literal. For in Chapter 40
we find the following:

> Now, Eulenspiegel had this custom whenever he did some
> mischief where he was not known: he took chalk or coal and
> drew an owl and a mirror over the door, and underneath wrote,
> in Latin, *Hic fuit.*

---

49. In *Jahrbuch des Vereins für niederdeutsche Sprachforschung*
(Hamburg, 1933), lviii/lix, pp. 104–114.

50. See, for example, Ernest Jeep, "Eulenspiegel," *Mitteilungen
des deutschen Sprachvereins* (1885), viii.

51. Schröder, "Gleitwort," pp. 29–30.

It may be true, as Schröder wishes to maintain, that the book gives us no explicit connection between the character of the hero and his name; but this description, which obviously connects his name with his customary behavior, suggests (a) that Eulenspiegel knew well enough what his name meant and (b) that his audience both knew what his name meant and probably expected, as a result, a certain sort of mischievous behavior from him. It ought also to be remembered that the volume usually presents us with semi-satire, in which understatement and a deliberate avoidance of definitions becomes essential if the work is to succeed. Two other points should be made. The first is that Chapter 94 describes Eulenspiegel's gravestone as having an owl and a mirror carved into it (two woodcuts, of Eulenspiegel himself, on the title page, and of his gravestone, also show the owl and the mirror; but these can only be considered evidence of a widespread interpretation of his name). The second is that Schröder and other scholars (such as Jeep and Lappenberg) who agree with him are obviously engaging in a self-contradictory argument. On the one hand they are willing to say that, despite a very limited number of mistranslations, the translator of the Low German text has done a very good job indeed; on the other hand they want to argue that the translator did not even know the meaning of the hero's name.

Of course Schröder's real interest is in attempting to prove that Eulenspiegel was a real person who really died in 1350 (if he can show that his name has no literary significance, his case for this is stronger). This is also the interest of Lappenberg, Jeep, and Krogmann.[52] I agree that Eulenspiegel was— and is — a real person, though in the more interesting literary, rather than historical, sense of "real": for any historical argument in this case must rest on weak premises at best. Lutz Mackensen's very good essay "Zur Entstehung des Volksbuches vom Eulenspiegel" speaks convincingly to the problem:

---

52. See Lappenberg, pp. 340–346; Jeep, "Eulenspiegel" (*op. cit.*, p. 265, n. 50); and Krogmann, "Ulenspiegel" (*op. cit.*, p. 265, n. 49).

Above all, one thing is clear: the hero of these jests did not live. It is also not the case that the man who put together the *Volksbuch* was writing the biography of a beloved folk-hero. Lappenberg had accepted this and attempted a demonstration of Eulenspiegel's existence, and subsequently repeated efforts were made to discover traces of his life. But what was produced thereby is not convincing. . . . It was early recognized that the jests of the *Volksbuch* diverge internally to such an extent that they could hardly refer to a single person. . . . Nonetheless, this last conjecture contains a genuine kernel, namely the recognition that we have before us in the Eulenspiegel book not a whole but an historical work, that there were, therefore, several adapters involved in the work before there emerged the unity of the High German edition of 1515.[53]

This must indeed be true. It is also worth adding that whether some actual Eulenspiegel served as the historical model for the tales or not, it is impossible that even a good portion of them are about him: about thirty-three per cent of the tales are derived from other authors (as has been mentioned above and as will be shown more fully in Section IV, below). The question of his historical existence is also neither very important nor very interesting; what is interesting is Eulenspiegel's present life in his book — with all of its unique emotional and intellectual vitality.

For Eulenspiegel is clearly more than a practical joker, though he can be enjoyed as one. Goethe's one recorded statement about him is quite to the point:

Eulenspiegel: alle Hauptspässe des
Buchs beruhen darauf, dass alle Menschen
figürlich sprechen und Eulenspiegel es
eigentlich nimmt.[54]

[Eulenspiegel: all the chief jests of
the book depend on this: that everybody
speaks figuratively and Eulenspiegel
takes it literally.]

---

53. Lutz Mackensen, "Zur Entstehung des Volksbuches vom Eulenspiegel," *Germanisch-Romanische Monatsschrift* (Heidelberg, 1936), vii/viii, pp. 242–243.

54. Johann Wolfgang von Goethe, *Maximen und Reflexionen* (Weimar, 1907), p. 218, number 1045.

Goethe's statement applies directly to about half the tales in the book, and in many of the remaining tales it is clear that figurative speech and Eulenspiegel's literal interpretation of it influences the action. He wins a barrel of beer from a priest who fails to shit, as he has said he would, in exactly the middle of his church (Chapter 12); he bakes owls and long-tailed monkeys for a baker who jokingly tells him to bake them (Chapter 19); he has his horse shod with gold shoes and silver nails because the King of Denmark promises him the "best" horseshoes (Chapter 23); he presents a soapy sausage to a priest who wants to eat till his mouth gets messy (Chapter 37); he breaks through the roof of a house of a smith who tells him to get up and out of his house (Chapter 39); he cuts animals out of the leather of a shoemaker who tells him to cut large and small shapes, like those the swineherd runs past the gate (Chapter 42); he sells twelve barrels full of human excrement to a shoemaker who wants to buy grease (Chapter 45); he brews a dog called Hops instead of hops (Chapter 46); he leaves his shit in a wool-weaver's dining room, because the wool-weaver tells him to put it "where no one will have it" (Chapter 50); and so on. When the reaction to this odd behavior is, as might be expected, a foul-faced explosion, his reply is invariably that he has done what he has been told. As has been suggested earlier, Eulenspiegel clearly understands two facts about the human condition: first, that it requires metaphors and dishonesty; and second, that liars, such as himself, are not always uninterested in the truth.

Enid Welsford's *The Fool: His Social and Literary History* (Cambridge, 1936) distinguishes neatly between the professional buffoon, the court fool and the mythical buffoon, as definite types.[55] The professional buffoon, or jester, whose

---

55. These subjects are cleverly, if not as sensitively and thoroughly, treated in Barbara Swain's *Fools and Folly* (New York, 1932). A weakness of Miss Swain's work is that she patronizes the fool without quite understanding him: she almost invariably treats any fool or clown as though he were somehow mentally deficient (see, for example, p. 1). This point of view is, as regards Eulenspiegel at least, unsupportable.

Western origins Miss Welsford correctly discovers in ancient Greece,[56] is the parasitical entertainer, willing to commit any absurdity on himself for a meal. He is "neither the unconscious fool, nor the conscious artist who portrays him; he is the conscious fool who shows himself up, chiefly for gain, but occasionally at least for the mere love of folly."[57] Examples of such historical figures are the German Hans Clawert and Friedrich Taubmann (both of the sixteenth century) and the Italian Fra Mariano (of the same century). The court fool, on the other hand, is one of three types: he is either a clever rogue, entertainer, and even sometimes politician; or he is no fool at all but instead the sort of pitiful incompetent whose physical or mental deformities would, in the twentieth century, probably require permanent medical attention; or he is the court dwarf. All three were kept as pets in a sense, though the first of these types no doubt enjoyed the freedom of his cleverness (Eulenspiegel frequently plays this sort of court fool).

The mythical buffoon, on the other hand, is, as Miss Welsford observes, a mostly fictional character.[58] He is also a more interesting person. For his peculiar, humorous, often vicious, and sometimes charming behavior results, as might reasonably be expected in good fiction, less from a desire to make a living than from his skepticism. And Eulenspiegel is precisely such a buffoon, rascal, and even philosopher. Miss Welsford's comments are worth quoting:

> Almost all of us feel an instinctive pleasure in an occasional reversal or topsyturvydom, an occasional reminder that no human barriers are unbreakable, no human judgments final. And so we get the Marcolfs and the Eulenspiegels, the incorrigibly impudent rogues, the irrepressible mischief-makers. There is one quality about this kind of buffoon, however, that is most disagreeable and that is his complete heartlessness. Regard Eulenspiegel as a real man, dealing with real men capable of feeling pain, and he becomes a purely odious figure. Buffoons can only flourish, jest-books can only be written in a

---

56. Welsford, p. 4.
57. Welsford, p. 27.
58. Welsford, p. 29 ff.

society where the general level of sensitiveness and sympathy is not very high. Nevertheless, although a certain amount of callousness must be assured if the book is to be enjoyed at all, yet the remarkable quality in Eulenspiegel is not his power of causing trouble, but his skill in evading consequences. To identify oneself with Eulenspiegel is to feel for a moment invulnerable. True, one must regard other men as puppets of sawdust, but then identification with Eulenspiegel does, for the time being, delude one into the intoxicating fancy that other men are made of sawdust, that sensation is not real, that fact is not inexorable, and that pain itself is comic.[59]

Despite the excellence of Miss Welsford's comments on the "topsyturvydom" of many of the tales, her notions about invulnerability cannot be considered quite accurate,[60] and her description of Eulenspiegel's "complete heartlessness" must be questioned. For what is unique about Eulenspiegel (in contrast to the sources of his tales, such as *Pfaffe Amis* and *Pfaffe vom Kalenberg*) is that, far from simply playing tricks on the naive, innocent, and gullible (though he does this too), he often sets out to deceive the dishonest, harsh, cruel, stupid, conceited, obnoxious, boring, and unjust. If his behavior is generally negative and sometimes sadistic, it is also, in this sense, moral: for a full exposure to his adventures affords us the rare pleasure, unobtainable in life but possible in art, of seeing wrongs perfectly righted and punishments perfectly suited to crimes. An interesting example of the moral concern of many of Eulenspiegel's adventures may be found in Chapter 17. In this chapter, Eulenspiegel poses as a doctor. He arrives at a hospital in Nürnberg and promises its director to make all his patients healthy. This is, of course, a deception, for what he actually means is that he intends to get all the patients out of the hospital — and he succeeds in doing so by threatening to kill them. What is odd, though, is the portrait we are given of the hospital's director. He is presented as a man who "would have been glad to be rid of these sick people and would hardly have

59. Welsford, pp. 50–51.
60. See p. 260, above, for a contrasting opinion of Eulenspiegel's invulnerability.

begrudged them their health" — a description which, with its implications of harshness and cruelty, causes us to side with Eulenspiegel here. For Eulenspiegel injures no one in this story but the director — whom he cheats out of a substantial amount of money. The patients eventually return and are cared for again. If, however, we compare the tale with its likely source, lines 805 through 931 of *Der Pfaffe Amis,* we realize at once that N., by describing his director as cruel, has introduced a moral interest into his version which is not to be found in the source. For the "director" of the hospital in the earlier tale is a duke, and he is portrayed (in lines 814 through 822) as a man worried about the illnesses of his patients. There is no suggestion of anger or cruelty; in fact the lines

> ich hân hie mâge unde man,
> den ich ir leides übele gan,
> der lît hie siech ein michel teil

> [I have relatives and people here,
> whose misery I by no means envy them —
> it's been here for so long]

may, without difficulty, be read as indicating the Duke's sincere concern for his patients. The Duke, in other words, is to be thought of as an innocent but foolish man, who allows himself to be cheated by Pfaffe Amis in precisely the manner in which Eulenspiegel cheats the director of the hospital at Nürnberg. But the point is that the director of the hospital at Nürnberg deserved to be cheated.

Is Eulenspiegel's behavior simply "heartless?" Or does it in fact have a moral motivation — one which is perhaps to be found again in Eulenspiegel's attitudes toward humanity, reality, and perhaps his own definition of "truth?" For great numbers of Eulenspiegel's tales — and especially those which have no apparent sources[61] — present us with similarly moral situations which involve some attempt at justice.

---

61. More than sixty per cent of the tales fall into this category. See p. 257, above. This fact is perhaps significant because it suggests that N. is both presenting original tales which have justice as a theme and modifying earlier tales to make justice their theme.

In Chapter 70, to take another tale with a source, justice displays an unusual symmetry, which becomes all the more absorbing once we compare the tale with stanzas 16 through 18 of the *Facecie del Gonella, composte per maestro Francesco, dicto maestro Raynaldo da Mantua.*[62] In the Italian version, Gonella, a court clown and buffoon, meets three blind men in a church. He feigns compassion for them, telling them he wishes to give them some money which they are to divide equally among themselves. The blind men thank him; but when they get home to make the division, they discover that each thinks the others have the money, and that they are really penniless. The tale ends with the rather sarcastic remark, "Questo è il diuarvo" ["This is the division."]. The cruelty of the tale destroys — for us, at any rate — the possible pleasure in the deception. And it did so for N., apparently, too. For N.'s version of Eulenspiegel's meeting with the blind men differs from the Italian tale chiefly in its effort to introduce human justice into the situation. In Chapter 70, Eulenspiegel, like Gonella, pretends to offer money to twelve blind men he has met. He sends them to an inn at Hanover, telling them to spend the money there "for his sake," until winter is over and they can go on their way again. The blind men soon arrive at the inn, where they inform the innkeeper of their great good luck in having been given money enough to survive for a while. The innkeeper, who makes the mistake of not asking for payment in advance, takes them in, and keeps them until the "money" is spent. When he presents his bill, however, the blind men discover, as in the Italian tale, that each thinks the next has the money — and that no one has it at all. So far N.'s account duplicates nearly exactly the action of the source. But at this point a number of things happen which change both the result and meaning of the story. The innkeeper, who wants his money and fears losing everything if he lets the blind men go, locks his former guests into his pigsty where he feeds them hay. At the same time, Eulenspiegel, who assumes

---

62. This work is discussed more fully in Section IV, The Sources, p. 283 f.

his "money" must have been used up by now, disguises himself and proceeds to the inn. When he discovers the blind men trapped helplessly in the pigsty, he accuses the innkeeper of cruelty and promises to find someone who will pay him what he wants. The greedy innkeeper is delighted. Eulenspiegel now visits a priest, informing him that the innkeeper has gone mad and is possessed by an evil spirit. Would the priest exorcize the spirit? Gladly, replies the priest; but, he adds (and we suddenly feel he is adding this hypocritically), one must wait two or three days. "One can't be in too much of a hurry about such things." Eulenspiegel now returns to the innkeeper, tells him he has found someone to pay him, and sees to it that the blind men are let go. He tricks the priest into telling the innkeeper's wife that he will "help" her husband — she does not know with what. At this point Eulenspiegel vanishes from the story. Two days later, the wife arrives and demands the promised payment; the priest, who has been told that he was to exorcize an evil spirit, naturally refuses. A violent argument ensues, followed by a pitched battle between the priest and the innkeeper. The story ends with the comment that "as long as they both lived" the innkeeper considered the priest a liar and the priest considered the innkeeper mad. But what has happened? Clearly, the blind men get off rather nicely: they have been sheltered for nothing and are eventually allowed to go where they please. What is interesting, though, is that (a) Eulenspiegel's behavior shows a rather genuine interest in protecting the helpless and innocent, and (b) his behavior makes possible both the exposure of hypocrites (the innkeeper and the priest) and their punishment (for they are caught up in a silly battle).[63] N. has thus turned a fatuously vicious adventure into a rather charming depiction

---

63. The innkeeper and priest are, of course, stock characters whom N. and his contemporaries would automatically have suspected of treachery in any case. Thus we are asked to dislike the innkeeper even though he treated the blind men well and is defrauded. N.'s audience would probably have enjoyed the ending here as much because the innkeeper is tricked as because he inflicts a too cruel punishment on his former guests and gets his just desserts.

of human nature and the possible nature of human justice. Again, this story is but one of many similar ones in which Eulenspiegel seems to behave in some sense morally.

If we now begin to put together what I think it is fair to describe as Eulenspiegel's clear interest in a certain sort of justice with his already established interest in "truth,"[64] we may begin to get some idea of what is happening in this book. For while Eulenspiegel seems to exhibit a genuine passion for justice and honesty in a large number of his adventures, he has his own definitions of these words. By "honest" and "just" he seems to mean not simply "well intentioned" or even "the truth, or justice of a situation, as one knows it," but truth and justice as a child's passion for logic and retribution would like them to be — and as an unjust world only rarely allows them to be. Where other, more acquiescent men are satisfied with metaphors and approximations of truth and justice, Eulenspiegel is content only with literal precision. He is, literally, a mathematician of human reality, believing as much in the absolute possible perfection of the human world as a mathematician must believe utterly in the absolute truth of, for example, the infinitesimal calculus. Eulenspiegel's (and N.'s) obsessions with "truth" and "justice" thus suggest that this is a *Volksbuch* with a more profound intellectual interest than has commonly been supposed. One of its intentions seems to be, in fact, to explore the effects of spoken language on human situations, and in doing so to illuminate how vast numbers of misunderstandings, arguments, and struggles between men result from errors in speech, as well as from the nature of language itself.

A brief digression. The reality of most speech — and most literature — is of course psychological rather than informational: it is more concerned to recreate and reveal states of mind than it is to communicate "facts." By doing so such speech intends, in the wonderful phrase of Richard Blackmur, to add to "the stock of available reality"[65] — with the emphasis here falling on the word "available" and on

---

64. See pp. 254–256, above.

65. R. P. Blackmur, *Form and Value in Modern Poetry* (New York, 1957), p. 337.

the notion that "reality" becomes available only when it is endowed with language. A meaningful literary, spoken, or musical language will thus possess some psychological, emotional, and intellectual relevance to those symmetries of our minds that may be alive at a given moment. For example, "A rose is a rose is a rose" neither makes, nor intends to make, any statement about roses. It is not informational. Neither is it foolish. Rather it is what may be called psychological and assertional: it reveals perfectly a state of mind, merely by asserting its existence, and regardless of our logical expectations. By causing us to look at that state of mind, the statement frees us of it. It helps us to enjoy ourselves. Hence its pleasure. It is, moreover, possible to argue without much difficulty that most of what we call conversation and imaginative literature operates in this way — that it is more concerned to reveal and fix for observation the infinite states of the human mind, as the human mind confronts itself in the outside world, than it is merely to reveal the outside world. Swift's *Gulliver's Travels*, Lear's raging that seems to produce an actual thunderstorm, and Dante's circles of Hell are all logically absurd, if we for a moment consider them as offering true propositions about conditions in the physical world. However, their intentions are not at all, of course, to offer logical or true propositions about that world; their interest instead lies in their attempts to reveal the possible conditions of our minds through depictions of their most naked movements.

The language of literature — and of most speech between people — is thus not the language of propositions. Indeed, the very word "proposition" seems — especially as it is used by certain philosophers[66] — too often to be confused with

---

66. Bertrand Russell's definition of this term, in "On Propositions: What They Are and How They Mean," is this: "A proposition may be defined as: *What we believe when we believe truly or falsely.*" But while this definition has, as Russell demonstrates, a perfect application to sentences *which explicitly demand true or false belief,* because they have to do with facts, it is questionable whether the definition remains compatible with our usual uses of "proposition" once we move into other areas, such as literature. This raises the problem whether Russell's definition has not been deliberately made so narrow as to exclude a

the word "assertion." Consider, for example, the sentence "The present king of France is bald," in which it is granted *a priori* (a) that there is no present king of France, and (b) that he cannot therefore be bald.[67] Such a sentence is not either true, false, or meaningless — as would, for instance, be the case with a statement such as "If x contains y, and y contains z, then x must contain z." For while the latter statement is propositional, because it proposes logical consequences which can be deduced from the very conditions of the sentence and the deduction of which requires our acquiescence in certain mental disciplines, the former statement is assertive because disdainful of all branches of disciplined thought, it makes a statement. What is the statement about? How are we to understand it? Clearly, it is not "about" the "outside" or physical world but about the "inside" world of our emotions — and it is there that we as readers are forced instantly to test its "truth." If the sentence makes us laugh, because we know that it cannot propositionally be true, then we seem in fact to be confirming its emotional "truth" or value. It is possible to go even further: sentences which contain propositional truth are most unlikely to contain also the emotional truth just defined; the two categories appear in most cases to be mutually exclusive. This is why art is deliberate nonsense and lying, in the conventional sense, and it is also why art must remain so. For

---

number of those areas of language which it could illuminate. Swift's *Gulliver's Travels*, for example, may be looked at as consisting of a series of propositions (i.e., statements in the indicative which propose, present, and propound). But are we to believe in these propositions as if they were simply true or false—or is another demand, a psychological and emotional one, unrelated to truth and falsehood, being made upon us? Is it Swift's intention to convince us that what he is saying is factually accurate or to change our way of looking at the world? And cannot language be used to do this? J. L. Austin, in *How to Do Things With Words* (Cambridge, Mass., 1962) proposes that words may be "performative" as well as true, false, and meaningless. This notion, which leads into the further notion of "assertive" language, outlined here, is an outgrowth of Russell's approach to propositions.

67. This sentence is Russell's famous one, from his essay "On Denoting," in which he advances the notion (modified in subsequent essays) that a proposition is either true, false, or meaningless.

art's exposure of how to perceive and feel the world seems to lie in its asserting conditions out of the emotional and psychological world rather than proposing them out of the inanimate world. Where science organizes what is speechless, art explores whoever is articulate. If a man can assert enough nonsensical but relevant conditions in a consistent enough and pleasing enough form, which because of their strength and also their shock to our emotions make us feel more wonderfully, meaningfully, wisely, and cleverly than before, we will probably call him an artistic genius. But his success — a success for which human beings hunger because they seem to need constantly to change how they feel — will result from just the opposite of the propositional thinker's success; and the two men, misunderstanding the differences between their activities, will frequently and for no reason be at odds with one another. The artist (and most men probably attempt to become artists in at least their conversational lives) is thus perhaps more concerned with a proposition's being right than with its being "true:" a revealing appropriateness to some given psychology is what counts.

But it is precisely this revealing appropriateness to human psychology that Eulenspiegel refuses to accept when he meets it in human speech. In all of those tales in which he reacts literally to metaphors or hyperboles or emotional speech he seems deliberately to disregard the psychological or assertional qualities of the language addressed to him; and in those chapters in which he seeks to impose a perfect "justice" on someone who has treated him harshly, he in fact often comments on the innocent cruelty of the psychological and assertional language which we all speak and which we cannot do without. A single example, of many possible ones, may illustrate what is meant by this. In Chapter 50 Eulenspiegel becomes a wool-weaver's apprentice, and performs his work absurdly, as is his habit. The wool-weaver tells him sarcastically, "If you want to beat the wool that way, you might as well do it sitting down on the roof instead of standing up here on this ladder." So Eulenspiegel climbs onto the roof and beats the wool there. When the wool-weaver catches him on the roof, he remarks, again with obvious sarcasm, "If you want to beat wool, beat it; if you want to fool around, fool around: climb off the roof and shit in the wool basket." So Eulenspiegel shits in the wool basket. But the point is that when Eulenspiegel takes the wool-weaver's "instructions" literally, he ignores their psychochological intent. For the purpose of the wool-weaver's statements is clearly to ridicule; it is not at all to inform or instruct. The wool-weaver, who is here using the assertive and psychological language of the artist (though admittedly on a rather inferior level), is himself ridiculed by someone who refuses to recognize the possibility of such language — and who in fact treats most language as if it were propositional, informational, and logical. And there can be no question but that Eulenspiegel does this by deliberation rather than out of stupidity: his cleverness and intelligence are too obviously aspects of his nature to need any illustration here.

What then are we to conclude? Clearly, that Eulenspiegel is terribly interested in speech, language and psychology: his usual rejection of assertional and psychological language simply emphasizes his keen sensitivity to it. Perhaps it is therefore correct to suggest that Eulenspiegel is, in this sense at least, a rather early and interesting linguistic philosopher.

For the more important modern linguistic philosophers, such as Bertrand Russell and Ludwig Wittgenstein, exhibit an interest in the relations between speech and psychology which, in a fascinating way, parallels Eulenspiegel's. Here, for example, are Russell's comments on the establishment of a definition of "one":

This development in the principles of mathematics suggested that philosophical puzzles are to be solved by patience and clear thinking, the result being, in very many cases, that the original question is shown to be nonsensical [because it has been proposed psychologically rather than logically]. Carnap maintained at one time that *all* philosophical problems arise from errors in syntax, and that, when these errors are corrected, the problems either disappear or are obviously not soluble by argument. I do not think he would still maintain quite so extreme a position, but there can be no doubt that correct logical syntax has an importance which was not formerly recognized, and which logical positivists have rightly emphasized.[68]

Clearly, the conflicts in many of Eulenspiegel's tales arise, as in the mathematical difficulty here described by Russell, because of nonsensical, or purely psychological, language. But is there, except in exclusively logical realms of human thought, such as mathematics, any alternative to such language? And would not any alternative be finally less meaningful and important to us personally than its psychological and assertional opposite? The dilemma is thus incapable of any solution, except perhaps the provisional solution of continuously remaining sensitive to its existence. And this is what Eulenspiegel seems to be. It may not be wrong to suggest that much of Eulenspiegel's life is spent in revealing the nature of the linguistic trap in which all men seem condemned to struggle. His life also reveals ways of becoming free within the trap — through his refusal to tolerate imprecision between people, through his frequent enthusiasm for the possibilities of justice between people, and through his apparent conviction that many of the fictional, or linguistic, confusions of human life can be made to vanish, or turn into pleasures, if only they are met with clear, accurate thinking.

---

68. Bertrand Russell, "Logical Positivism," *Logic and Knowledge* (New York, 1956), p. 370. It should be added that much of Russell's great achievement in philosophy consists, as is well known, of clarifications of what were supposed to be genuine intellectual problems, through an elimination of their psychological terminology, with the result that, as he here remarks, "the original question is shown to be nonsensical." Thus in "On the Notion of Cause," as published in *Mysticism and Logic* (New York, 1957), p. 174 f., he demonstrates not only that science does not deal with "cause and effect," but that the concept of "cause and effect" is itself fallacious; in "The Relation of Sense Data to Physics," *ibid.*, p. 169 f., he shows how the term "existence" is meaningless when used in metaphysics; and in "Logical Atomism," in *Logic and Knowledge*, p. 328, he writes, "The ontological argument and most of its refutations are found to depend upon bad grammar."

Whoever wrote Eulenspiegel must have been either widely read or a good listener: thirty-three of the tales appear to have been taken directly from earlier authors, and many of the rest contain echoes, phrases, and popular expressions from earlier authors. Lappenberg traces the derived tales to eight sources: Pfaffe Amis, Pfaffe vom Kalenberg, Gonella, Poggio, *Le cento novelle antiche*, Morlini, Heinrich Bebel, and *Les repues franches*.[69] Kadlec, in his investigations of the sources, usually follows Lappenberg: his improvements are greater thoroughness and sometimes greater accuracy of critical judgment — these due chiefly to the revisions of opinion necessitated by Schröder's discovery of Grieninger's edition of 1515 and the publication of Schröder's facsimile.

Pfaffe vom Kalenberg (who, along with Pfaffe Amis, is mentioned by N. himself at the close of his "Foreword" as being one of his sources) is the hero of the rhymed *Volksbuch* bearing his name, which first began to be widely circulated toward the end of the fifteenth century.[70] Whether Pfaffe vom Kalenberg actually lived, is, as Lappenberg admits, neither known nor important: probably, like Eulenspiegel, he is a mostly mythical figure. Kadlec (p. 9) proposes that Chapters 14 and 23 derive from his history, while Chapters 17, 27, 28, 29, and 31 can be traced to *Der Pfaffe Amis*, the rhymed *Volksbuch* which belongs to either the thirteenth or fourteenth century.[71] Kadlec adds, though:

> A literary borrowing from the two Kalenberg tales is, however, scarcely to be considered. For a glimmering-through of the source, whether in rhymes or also only in the vocabulary,

---

69. See Lappenberg, p. 352 ff.

70. See Lappenberg, pp. 354–355. A good, modern reprint of Pfaffe vom Kalenberg's *Volksbuch* is to be found in Felix Bobertag's *Narrenbuch* (Darmstadt, 1964), pp. 7–86.

71. See Lappenberg, p. 353. "Der Pfaffe Amis von dem Stricker" has been reprinted in Hans Lambel ed., *Deutsche Classiker des Mittelalters: Erzählungen und Schwänke* (Leipzig, 1883), pp. 22–102.

is not to be observed. The tone of the adaptation is, moreover, thoroughly altered in opposition to the source. Conciseness and plainness distinguish our author. How simple and yet satirically exquisite sounds the speech of Ulenspiegel in comparison to the rather unsalty speech of the Viennese peasant priest. The other history is also sharper and more straightforward. The long speeches in the source are altogether missing here or reduced to a few words, perhaps not always to the advantage of our *Volksbuch*.[72]

These arguments are not very convincing. Changes of tone or intention do not necessarily indicate a lack of literary influence: indeed, one need only reflect on the probable relations of Holinshed to Shakespeare to realize the difficulties of such an hypothesis. In addition, the tone, and even the content, of N.'s "Foreword" seems to parallel that of the *Pfaffe vom Kalenberg*. Here are the first nineteen lines of *Die Geschicht des Pfaffe vom Kalenberg:*

Het ich der bůcher vil gelesen,
das wer mir nie so not gewesen!
Wer ich der kunst ein weiss man,
ein dicht das wolt ich fahen an,
und das auch gut zu horen wer.   5
Mein zung die ist mir zu schwer,
das ich nit hab auff disse fart
suptile und gelůmpte wart,
alss die rethorica hat in ir,
iedoch so stet meines hertzen gir   10
noch lobes preiss und hoher kunst,
darnach so reůcht meines hertzen dunst,
Bin ich der bůcher ungelart
dennoch richt ich mich auff die fart
noch meisterschafft und klugem dicht,   15
darnach mein sin und hertz sich richt,
das ich kum auf der kunsten pan,
do mit heb ich mein red hie an,
ich hoff, es pleib on allen zorn.[73]

[If I had done much reading of books —
that wouldn't have been any misery for me!

---

72. Kadlec, p. 11.
73. Bóbertag, *Narrenbuch*, p. 7.

If I were a clever man of the arts,
I'd certainly be able to start a poem —
and it would even be good to hear.   5
But my tongue is too heavy for me,
so I don't have, in this endeavor,
subtle and flowery words,
such as rhetoric contains.
But anyhow my heart's desire   10
is for the prize of praise and of high art —
My heart's passion reaches for it.
If I'm unlearned in books,
still I point myself along the path
of mastery and bright poetry: 15
my soul and heart point themselves toward it,
so I may achieve art's course.
With that, I here begin my account —
I hope it remains without all censure.]

What is striking here is both the stylistic and verbal paral-
lelism. The author refers to himself as someone who has not
read widely (line 1), who has no skill (lines 2-5), who
cannot speak well (line 6) — all of which are rather neatly
echoed on N.'s introductory sentences. In line 8 the author
uses the word "suptile;" this word, in a similar context,
appears in N.'s "Foreword," in which he says, "Es ist auch
in disem meinem schlechtē schreiben kein kunst oder sub-
teilichkeit." In line 9 the Greco-Latinate "rethorica," which
is tossed in almost casually, performs an ironic task not dis-
similar to the task which N. assigns his occasional Latinates:
it lets the reader know that the author is much more sophisticated than he pretends to be and that his book must somehow be a joke. Because of these correspondences, it seems
inadequate to argue that N. had definitely not read the
Pfaffe vom Kalenberg: for there is the further evidence of
the parallel tales to be considered. I am not attempting to
prove here that the author of Eulenspiegel's tales either had
or had not read the *Pfaffe vom Kalenberg* — only that the
possibility is great that he had and that it is odd of Kadlec
to insist that he had not. It may be added (as Kadlec himself observes on page 8) that Pfaffe vom Kalenberg's tales,

in either manuscript or print, were well known throughout Alsace during the fifteenth and sixteenth centuries.

Kadlec believes that Chapters 24, 26, 35, 70, and 86 are similar to certain adventures attributed to Gonella, the court fool of Count Niccolo d' Este and his son Borso, Duke of Ferrara; these adventures were collected in *Facecie del Gonella composte per maestro Francesco, dicto maestro Raynaldo da Mantua.*[74] The adventures are indeed similar — and Gonella's encounter with the Duke of Ferrara's servant (stanzas 3–9), which is to be compared with Eulenspiegel's adventure at the court of the King of Poland (Chapter 26), is a good example of how. Gonella, in this *facezia*, is a boy of seven and already a favorite of the Duke's. The boy falls ill and the Duke asks him what he wants. Gonella at first refuses to tell him, but when pressed, answers, "Voria de un stronzo, habenche e disonesto"[75] ["I'd like some of a shit, even though it's disgusting."]. But the Duke's servant, so he complains, would never fulfill his request. The Duke summons his servant, terrifies him with threats of torture, and forces him to do whatever Gonella wants. Gonella naturally asks for the "stronzo," which, after some delay, the servant manages to produce. Gonella then orders the servant to chew the "stronzo" a bit to prepare it for him — and the servant does this too. But when he finally tries to present the awful stuff to Gonella, the buffoon, much to the delight of the Duke and his household, says

> "Tu li ciciasti ogni sapore,
> Et or a me me porgi la vinaza.
> Mo mangial tu; che'l mal pro si te faza!"[76]

> ["You've chewed up every relish here,
> And now you offer me the refuse.
> Better you eat it. May it give you indigestion!"]

Kadlec describes — correctly, I think — the parallels be-

---

74. Bologna per Justiniano da Rubiera, 1506.
75. Lappenberg, p. 427. It has been impossible to obtain the edition of Gonella referred to here. I have used Lappenberg's reprinting of it, which appears on pp. 426–434.
76. Lappenberg, p. 428.

tween this tale and Chapter 26 of Eulenspiegel's adventures: the competition between two servants, both of whom are eager for a reward from a powerful noble; the noble's recklessness, his willingness to allow any sort of behavior; the focusing of the reader's attention on the servants, with the noble and his household functioning as mere necessary background figures; the eating of human excrement as an ultimate test; and finally the triumph of the rogue. While it is impossible to prove any direct relationship between Gonella and Eulenspiegel (the differences between the episodes are all too apparent), it is nonetheless possible that some influence, whether direct or indirect, is present here.[77]

Lappenberg and Kadlec both discover similarities between a number of Eulenspiegel's tales and those of Poggio Bracciolini, the Italian author who died in 1459.[78] Poggio's *Facetiae* had already been published in Nürnberg during the 1470s, and shortly afterwards it became widely known through Germany, printed versions of it appearing in Strassburg by 1511.[79] Kadlec (p. 56) describes the influence of Poggio on German *Schwankliteratur* of the sixteenth century as enormous, and in this he is probably right. The influence on Eulenspiegel, however, appears to extend to just four tales — Chapters 14, 17, 29, and 61 — and even here the relations are probable rather than provable: the authors of the tales of Pfaffe Amis and Pfaffe vom Kalenberg seem to have read Poggio. Whether N. himself read Poggio is ques-

---

77. Kadlec again denies any influence. It becomes rapidly clear, however, that Kadlec's constant denials of perfectly possible literary influences are themselves suspect. Indeed, his otherwise superior scholarship appears shadowed by his desire to prove, at all costs, that the author of Eulenspiegel's adventures was somehow "a man of the people" — a *Volksmund* — whose work reflects a "popular consciousness" rather than any indebtedness to other artists. It is, of course, most doubtful whether the term "*Volksmund*" means anything at all — and most questionable whether *Volksbücher* such as Eulenspiegel's are in any sense creations of "the people," as Kadlec wishes to suggest. I would like to return to these problems, and to the nature of the *Volksbuch* as art, in a moment.

78. See Kadlec, p. 56.

79. See Riccardo Fubini, "Premessa," *Poggius Bracciolini: Opera Omnia* (Torino, 1964), p. v n.

tionable, though it is hard to see how he could at the very least have escaped hearing about his work.

Le cento novelle antiche, also known as *Il novellino*, the Italian collection of tales, perhaps by more than one author, which dates from the last decade of the thirteenth century, seems also to have some influence. Lappenberg doubts that N. had actually read this book, though he does not dismiss the posssibility.[80] Kadlec discovers relations between "Novella IX" and Chapter 79 of Eulenspiegel's tales, as well as between "Novella X" and Chapter 90 of the edition of the tales published in Erfurt in 1532 (this chapter does not appear in Grieninger's edition of 1515, and is therefore part of the *"Zusatzgeschichten"*). Kadlec traces Chapter 79, in which Eulenspiegel pays an innkeeper with the sound of his money, even further back: to Plutarch and to India.[81]

Another detectable influence is that of Morlini, whose exceedingly rare *Opus Morlini complectans novellas, fabulas et comoediam* was first published in Naples in 1520.[82] Lappenberg believes that Chapter 2 of Eulenspiegel's tales is a modified version of Morlini's "Novella XLIV," and that various tales of Eulenspiegel bear comparison with Morlini's "Novella LXXIII," in which a servant interprets his master's instructions literally.[83] Kadlec, who notes both similarities and differences between these tales, rather predictably argues against any literary borrowings.[84] He also rejects Lappenberg's suggestion (p. 248) that Chapter 34, in which Eulenspiegel meets the Pope, has any literary relation to Morlini's "Novella XII," "De colono, qui ut regem alloqui posset, quadrupedem se fecit." It is impossible to tell whether Kadlec is right in this — but it is true that both motifs are common to early folktales of many parts of Europe, among them Hungary and England.[85]

Heinrich Bebel, the self-educated humanist, professor at

80. See Lappenberg, p. 360.
81. See Kadlec, pp. 85–86.
82. Reprinted in Paris, 1885, as: Morlini, Hieronymi, *Novellae, Fabulae, Comoedia*.
83. See Lappenberg, p. 360 ff.
84. See Kadlec, p. 73 ff.
85. See Kadlec, p. 77.

Tübingen, and author (who died in 1514), exerted, according to both Lappenberg and Kadlec, a profound influence on German *Schwankliteratur* of the fifteenth and sixteenth centuries — and possibly on the tales of Eulenspiegel as well. Kadlec ranks Bebel with Poggio and Boccaccio, as a master humorist and writer; but while Lappenberg believes in Bebel's influence on Eulenspiegel, Kadlec suggests that the influence ran the other way, with Eulenspiegel's tales supplying some materials (those of Chapters 35, 69, 79, and 81) for the three volumes of Bebel's *Facetiae*, which were first published in 1512.[86] Kadlec's argument, which is perfectly acceptable, is that Bebel knew either the translation of Eulenspiegel made in 1500 or the Low German text made in the 1480s.

The last source to be considered here is *Les repues franches,* an anonymous collection of tales, with the poet François Villon as hero, first published before 1493.[87] Lappenberg believes that Chapters 6, 57, 61, 62, and 72 were drawn from this work.[88] Kadlec agrees to similarities between these chapters and certain tales in the French work, but he rejects the notion of any literary relationship.[89] Joseph Bédier apparently believes in a literary relationship of some sort.[90]

Two issues now remain. The first, which is minor, is to reassert what I hope has become rather obvious from this study: that Eulenspiegel, far from being a purely German or "democratic, people's" book, is most likely the imaginative, clever, and perceptive effort of a single gifted author who has introduced his own voice into both his own and others'

---

86. See Kadlec, p. 57 ff. The *Facetiae* was republished in Paris in 1516, as *Opuscula nova et adolescentiae labores.* I have used both this Paris edition and a very good critical translation into modern German: Albert Wesselski (ed.), *Heinrich Bebels Schwänke,* 2 vols. (Munich and Leipzig, 1907).

87. See Kadlec, p. 41. I have used a nineteenth-century edition, *Oeuvres de maître François Villon* (Paris, 1832).

88. See Lappenberg, p. 362.

89. See Kadlec, p. 41 ff.

90. See Joseph Bédier, *Les Fabliaux: études de littérature et d'histoire littéraire du moyen âge,* 4th ed. (Paris, 1925), p. 447.

tales.[91] The second issue, somewhat more complicated, is to try to discover what we ought to mean by the term *"Volksbuch"* when we apply it both to all *Volksbücher* and, uniquely, to this *Volksbuch*. To get at the heart of the meaning of this word will be perhaps to illuminate more clearly *Eulenspiegel's* place in literature, while describing more clearly the reasons for *Eulenspiegel's* enduring popularity. For the least we must mean when we call this a *Volksbuch* is that it is, and has been, immensely popular. The word itself implies this. But with whom? And why? If, as these pages have tried to maintain, *Volksbücher* are called *Volksbücher* not because they "spring" from "the people," but because they appeal to "the people," do they not perhaps make their appeals in ways which are largely different from the ways of other books, plays, and poems?

Enid Welsford's comments on Eulenspiegel's "skill in evading consequences"[92] may be helpful here. For if Eulenspiegel and the heroes of the sources of his tales have anything in common, it is that they meet and generally triumph over precisely those economic and social hardships which constantly confront people of the middle and lower classes. Other heroes — in plays, poems, satires, and novels — may do this too, but not with such a vengeance that they succeed in turning the dull routines of much middle-class and lower-class life into a Never Never Land of infinite humor and endless opportunities for fun. It is, perhaps, particularly important and useful for purposes of definition to emphasize the apparent economic aspect of these *Volksbücher*. For heroes such as Pfaffe Amis, Pfaffe vom Kalenberg, and Eulenspiegel are obviously concerned, in the vast majority of their adventures, with questions such as: "How do I survive now?" and "How can I make money in this or that situation?" While it is true that Eulenspiegel (as has been discussed above) exhibits deep interests in other questions — which have to do with "truth" and "justice" — he, too, seems to care a great

---

91. This point is one of the theses of Section II, The Author, above.

92. See p. 270, above.

deal about simply surviving. In doing so he shares much with Pfaffe Amis and Pfaffe vom Kalenberg. It ought, however, to be added that while these heroes are constantly preoccupied with making a living, they are not preoccupied only with that. They want to make a living without working and, more important, without enduring obligations. Invariably, after they have made their money in one place, they leave to go on to another. They seem not only to ignore the "virtues" of the usual economic loyalties of the middle class but also to be indifferent to them. The notion that one ought to continue to work for the same employer, or even continue in the same line of work, would no doubt strike them as pointless. In this sense, Pfaffe Amis, Pfaffe vom Kalenberg, and Eulenspiegel may be considered social and economic "outsiders." They move freely from opportunity to opportunity within their society, but never acquire an economically secure role within it. Nor do they want one. This fact may account for part of their appeal. For while they engage in a typically middle-class struggle (the struggle to earn a living), they succeed in gaining a certain physical freedom — thus becoming, perhaps, the natural heroes of an audience whose members own no productive property but must work for those who do. Perhaps such *Volksbücher* may then be characterized as the literature of middle-class and lower-class economic and social escape: their heroes seem to win victories over the frequent drabness of middle-class and lower-class existence.[93] This may also be why such books reveal such large obsessions with deceit, trickery, sadism, and the delights of deceptive language; for these must certainly be the most convenient, if not the most moral, instruments of economic and social

---

93. I do not wish to imply, of course, that all folk-literature is of a type with Eulenspiegel's. The term necessarily covers a vast area. It includes certain fables, homilies, tales, and elements of epic poems — though even these, in their written forms (as is well known), prove generally to have been re-made by individual artists to such an extent that they can no longer be described as having "sprung from the people," if indeed they ever did. The term *Volksbuch*, as I wish to define it here, is rather to be applied only to "jest-cycles" (see p. 251, above), or those collections of folk-tales which, having gathered around a single hero, achieve written form.

escape among people caught either at the bottom or in the economic middle of their society. It would no doubt be wrong, however, to assert that the audience for these *Volksbücher* is, or ever has been, exclusively limited to lower-class and middle-class people. Such people may have formed a primary audience, though even this is most questionable; but it is not at all hard to imagine priests, lords, and princes — the very people whom Eulenspiegel frequently ridicules — enjoying his fictional exploits as well. In fact the rich and immune probably laughed over his nonsense, even at their own expense, as much as those who were poorer and more vulnerable. The distinguishing feature of such books, though, is that they seem to depict an escapist version of lower-class and middle-class economic life, regardless of the nature of their audience. Their delight for any audience thus lies in their brash treatment of serious circumstances.

But if *Volksbücher* such as *Pfaffe Amis* and *Pfaffe vom Kalenberg* are depictions of middle-class and lower-class brashness and impudence, *Eulenspiegel* both belongs with them and profoundly differs from them — differing perhaps most in its elaboration of their comic devices and in its depth. Where these other *Volksbücher* exhibit a merely casual interest in the possibilities of deceptive language, *Eulenspiegel* appears (as has been discussed in Sections II and III, above) to display an even philosophical curiosity about its broadest and most significant implications. The hero's curiosity about such language is complemented, moreover, by his fascination with deceit as a fine art. For in contrast to both the sources of his tales and to other comparable books, one of Eulenspiegel's chief activities is play-acting. Where Pfaffe Amis and Pfaffe vom Kalenberg almost always play themselves, Eulenspiegel (in more than thirty-six tales) either acts a part or pretends to be someone he is not. On various occasions he plays page-boy, barber's boy, painter, scholar, wandering monk, salesman of religious articles, cleaner of pelts, Abbess' scribe, dying man, blacksmith's boy, shoemaker's apprentice, brewer's apprentice, furrier's apprentice, tanner, carpenter, optician, cook, horse-dealer, and sacristan. He deeply enjoys role-playing — often, it appears, for its own sake. And role-playing is after all both an ultimate instrument of revelation and an ultimate escape from oneself. Acting both allows Eulenspiegel to expose human pretensions and to be free. For Eulenspiegel is a much more complicated character than either Pfaffe Amis or Pfaffe vom Kalenberg. He operates on many levels of human psychology — and this may be another of the reasons that he has been so well liked by his German audience. If he is a devil, he is also a philosopher of language; if he delights in clowning, deceiving, and provoking, he also delights not infrequently in setting matters straight between men and women. The final pleasure of Till Eulenspiegel seems in fact to lie in his uniquely various ways of exposing human pretensions. For he exposes them through language that means what it says, through behavior that speaks for itself because it refuses to be polite, and often through an aggressive use of human excrement.[94] Eulenspiegel's ambition — if he believes that any ambition is worth anything — is thus perhaps to humble, charm, and amuse us by constantly showing us that we are all linguistically and emotionally clumsy animals — animals who always fall on their faces and begin to babble when they aspire to become gods.

---

94. The possible significance of excrement in the tales is discussed in Section II, above.

Bibliography

TEXTS

Ein kurzweilig lesen von Dyl/Ulenspiegel geborē uss dem land zû Brunsswick. Wie/er sein leben volbracht hatt. xcvi seiner geschichten. Anon. Text. Brit. Mus. cat. no.: C. 57 C. 23. Johannes Grieninger, Strassburg, 1515.

Schröder, Edward (ed.) *Ein kurzweilig lesen von Dyl/Ulenspiegel geborē uss dem land zû Brunsswick. Wie/er sein leben volbracht hatt. xcvi seiner geschichten.* Photographic facsimile. Inselverlag, Leipzig, 1911.

SECONDARY WORKS

Aickol, Johannes. *Till Eulenspiegels Streiche.* Düsseldorf, 1903.

Ashe, Geoffrey. *Land to the West.* The Viking Press, New York, 1962.

Austin, J. L. *How to do things with Words,* ed. J. O. Urmson. Harvard University Press, Cambridge, Mass., 1962.

Bebel, Heinrich. *Heinrich Bebels Schwänke,* ed. A. Wesselski. 2 vols. Munich, 1907.

Bebel, Heinrich. *Opuscula nova et adolescentiae labores.* Paris, 1516.

Bédier, Joseph. *Les Fabliaux: études de littérature populaire et d'histoire littéraire du moyen âge.* Champion, Paris, 1925.

Benz, Dr. Richard. *Geschichte und Ästhetik des deutschen Volksbuchs.* Diederichs, Jena, 1924.

Blackmur, R. P. *Form and Value in Modern Poetry.* Doubleday, New York, 1957.

Bobertag, Felix. *Narrenbuch.* Wissenschaftliche Buchgesellschaft, Darmstadt, 1964.

Brie, Friedrich W. D. *Eulenspiegel in England.* Mayer & Müller, Berlin, 1903.

Brown, Norman O. *Life Against Death.* Wesleyan University Press, Middletown, 1959.

Chute, Marchette. *Ben Jonson of Westminster.* Dutton, New York, 1953.

de Coster, Charles Theodore Henry. *Ulenspiegel.* Brussels, 1867.

Faral, Edmond. *Les arts poétiques du XIIe et du XIIIe siècle.* Champion, Paris, 1925.

Flögel, Karl Friedrich. *Geschichte der Hofnarren.* D. Siegert, Liegnitz & Leipzig, 1789.

Fournier, Paul. "The Kingdom of Burgundy or Arles from the Eleventh to the Fifteenth Century," *The Cambridge Medieval History,* VIII, Cambridge University Press (Cambridge, 1959), 306–331.

Fubini, Riccardo (ed.). *Poggius Bracciolini: Opera Omnia.* Bottega d'Erasmo, Torino, 1964.

Goethe, Johann Wolfgang von. *Maximen und Reflexionen.* Goethegesellschaft, Weimar, 1907.

Henning, Wilhelm. *Die Geschicht des Pfarrers vom Kalenberg, Hans Clawerts werkliche Historien, Das Lalebuch: Drei altdeutsche Schwankbücher.* Munich, 1962.

Jeep, Ernest. "Eulenspiegel," *Mitteilungen des deutschen Sprachvereins,* VIII (1885).

Kadlec, Dr. Eduard. "Untersuchungen zum Volksbuch von Ulenspiegel," *Prager Deutsche Studien,* 26. Koppe-Bellmann, Prague, 1916.

Kristeller, Paul. *Die Strassburger Bücher Illustration im XV. und im Anfange des XVI. Jahrhunderts.* Bär & Hermann, Leipzig, 1888.

Krofta, Dr. Kamil. "John Huss," *The Cambridge Medieval History,* VIII, Cambridge University Press (Cambridge, 1959), 45–155.

Krogmann, W. "Ulenspiegel," *Jahrbuch des Vereins für niederdeutsche Sprachforschung,* LVIII/LIX (Hamburg, 1933), 104–114.

Lambel, Hans (ed.). *Deutsche Classiker des Mittelalters.* XII. *Erzählungen und Schwänke.* 2nd ed. F. A. Brockhaus, Leipzig, 1883.

Lappenberg, J. M. *Dr. Thomas Murners Ulenspiegel.* T. O. Weigel, Leipzig, 1854.

Lemcke, H. *Der hochdeutsche Eulenspiegel.* Freiburg, 1908.

Lewis, C. S. *The Discarded Image.* Cambridge University Press, Cambridge, 1964.

Mackensen, Lutz. "Zur Entstehung des Volksbuches vom Eulenspiegel," *Germanisch-Romanische Monatsschrift,* VII/VIII (Heidelberg, 1936), 241–269.

Major, Emil, and Gradmann, Erwin. *Vrs Graf.* Holbein-Verlag, Basel, 1943.

McDonnell, Ernest W. *The Beguines and Beghards in Medieval Culture*. Rutgers University Press, New Brunswick, 1954.

Meiners, Irmgard. *Schelm und Dümmling in Erzählungen des deutschen Mittelalters*. C. H. Beck, Munich, 1967.

Meyer, Albert. *Lustige Streiche Till Eulenspiegels*. Wolfenbüttel, 1921.

Morlini, Hieronymi. *Novellae, Fabulae, Comoedia*. 3rd ed. P. Jannet, Paris, 1855.

Musper, H. Th. *Der Holzschnitt in fünf Jahrhunderten*. W. Kohlhammer, Stuttgart, 1964.

Oeuvres de maître François Villon, par Prompsault. Paris, 1832.

Opus Morlini complectens novellas, fabulas et comoediam. Paris, 1799.

Paul, Herman, and Mitzka, Walther. *Mittelhochdeutsche Grammatik*. M. Niemeyer, Tübingen, 1963.

Pauli, Johannes. *Schimpf und Ernst*, ed. Hermann Österly. Stuttgart literarischer Verein, Stuttgart, 1866.

Phillips, Dayton. *Beguines in Medieval Strassburg*. Stanford University Press, Stanford, 1941.

Poggio. *Facezie di Poggio Fiorentino*. Rome, 1885.

Poggius Bracciolini. *Opera Omnia*, con una premessa di Riccardo Fubini. Bottega d'Erasmo, Torino, 1964.

Roloff, E. A. *Ewiger Eulenspiegel*. Braunschweig, 1940.

Russell, Bertrand. *Logic and Knowledge*, ed. Robert Charles Marsh. Doubleday, New York, 1956.

Russell, Bertrand. *Mysticism and Logic*. Doubleday, New York, 1957.

von Schacking, Otto. *Till Eulenspiegel*. Regensburg, 1914.

Splittgerber, Walter. *Die französischen Nachahmungen des Eulenspiegel in ihrem Verhältnis unter sich und zum deutschen Volksbuch*. Abel, Greifswald, 1920.

Swain, Barbara. *Fools and Folly during the Middle Ages and the Renaissance*. Columbia University Press, New York, 1932.

Voulliéme, E. *Die deutschen Drucker des fünfzehnten Jahrhunderts*. Reichsdruckerei, Berlin, 1922.

Welsford, Enid. *The Fool: His Social and Literary History*. Farrar & Rinehart, Murray Hill, New York, 1936.